BEYOND THE
ASPEN GROVE

BOOKS BY ANN ZWINGER

*Beyond the Aspen Grove**
*A Desert Country Near the Sea**
John Xántus: The Fort Tejon Letters (editor)*
Land Above the Trees (with Beatrice E. Willard)
*Run, River, Run**
*Wind in the Rock**

* Available from the University of Arizona Press

BEYOND THE ASPEN GROVE

ANN ZWINGER

WITH DRAWINGS BY THE AUTHOR

THE UNIVERSITY OF ARIZONA PRESS
TUCSON

THE UNIVERSITY OF ARIZONA PRESS
Copyright © 1988
The Arizona Board of Regents
Manufactured in the U.S.A.

93 92 91 90 89 88

5 4 3 2 1

Library of Congress Cataloging-in-Publication Data

Zwinger, Ann.
    Beyond the aspen grove.

    Bibliography: p.
    Includes index.
    1. Nature. 2. Natural history—Rocky Mountains.
3. Natural history—Colorado. I. Title.
QH81.Z9 1988   508.788'3   87-34274
ISBN 0-8165-1054-7 (alk. paper)

British Library Cataloguing in Publication data are available.

For Herman, who understands

For Susan, Jane and Sara, who will someday understand

For my parents, who understood

Contents

Preface to 1988 Edition

The reprinting of a book involves a careful reading for changes that have come about, for facts that may have been superseded by newer research, for errors that can now be corrected. Re-reading *Beyond the Aspen Grove*, my delineations of the heart, has left me floating in the sky like one of Marc Chagall's amorphous figures, watching myself cooking on the wood stove, watching myself watching the children splashing in the lake, watching a woman somehow scarcely familiar. The characters have changed, and so has the set.

As Edwin Way Teale once wrote, nature writing preserves a time and place in the same detail with which a fly is preserved in amber. In the re-reading it all came back, the smells of a ponderosa summer, the taste of an over-tart wild raspberry, the sound of fall through the aspen leaves, the softness of snow on a frozen pond. But most of all, the sound of children's voices.

Constant Friendship came into our lives at the right time for us as a family. For me, becoming acquainted with the land became a period of opening doors, of discovery, of learning—and thus it has remained. No matter how much other work now takes me away, it remains the keystone of my existence as a human being and as a writer. Because of this forty acres, the life of a dedicated housewife and mother was changed irrevocably. My world tilted and has remained off the horizontal ever since, a kind of seismic psychological rearrangement.

It happened so simply. Nancy Wood, a friend of mine and a fine writer, called up one spring day and said, "My agent is here visiting and I'm running out of things to do with her. Would you take us up to the mountains?" Of course. Such things fit easily into the life of an unscheduled unstructured housewife.

Marie Rodell rode to the mountains with me, asking questions about the wildflowers gracing the meadows. We had belonged to Constant Friendship for four years and I had been keeping a notebook, sketching the flowers, all of which were new to me, as a mnemonic device (which I still do). Doing so gave me great pleasure as well as serving to cement them in my mind, trying to be as accurate as possible, noting both my own observations and botanical notes on the page. When Marie asked me to identify a plant, I referred her to that notebook.

After more questions, more explorations, out of the blue Marie said, "Why don't you do a book on Colorado ecology?" I remember it, oddly, as a statement, not a question. I chuckled. "What's for dinner" was about as far ahead as my planning went.

We went for a long walk. There was a hawksbeard with very long hairs on the leaves that I identified as a (God forgive me) sundrop. Marie blanched, corrected me, and, miraculously, brought the subject of a book up again. I scarcely noticed.

The next day Nancy called me. "Do you know who SHE is?" she demanded and, without waiting for an answer, proceeded to tell me. "Listen, she's one of the best agents in New York, she specializes in nature writers, she was Rachel Carson's friend and is her literary executor. [Since my favorite book was *The Edge of the Sea*, my ears pricked up.] She represents any nature writer who's anybody. And she *asked* you. [Nancy didn't add "you idiot" but the inflection was there.] Are you going to do it?"

I demurred. It was too outrageous.

But, like all outrageous thoughts, it took hold, insidiously, irrevocably, and I realized that was precisely what I wanted to do. I wrote Marie and asked her how to proceed. She advised an outline and several full chapters.

I went to the dime store and bought a new typewriter ribbon and a twenty-five−cent packet of typewriter paper and thought I was in business. I naively typed a one-page outline and a two-page chapter and sent them off. My excuse is that I simply didn't know any better.

No word from Marie. The waiting stiffened my resolve. Finally, a call came. She apologized, she'd been ill, she'd had lunch with an editor who asked if she had any new natural history material, and she had pulled my meager pages out of her purse, "against my better judgment." She was leaving town and "when I get it back, I'll return it to you with a detailed commentary of what you need to do." (Marie was an uncommonly fine editor.)

That was late 1967. On Leap Year Day, 1968, the telephone rang. Marie had a rather high quavery voice, and it was a mite higher and perceptibly more quavery than usual. "My dear," she said, "Random House has taken your book." Then there was a long silence. I realized that she was even more astounded than I.

It took about nine months to write *Beyond the Aspen Grove*, a figure that has not escaped comment (books now take me two to five years). I resurrected every research skill I had learned at Wellesley and in graduate school as an art historian. Art history is a very visual discipline and that was precisely what I needed. I spent much time at Constant Friendship learning the discipline of fieldwork. I realized, with considerable concern, that I hadn't had a biology class since ninth grade (I had my first botany course five years ago). Looking back, I wonder that I could have been so innocent of the work involved or of the commitment that nature writing involves—the search for the holy grail of accuracy, the research that involves more questions than answers, and the intricacy of words, the joy of words, the misery of words, the am-I-saying-what-I-want-to-say of words, all the frustrations of writing. As an eighth-century scribe put it, "Writing is excessive drudgery. It crooks your back, dims your sight, twists your stomach and your sides. Three fingers write, but the whole body labors."

I sometimes have the best conversations in the world while I am drawing. It's the busy-hands syndrome (dishwashing with someone else accomplishes the same thing), the task that occupies the hands while leaving the mind free to roam the hills and valleys of thought.

But one cannot converse and get words down on paper at the same time. Concentration needs isolation. Because of this I am doubly grateful for the saving grace of writing natural history, which provides the constant recharge and good health of the out-of-doors.

I was helped tremendously on *Beyond the Aspen Grove* by having an editor who was a real city girl, Nan Talese, whose idea of wildlife was pigeons on the windowsill of the fifteenth floor of Random House. To convey to her what was going on at 8,300 feet in the Colorado Mountains demanded clarity and organization. If I could explain it to Nan Talese, I could explain it to anyone. I have continued to be blessed with wonderful editors who have patiently taught this late bloomer her craft.

I also cut my teeth on illustrating with *Beyond the Aspen Grove*, a hard lesson I am still learning. I simply drew what I wanted to draw. I didn't know about how a proper one-quarter reduction sharpens the image, how enlarging coarsens—when I look at the illustrations, I would like to do them all over again.

When a book is printed, the first two copies go to the editor who immediately ships one bound copy to the author who, by this time, is wondering whatever happened to that book she wrote. Mine came, unannounced, in the afternoon mail. Sara was just home from school, glass of grape juice in hand, when the telephone rang. She answered. It was for me. I put my pristine copy on the table and took the call. When I came back, I found a firm lavender circle in the middle of the cover and a very contrite daughter. "Oh Mom, I'm *so* sorry—I didn't want to put my glass down on the table—it might have left a ring!" That cover is one of my most cherished possessions. It reminds me where my priorities lie.

The three ankle-biters in *Beyond the Aspen Grove* are now young women of considerable talent and accomplishment and independence. Constant Friendship has remained in their lives in various ways, reflected in their continuing love of the out-of-doors. When I wrote *Beyond the Aspen Grove* (or BTAG, as my favorite bookstore refers to it), I received so many letters from people recalling how important had been their parents' taking them out into nature, giving them an at-homeness, an ease that had remained with them to adulthood. Reading *Beyond the Aspen Grove* brought back that appreciation and made me realize how much we teach our children, not by deliberate intent but by osmosis, by passing on what it is we love in living.

In the interim I have listened, more often than I'd like, to "I wish you'd write anther *Beyond the Aspen Grove*." That is, of course, impossible. That would preclude children growing up, my growing up, the chance to expand and to change. Thomas Wolfe's phrase is apt: "You can never go home again."

That was eighteen years ago and a lot happens in two decades. In twenty years the cast of dogs has changed. Dear Folly and rambunctious Graf have gone to the big kennel in the sky where they have endless dog bones. My years there have been graced with my beloved Nana, a long-haired German shepherd, gracious of disposition, loving of mien, whose leaving has made the coming summer loom empty. And now there is silly Tosca, a blackberry of a retriever who will sample the lake during this, her first summer at Constant Friendship.

We have had beavers, at first joyfully welcomed tenants, and then a scourge—they felled over 200 aspen, decimating the small grove between the cabin and the lake that had grown from five feet to fifteen. Unable to get someone to trap and relocate them, Herman was forced to shoot them. Their damage was massive, the cure was draconian, a trauma I am still working through for it brought about, for me, a somber rethinking of my place in nature.

There have been wet years and dry, deep winter snows and nearly none, and the first Calypso orchids always bloom the first week in June while the Pasque flowers, full of vagarious genes, appear between the end of March and the middle of April. I have seen enough of the seasons to know when the brown-capped rosy finches will blow down from a tundra storm, when the female mallard will first drop onto the lake, a surprisingly similar date each year. And there have been seasons of the heart and mind here, of children growing up, going away, of accommodations and shifts and new occupations and challenges and stumbling blocks. Thank heaven for stumbling blocks.

Eighteen years and ten books later, I have only one regret: that my parents never saw this book, that my mother who always saw to it that I had drawing lessons as a child, that my gentle father whose meticulous mind is reflected in my love of detail, never could see where their willful daughter found home.

In all other ways, this book has brought me great joy because it taught me to fly, reaffirmed the value of learning, and took a very circumscribed housewife, picked her up by the heels and shook her, set her up on her feet and opened a whole world of wonder. I did not begin as a natural historian. I was the kid who hated camp. That I have become a naturalist is not of my choosing—but here in this land I find all the answers I need. Here there is rollicking good health, and laughter in clouds, and happiness in bee flies, and delight in falling stars. Here I discovered the joys of wandering. This land has granted so much to me that it is my measure of how much I owe it, owe it and all of this best of all possible natural worlds, and of what my obligations are to northern anemones and mountain candytuft. *Beyond the Aspen Grove* held and holds many beginnings. It ties me to a tradition of nature writing that ballasts my life, gives me joy, orders my reality.

As William Cowper wrote two centuries ago: "My descriptions are all from nature: not one of them second-handed. My delineations of the heart are from my own experience: not one of them borrowed, or in the least conjectural."

ANN HAYMOND ZWINGER
Constant Friendship
1987

Acknowledgments

Without the generosity and graciousness of these knowledgeable people who shared with me their love of the out-of-doors, I could not have finished this book.

Dr. Richard Beidleman, head of the biology and zoology departments at Colorado College, carefully read, checked, and commented on the manuscript. Since he is both ecologist and writer, his time, skill, and experience in the ecology of this area were invaluable. Dr. Beidleman carefully read the appendix and brought it up to date with current taxonomic thinking. I am most indebted to Dr. Beatrice Willard of the Thorne Ecological Foundation in Boulder, Colorado; she not only read the manuscript in preparation but checked drawings and plant identification. Both helped extensively with the list of references. Dr. and Mrs. S. H. McFarlane camped at Constant Friendship; both are teaching biologists at Aurora College and I count myself privileged to be one of their students.

Mr. Edwin Engle of the Soil Conservation Service identified the many grasses that grow on our land and explained dam construction; he made available many publications to which I would not otherwise have had access. I thank Mr. Lynn Larson, of the U. S. Department of Agriculture, for clearly explaining the soil survey he made of the land. James Ratliff, a teacher and consulting geologist, and Dr. John Lewis,

Professor of Geology at Colorado College, walked the area and explained the geology. Clark Corbridge, a young teacher of mathematics—with his wife, Marty, and me as questionable helpers—did the surveying. His patience was as great as his skill. I also appreciate the hospitality extended by those at Pike National Forest Headquarters, particularly Mr. Robert Poole. I thank the Cripple Creek Record Office, especially Mr. Ralph Dial, for helping us trace the history of the land. Mr. and Mrs. Richard Noyes of the Chinook Bookshop made bibliography recommendations, and their staff was always helpful.

All the drawings were done from nature, most *in situ*. Vivian and Sidney Novis kindly gave advice on materials and technique.

Scientific plant names are based on the authority of Dr. William Weber's *Rocky Mountain Flora*; I am indebted to Dr. Weber for helping me with some of the identifications. Common names used are my preference of those listed in Ruth Ashton Nelson's *Handbook of Rocky Mountain Plants*. Dr. and Mrs. Robert Smith checked mushroom identification.

Many friends have read the manuscript at various stages; their interest, affection, and honesty make their friendship much cherished: Maryette and Henry Beers, Lorraine and Guy Burgess, Anne Cross, John Eastham, Eni Jaspersen, Janet LeCompte, Sam and Lea Levenson, Audrey and Robert Powers, Dorothy and Bob Olds, George and Virginia Pierce, Timilou and Richard Rixon, Joy Rucker, June Smith, Nancy Wood and, in remembrance, Irene Musick. There are others who have shared sunny days at Constant Friendship, some of whom are in these pages; I wish there were space to thank each one. And I appreciate Harry Bruton's proofreading advice.

Marie Rodell has provided guidance all the way through; it was at her suggestion that this book was undertaken and through her encouragement that it was completed. No words can express my appreciation for that.

Of course, this book would not exist without my family, and I thank them officially for putting up with a somewhat absent-minded mother who wrote grocery lists on the back of manuscript pages and kept a dead hummingbird in the dining room. Susan's love of the land and her own experience as a writer and artist gave me much pleasure and help. Jane caught all the insects, and identified and mounted all the butterflies. Sara tirelessly stacked typing paper and carbons for me, and her cheery note "Glad to do it!" is sheer sunshine posted on my bulletin board.

Herman's photographs gave off-season accuracy, and their beauty and sensitivity helped me to see Constant Friendship through other eyes. But most of all, I thank him for my wood stove and the many happy years shared at Constant Friendship.

Illustrations

Plate

1 ❦ ❦ To Constant Friendship

As many times as I have opened this gate, there is always the sense of coming home, a feeling of belonging. No matter that we spend only part of our year here, this wild mountain land is home in a way that no city house can ever be.

The familiar vistas are framed through the gate, always constant, yet always changing. The gate creaks as I walk it open and I unconsciously note the progress of the season. The rough notched curve of the meadow, the sentinel ponderosa pines and Douglasfirs, the vast stretch of sky are always there. But where there was snow last week, there is today a delicate Pasque flower, so pale as to seem formed of snow crystals. Where the meadow was sere and bleak, bearded with dry grasses, today wild candytuft and early daisies sprig the returning green. Or, in the warming sunshine of summer, the magenta and silver green Colorado locoweed is in full bloom in the middle of the road, like Thoreau's flower between the wagon tracks. Or, where there was a meadow ablaze with purple asters, there is now snow a foot deep.

This land is a place of all seasons, for even in winter there is the promise of spring, and in spring, the foretaste of summer. The white of snow becomes the white of summer clouds; the resonant green of spruce becomes the green head of drake mallard; the gray of rock and lichen endures in the gray of lowering winter skies; the same orange-red of Indian paintbrush bars the blackbird's wing and stains the western tanager's head. Here part of each season is contained in every other. The tight-woven knowledge from all our yesterdays at this land is held in the stern simplicity of tree and sky and flower and rock, a certainty of tomorrow.

✿

To understand this mountain world, one must start far away at the Mississippi River where the Great Plains begin to slope toward the Rocky Mountains, come west across Missouri to Kansas, where there is more space than there are towns, where the horizon line is blurred by tall grass and grain, punctuated by silos, church spires, and cottonwoods growing along streams. The rise is so gradual that it goes almost unnoticed, but the western border of Kansas is three thousand feet higher than the eastern. Within a hundred miles, after crossing the Colorado border, you will have a glimpse of Pikes Peak, distant as a mountain in a Japanese woodcut, perhaps as Lieutenant Zebulon Pike first saw it in 1806.

The grasslands persist, but now the grasses are shorter. Scrubby buffalo grass and hairy grama tell of sandy soil and rains which penetrate only the top two or three inches of soil. By mid-Colorado, at an altitude of 5600 feet, there is not enough rain for forest, and the grasses choke out tree seedlings. Pike called these desolate grasslands a barrier "placed by Providence" to keep Easterners from coming West, a prophecy that has hardly proved true. A taste of dust dries the mouth when the wind scrapes across the flat open fields. The wind fiercely and persistently roiling down out of the mountains, unchecked by trees or towns, leaves miles of tumbleweed caught in the fences.

And then, rising fast out of the western horizon, there is the Front Range of the Rocky Mountains. This easternmost extension of the Rockies is a knucklehold connecting the high plains to the Continental Divide. The Front Range springs far over the horizon; its southern anchor is Pikes Peak, hanging blue-gray and cool over the dusty plains. Closer, the mountains become greener in the crystalline clarity of mountain air. In the winter they are sprinkled with snow like powdered sugar, and the ridges are sharp and bright against the deep winter-blue sky. I cherish this horizon, so different from the level horizons of other years. The mountains are no longer intimations. They are presences.

The highway, so long followed across desolate miles, tames to a city street at the base of the foothills. Here, strung out like beads against the slopes, are the major population centers of Colorado: Ft. Collins, Greeley, Boulder, Denver, Colorado Springs, Pueblo. Just west of Colorado Springs the highway loops into a low northwest passageway through the Foothill Zone, grading from 6000 to 8000 feet. Ute Pass was the way of the Ute Indians and of the early settlers, going to South Park and the towns beyond with the romantic names of Cripple Creek, Fairplay, and Leadville. Now the Pass is a four-lane highway, cut between lunettes of sandstone and Pikes Peak granite, traveled at all seasons of the year.

The Pass is the result of a fault, a sharp break where monstrous blocks of rock have shifted, leaving a cleavage through the mountain wall of the Front Range. You can see the notch from miles to the east, chiseled in the rocky phalanx. To the right, against a pre-Cambrian granite cliff, is a remnant of the original wagon trail. Along the left runs the mute roadbed of the Colorado Midland Railway on which gold ore was shipped down from Cripple Creek to the mill at Colorado Springs. Winding upward, there is a vocabulary of rock formations, telling of a time before people, before animals, before plants.

The Pass is an introduction to the high mountains, to the abrupt changes in vegetation created by altitude. At the base of the Pass, vegetation is low: scrub oak, yucca, silver sage, piñon and juniper, all plants able to survive the dryness of the steep well-drained graveled slopes. Tall cottonwood trees, cousins of mountain aspen, grow only in the wet path of the stream running beside the highway. Only small ponderosa pine grow on the sunny south-facing slopes. To your left, the north-facing slopes, which are shaded most of the day, begin to bear trees as the road rises: white fir, ponderosa, Douglasfir and Colorado blue spruce. Around the last curve of the Pass the view is suddenly blocked by a horizon full of forested mountain: the beginning of the Montane Zone at 8000 feet.

Continuing upward and westward the Pass opens out, running in a meadowed montane valley bracketed by steep hills. On the east is the back of the Rampart Range, a local spur of the Front Range. On the west are the ridges culminating in the majestic mass of Pikes Peak. The granite of the mountain summit stands bare above the wooded ridges, a monadnock, remnant of a larger rock mass which has since been eroded away, leaving only the resistant core. The hard granite that remains is known as Pikes Peak granite and underlies this whole area. Formed and cooled perhaps twenty or thirty miles below the surface, the molten rock solidified into the pinkish gray rock whose outcroppings you can see along the roadside.

The road, now running more north than west, lies at 8000 feet and marks the beginning of an up-again down-again rise to the Continental Divide, less than a hundred miles to the west. In the summer the valley's meadows are enameled with penstemons as magnificently blue as a Colorado sky, intensified by the contrasting red-orange of Indian paintbrush. Big, fat bee-laden thistles and clumps of bright purple-pink locoweeds and scarlet gilia shimmer against the grasses. Scrub oak comes to leaf in opaque thickets which burn bronze in September, the same time that pockets of golden aspen spatter the somber olive-green pine. The evergreen watermark now begins to stain lower on the slopes as the valley begins to rise.

The highway angles through Woodland Park and then turns due north. There is a brief glimpse of the snow-covered Tarryall Mountains fifty miles to the west, and then the open vistas are blocked by evergreen screens. Ponderosa pines tiger-stripe the macadam with sun and shadow, three times, or more, taller than their counterparts down the Pass. Darker pointed spruce and pale-boled aspen intermingle with them. Houses are single and far apart. A startling black squirrel with ears almost as big as his tail darts across the road and scuttles up a tall ponderosa. The air smells of sun-warmed pine.

It is time to turn off the highway and take the road to our land. The narrow dirt road meanders back and down a bit, south and west. It is not a mountain road in the sense of back-up

turns and sharp drops, but more a backwoods road, threaded
between pine and aspen, over short sharp hills, through small
open meadows and closed woods, cattle gates, past "No Hunt-
ing" signs and fences strung on aspen posts. One more short
rise and a sharp turn reaches our gate, but only if it is raining
will you see this land as we first saw it.

❦

Herman and I came to this land in the midst of a summer
downpour. We had been looking for mountain land for months.
A military family, we had enjoyed the Florida ocean, an Arkan-
sas farm, the big city and the small town, the bests of many
worlds. But here in Colorado we had felt an openness and
freedom that promised the kind of life we wished for ourselves
and our children.

I had driven miles on rutted dusty roads in quest of a place
that would meet Herman's criterion that "it must have water"
and mine that "it must be far from civilization." I saw this land
on a bright, impeccable May day. It was not yet spring in the
mountains, but the air was so full of joy and birdsong that as
I stood in the high rough meadow I felt as if spring were per-
meating my veins just as it infused those of the plants greening
at my feet.

And so I went home and wrote Herman a long letter and
mailed it. Whenever there is anything of major importance and
I want his undivided attention, I write a letter, a struggled-over,
persuasive, thoroughly researched, painfully produced document.
The answer was that Herman was intrigued. So I made arrange-
ments to leave our children with a friend one Saturday morning,
and hoping for a beautiful day, we set off. To my disappoint-
ment it was pouring when we reached the mountains.

The rain fell in curtains of lead beads. Lake surface and
sky intermeshed. The meadow was awash. Grasses and flowers
shattered. Even the pine branches dripped, and the duff beneath
was soggy with needle-sieved rain. Vignettes of pine forest, aspen
grove, rushing stream, open meadow, granite outcropping, flick-
ered into focus as the rain alternately blackened and lightened.
Willows dripped with insistent monotonous regularity. The rain
ran down our cheeks and dripped off our noses. Momentarily the

rain thinned to a fine mist. A mule deer entered the near meadow, paused, looked solemnly at the interlopers, and with a flick of tail, merged back into the shadowy woods—a good omen for those looking for good omens. We went home and signed the preliminary papers.

We brought our children here a week later, on a bright sunny June day. I remember that day as an Impressionist painting, full of light, animated with short brushstrokes of bright color: a trio of two small figures and one taller one, brushed against blue of sky and lake, green of tree, charging the landscape with their vitality and curiosity. Susan was in her teens, Jane and Sara still in elementary school. They stood clustered on a large sun-warmed rock, overlooking the lake, somewhat hesitant about all these woods for roaming, but letting it all soak in: city girls faced with the forest primeval. Then Sara, who has always been one for immediate and enthusiastic reactions, bounced up and down with the idea, pulled off sneakers, rolled up jeans, and went wading in the lake. Jane stood, pensive, absorbing it all, registering each facet of the terrain. Then she too sat down, took off her shoes, and joined Sara, splashing as she went.

Susan, who had just completed an English assignment which involved research about her family, immediately suggested a name for the land. Her great-great-great-great-great-grandfather, John Haymond, came to this country from England some time in the early 1730's. As a carpenter, or "joiner," he came to build a house for a wealthy Maryland planter. He remained in this country and settled on a large tract of land which he called Constant Friendship. Having contributed the perfect name, Susan went exploring the new domain.

❧

And so Herman and I signed the final papers and assumed, in our innocence, that we had bought and therefore now owned these forty up-and-down acres. It has since turned out to be precisely the other way around. It is we who belong to the land. Beginning to know these mountain acres has been to discover a puzzle with a million pieces already set out on a table. Occasionally a few pieces fit together and we gain another awareness of the land's total pattern of existence, of its intricate interdependencies, enhanced by knowing that the puzzle will never be completed. There will always be something new to discover: a minute moss never found before, a rabbit eating birdseed with the birds on a hungry November day, a bittern that stays only long enough to be remembered.

But to "own" this land in a sense of control, as one owns a book or a pot or pan, is simply impossible. We own it only as it becomes a part of the experience of each one of us. It is its own reason for being. Human values are extraneous. The life of the wood, meadow, and lake go on with or without us. Flowers bloom, set seed and die back; squirrels hide nuts in the fall and scold all year long; bobcats track the snowy lake in winter; deer browse the willow shoots in spring. Humans are but intruders who have presumed the right to be observers, and who, out of observation, find understanding.

And as each season passes, we have come to know how our ancestors felt about the preciousness of their land, a land as unsettled and new to them as this land is to us.

❦

Our Constant Friendship is a generous mile and a half higher in altitude than the original in Maryland. Ours was not surveyed until the original had been lived on for nearly a hundred and forty years. Included in the Louisiana Purchase of 1803, our area was first sectioned in 1869. Under the impetus of the Homestead Act, Congress established a rectangular survey system to be used on the newly opened western lands. Our township map, embellished with nineteenth-century calligraphy, shows sections divided into quarters of 160 acres, the size of a single homestead. It is a simple line map with no contouring; one of our streams is sketched in as a landmark only.

By 1840 most of the land east of the Mississippi River had been explored and settled, platted, plowed and planted, but the western wilderness was little more familiar than when Lewis and Clark traversed it in 1805. Not until the push of civilization, the impetus of gold discovery in California, crowded conditions in cities, and post-Civil War restlessness were these lands traveled by any but the "mountain men." By the 1880's homes and trading posts were established throughout the West. In 1910, when over a million acres were set aside for Pike National Forest, some 160,000 acres within its boundaries had been either homesteaded or staked with claims. Constant Friendship was one of these pockets of private land.

Out of curiosity we have traced the sale of our land. Large gray duckbound volumes, cornered with maroon leather, hold the Teller County records back to 1899, when the county was established. Entries, beautifully written in Spencerian script, list tax sales, lode claims, deeds, and the transactions of an area largely concerned with mining. In 1910, our land, then part of a larger parcel, was bought for delinquent taxes. The Little Carlyle Mining and Milling Company owed $10 on two quarter sections, or 320 acres. The bid and paid amount was $16.99!

❧

When we first came here, we solemnly promised each other that we would never build anything to change the smallest aspect of the land. No cutting of trees, no fencing, no human imprint at all.

So we camped and loved the sound of rain on the tent top. It was somewhat less romantic when it sounded for hours on top of the canvas dining fly with all five of us huddled beneath. I cooked over an open fire and counted smoke inhalation as part of the privilege of being out-of-doors. And each time we came we left something else under a tarpaulin for the next time: a sturdy grill, a folding table, a stack of cooking pots.

But we had not reckoned with Herman's penchant for building, the neighboring cattle's affection for our lake, and my penchant for creature comforts, nor my awakening interest in the land itself which made me somewhat less than enthusiastic about spending all day kneeling beside an open fire waiting for water to boil, which seems to take all day at this altitude.

So first we built a gazebo, open to the world and the wind, but large enough so that we could all sleep under shelter if need be. Then with the donation of some windows, it became a kitchen-cabin with a loft. My prized Valentine present that year was an ancient wood stove from the Salvation Army store, a stove of grandiose proportions and comforting mien. Next we added a deck. And then we enlarged the cabin with an upstairs studio-bunk room and a living room. And which, as all good projects go, will never be finished. Three years later, I still have three upstairs windows to frame, and Herman is talking about another deck, since we always seem to be overflowing the one we have. The presence of the cabin has helped us to become more a part of the land because we can now spend time here throughout the year, regardless of weather. And we have had the joy of building shelter with our own hands. And the mashed thumbs.

We chose not to have electricity even when it became available, and so we read by oil lamps, which I am always, much to Herman's annoyance, forgetting to watch and letting the chimneys blacken. We have stained the rough cedar boards and battens the color of the aspen grove in which it stands. Except for a furtive glint of sun on window pane, it is as camouflaged as a deer.

❧

There are many ways to view this land. Flying over, the whole topography is available at a glance, the lake looking like a scrap of shiny metal in the midst of deceptively soft-looking folds of cloth. As a child confined to bed plays with the crumpled covers to make hills and valleys, so a giant's restless child seems to have arranged the land in folds of green baize.

A long walk communicates the steepness of the ridges to your leg muscles and gives an intimate sense of the different aspects of the land as measured by foot lengths. I have watched a soil survey being made; it is a fascinating way to see and feel the land. Each handful of soil communicates, in the variations of color and texture and moisture, information about cactus-dry slopes, damp spruce hillsides, and fertile grass and wildflower-quilted loam.

But the most thorough way is to be part of a survey team. When I began writing this book, I wanted to know as much as I could about the precise convolutions of this land. I was reading everything I could about ecology—the relationship of plants and animals to their environment—and I wanted to discover the visible truths of all I saw in print. When a young friend of ours was interested in surveying, the idea of a few day's work seemed attractive. When we finished some six weeks later, I did indeed have an awareness of this land and the sure knowledge that I would never ever know all I wanted to know.

❧

The theory of surveying is to project an imaginary horizontal grid on the land surface beneath. We used a hundred-foot grid, marking each corner point with an accurately placed stake, pounded solidly into the ground, laboriously checked and double-checked and labeled. Each stake was identified by a tall lath, tied with a bright orange tape, making the meadows look as festive as a medieval fair.

On even terrain it is simple to pull the survey chain taut on the ground. On uneven terrain the chain must be held in such a way that it is horizontal, regardless of the ground's slant. Sometimes a steep slope reading involved quite a stretch for me, holding the chain at arm's length overhead and trying to mark a pinpoint at my feet with a plumb bob that swung like the pendulum of a grandfather clock. Stretching the chain tight on a downhill slope meant digging in my boots and the ever-present possibility of going tailbone over teacup down the slope when the chain went slack.

On our steep slopes almost every reading had to be recalculated to give accurate vertical projection. The chain constantly tangled in the deadfall of the forest, and always the most stately trees blocked the transit's straight view. Often we began readings all over again from a previous point to avoid cutting down a beautiful old pine or spruce.

On uneven ground it takes time to set up and level a transit. These minutes provided a wonderful time for exploration. The systematic progression across the land brought me to new areas which were often unfamiliar. The discoveries were many: a row of Calypso orchids studding a decaying log, a new gentian by the north stream, a hummingbird whose thicket of bush honeysuckle we invaded and who took my red shirt for a new variety of flower.

To make a topographical map from such a grid, elevation readings are taken at grid intersections and other significant points, such as the highest and lowest points on the land. Readings are made on a calibrated level rod. Again, there was seldom a straightforward progression from point to point. Even in the meadows, which look deceptively even, there are gullies and washes and draws which make it impossible to take elevation readings more than thirty feet apart. In the steep woods, readings are even more frequent and time-consuming.

The last day we worked I stood on a ridge-top in a wildly thundering mountain storm, water streaming down my face and running under my collar, holding up the fully extended level rod. Lightning was crackling all around and I tried not to be aware of the rod's metal tip. But it was that or begin readings up the long slope all over again, and I was quite willing at that point to stand up to the lightning as the less bothersome alternative.

All this imprinted an immediate physical awareness of this land that no map can convey. When I drew the map, first interpolating the readings for ten-foot contour intervals, and then drawing the connecting contour lines, I could only think how innocent it all looked on paper. Still, the closeness of the lines repeat that this is "bear went over the mountain" country, and all that you can see when you get over one ridge is another ridge, and that you can run out of leg muscles and breath before you run out of wooded ridges.

❦

Fortunately for the middle aged surveyor or the lowland hiker, the exertions of up-and down hiking are forgotten in the pleasantly cool dry mountain air. Although we are at the same latitude as Washington, D. C., our altitude of 8300 feet creates a climate more like that of Lake Louise in Canada. There is less atmosphere between us and the sun, and this "thin" mountain air holds little moisture, as the skier who forgets his lip pomade is soon painfully aware. The thin air filters out less of the ultraviolet rays, so sunburns are surprisingly quick. There is a little more than two-thirds as much atmospheric pressure than at sea level, causing water to boil at a lower temperature and taking longer for food to cook. Herman says we haven't had "done" potatoes in years. And it makes unacclimated lowlanders quickly breathless after even modest exertion.

Nevertheless, this is invigorating country for walking; it is varied and unfrequented, and full of treasures for the bright-eyed. Jane finds a porcupine skull, complete with long yellow ponderosa-scraping incisors. Sara discovers a nest, tumbled to the ground in a recent storm, lying beside an unfamiliar wildflower. Susan picks up a weathered tree knot that looks like a bird. Or perhaps a whale, depending upon which way you hold it.

Often, on our family walks, one of our two dogs goes along. If it is Graf, the German shepherd, he pretends that the pine cones are rats and kills them before they can bite back. Anything we lean down to look at he assumes is to be thrown for his chasing, and just to help out, gets his big black muzzle there first. He crashes up and down the ridges on four pogo-stick legs, quite wearing everyone out with his energy.

If it is Folly, ponderously basset of body, short and crooked of leg, she is thankful only to keep up with her humans and scarcely notices the rabbit bounding just ahead. It is beneath her dignity to make a mad scattered dash as Graf would do. Her tongue lolls down as far as her drooping ears that swing from side to side with her rolling sailor's gait. Her coat is covered with seeds and dry leaves, but it is enough for her to keep up and keep walking, and she won't shake herself clean until after a long and well-deserved nap.

In the cold of winter, these summer walks are what I remember most. Not that winter walks aren't exciting—tracks in the snow, a pile of spruce cones' scales where a squirrel break-fasted, red kinnikinnik berries against white snow, and blue, blue sky—but summer walks have an ease and grace about them. Winter walks are hard work, with snow often hip deep. Perhaps we don't appreciate the summer walks as we should because there is always "next summer" at Constant Friendship.

🌿

Each of us has favored places that we visit again and again, depending upon season or fancy.

Sara loves the lake, and in the summer she takes a book out to the raft to read in uninterrupted quiet. The rowboat's gentle bumping against the raft steps tells me where she is without even looking. In the winter the lake becomes her private giant ice rink. Having practiced for years in an indoor rink where "patch" space is carefully allotted, she loves the freedom to do jumps and spins and spirals and school figures with no one to bump into.

Jane's favorite place as a child was a cavernous heaping of rocks below the dam through which the stream falls in glistening splinters to run over a clear gravel bed. She named it the Whale's Mouth. It is cool and damp, full of ferns and mosses, and very special. But now that she is older she goes wandering, to far ridges and higher meadows.

Susan loves to roam the far horizons too, bringing back pocketfuls of mountain memorabilia. She returns, followed by an exhausted Graf, draws us a map in the dirt of where she has been and shares her vistas with those of us who only sit on the deck and peel potatoes.

Herman likes to sit on the rock by the boat dock where the water is shallow and clear and he can watch the trout lurking in the shoals. There he ponders his next building project: a larger deck? an upstairs balcony? an ice house dug in the hill-side, perhaps combined with a summer wine cellar? And he thinks about just how much he can persuade me to participate and how many hours he can lure me away from the microscope and still not infringe on cooking time, and how much he'll have to teach me. Although I've developed into a fairly good "joiner" in the tradition of my ancestor, Herman hasn't yet gotten over having to teach me how to pound a nail and climb a ladder.

One of my chosen places is the other lake rock, an exposed stump of granite about eight feet from shore. Reached by a cat-walk, it can be a wonderful place to sit and absorb the order of mountain life. Another favorite is a particular quiet hilltop high above the lake. Here the sunlight is filtered just enough to mel-low the crisp white anemones into pearly opalescence. Yellow-flowered stonecrop is made of drops of molten gold. Boletus mushrooms are welded of brass and bronze. Carnelion kinnikin-nik berries hang pendent beneath dark jade leaves. Old logs, tufted with lichen and inlaid with moss, provide comfortable seating. Ruby anemone, amethyst gentians, death camas remain later in this gentle spot.

From the beginning I have felt a special pleasure in this

quiet jewel box of mountain treasures. Perhaps my first curiosity about this new world began here, for I knew few of the flowers and I was curious about the mosses and gray curls that iced the soil. And so I began looking up names and descriptions, and each time I learned another new plant, my eyes were sharpened and I saw another. Each answer led to a new question, to the beginning perception of a new order and reason.

My view of the lake far below is barred with thin aspen boles and macraméed with pine needles. It is there, in the shining oval of the lake, much of what I know of the world of Constant Friendship begins.

2 ❧ ❧ The Lake

At six o'clock on a summer's morning the sun is still so low that its slanting rays only glaze the lake. I walk the lake path before anyone else is awake. Mists vacillate a foot above the surface, evanescing in the coming light like ghosts reluctantly fleeing before the day. Indians call them cloud spirits and believe that they rise from the water each morning. Trout skirt the shallows, seeking midges trapped on the silvered surface of the water. Pendent drops of moisture tremble and sparkle and glitter on the sedges at the lake edge. No wind shatters their crystal chandeliers. Time seems suspended in quiet.

The sun appears over the Rampart Range to the east. Mists clear. Where there were blurred outlines there is now clarity. A quick breeze draws ruffles across the surface of the lake. The heat of the emerging sun feels warm on my shoulders. A dragonfly zigzags by, sewing dawn to morning. A trout jumps out of the water and catches a fly whose wing muscles are not yet warm enough to make him agile. A day of feeding and flying has begun.

This lake is the eye of the land. The land's changes are seasonal, expected; the lake's are swift, expressive, momentary, subtle. The lake changes from rain-dimpled to sparkling blue to flat brown within the hour, from misty sheen to bottomless black within the day. Looking down from my ridge above the lake, I see the water, dark, clear, and deep. Sitting among the sedges at the edge, the surface gleams wide, flat, and opaque.

❧

The deepest part of the lake is about twelve feet and lies off center, toward the dam. The dam was built long before we came here, across the narrows of a ravine where a beaver dam had been. The beavers have moved on, deeper into the wilderness where you can still see their meshed steps of sticks which terrace the mountain streams.

The terminology of "pond" and "lake" is somewhat confusing. Technically ponds are shallow enough for plants to grow across the whole area rooted in the bottom. A lake has a deeper area in which no plants can grow because of insufficient light. In this sense, ours is a lake. To the Soil Conservation Service it is a "fish pond." The word "lake" also carries the connotation of the large summer lakes of childhood vacations, filled with sailboats and motorboats and water skiers. In this sense, ours is a pond, for all that traverses it is a small rowboat named the *Andrea Doria*, a brace of itinerant mallards, and Mad Ludwig, our muskrat-in-residence. "Lake" and "stream" are western usage for what an Easterner calls "pond" and "creek."

The beavers would scarcely recognize the dam that stands where theirs once was. To construct an earth dam, soil is removed down to bedrock or solid compacted earth. As the dam is built up, all rocks, sticks, and roots are removed from the soil, and the earth is tamped down every eight inches to prevent the formation of air pockets. The completed dam and the barrow area, from which the soil for the dam was taken, are planted with native grasses. The straight line of the dam is an unnatural line in an otherwise flowing landscape, and the brome and wheatgrasses which feather its top, and the brilliant yellow of blooming golden banner, scarcely soften its severity.

We can plant nothing, however, to break the artificial line, for tree and shrub roots loosen the soil and weaken the dam. Two willows, now about four feet high, have established them-

SEED POD

GOLDEN BANNER
(*Thermopsis divaricarpa*)

Plate 1

selves at the water's edge, and we must remove them if we wish to keep the dam and the lake. Ludwig has tunneled into its slope and we must persuade him to find more appropriate quarters.

A "rip rap" of rocks is piled at the end of the dam to serve as ballast and to prevent washing into the adjacent floodway. Fireweed and flax, cinquefoil and rose are tangled in among the rocks, having moved in as soon as the ground was disturbed. The floodway is about thirty feet across, so that it can handle a peak runoff. It must drain, in emergency, not only our lake's runoff, but that from several thousand upland acres. Gullies tell of overflows before our time and should be filled in to prevent further erosion. I mention this every spring to the girls and am now resigned that it will be a mother-hen project.

❦

The lake is very much a part of our existence at Constant Friendship, even though our first experience with it was a difficult one. Sticks and branches were wedged deep in the bottom of the standpipe. Enough had accumulated to block drainage and the lake had risen several inches. Herman tried all sorts of ingenious devices to dislodge the debris, most of which required maneuvering from the stern of an unstable rowboat, and all of which were unsuccessful. When patience ran thin, he lowered the lake by opening the outlet valve, hoping that the rush of water would flush out the obstructions.

Trout were swept through, but no branches. To keep the trout from being lost in the runoff stream, Herman would sidestep down the dam, which is about twenty feet nearly straight down on the downstream side, to catch the trout coming through the outflow pipe. Then he would dash back up again, a protesting wriggling trout in each upraised hand, their white undersides gleaming in the sun, tails flipping in indignation. Exhausting as it was for the human, it must have been traumatic for the fish, but so far as we know, we lost not a single trout.

The third attempt at clearing the pipe was successful. A long pole with a meat spike on the end penetrated and held the slippery waterlogged sticks. One by one they could be pulled up. We followed the Soil Conservation Service's recommendation and capped the standpipe with a heavy wire basket to avoid further trauma for the trout.

And Herman.

❧

It is a lake for people to be in as well as fish. After a strenuous afternoon of woodchopping, Herman assures me that there is nothing so refreshing as a quick swim. Swimmers are divided into the brave and the prudent. There are a few hardy souls who stand on the lake rock and dive in, but they seldom do it twice. Temperatures that are good for rainbow trout are a shock to the human system. Then there are those who stand on the ladder and inch in, protesting, shivering, vocal people who share their suffering with those who still wait. And who after that often continue to wait and never do go in!

But the one who finally and actually swims out to the raft is rewarded by a feeling not only of invigoration but of primitive survival. I prefer to embark from the shore on the questionable security of an air mattress. I feel a pleasant identification with the environment when being blown about like a leaf on a world as old as time. The surface of the lake is sun-warmed and pleasant, but twelve inches below the water is icy, so floating has its purpose. But one who only rides an air mattress is also subject to the bullying of those of her family who actually swim. I have long since chosen to be warm and ridiculed rather than cold and brave.

Some summers the swimming is not so fine, indeed not even advisable. Late in a very dry summer the inflow from the streams is not sufficient to balance the water lost by evaporation. The streams are mere trickles. No rainfall comes to drain down the meadow into the lake. The lake slowly and unpleasantly drops below the top of the standpipe. We watch the visible measure of lessening flow with concern. The noisy waterfall down the standpipe, a background noise the rest of the year, is silent. In the unfamiliar stillness the clatter of grasshoppers is loud. A scum of algae clogs the lake edges. Feet of mud are exposed on the shallow west side. Water striders, who took shelter in grasses along this lake edge, seek new shores. There are no morning mists. The lake retreats into itself.

A dead trout appears on the surface, floating white belly up. Other animals which we cannot see die and drift to the bottom. Their decomposition, encouraged by the warm weather and the warming water, hastens the depletion of the lake's oxygen supply. Unlike land animals, the fish cannot migrate. They can only remain and die. The smooth surface of the pond absorbs more and more of the sun's rays, welcome in May but deadly in August.

We bury the dead fish at the edge of the lake, only to have it dug up by the muskrat who leaves long clawmarks in the mud. Every time the breeze catches the dry aspen leaves it sounds like rain, but none comes. Then, early in September, there is a spatter on the tin roof. I stop whatever I'm doing to go outside and confirm the sound. The rain begins to thicken. It runs in rivulets down the road, making gullies in the dry dirt. It rattles like gravel on the tin roof, like beans in a pod. It sweeps through the meadow, refreshing the lake, and the lake begins to live again.

But the rain also washes in the end of summer. As the yellow leaves of the willows float across the water, they take the bright colors of summer with them. Waterlogged, dead brown, they sink to the bottom. October is deceptive: the days are halcyon, but no birds sing; the sun is warm, but no flowers bud. The wind tugs at my jacket, like an impatient child wanting attention.

❧

Late one October, before we built the cabin, we slept in a small two-man mountain tent in the aspen grove. It is terribly still on an October night, and breathtakingly chill. Whispering night leaves of summer are gone. Trout no longer broach the surface of the lake for a midnight snack. No frogs jump and plop. Even mosquito buzzings are stilled. Breath condenses on the tent ceiling. Everything hangs suspended with cold. I could almost hear the water freezing in the wash pan. It is too quiet, the silence of a land waiting for the executioner of winter.

I was not sleeping well, trying to avoid the cold spots in the sleeping bag. I had just huddled myself to sleep when from afar and above came a reverberating, maniacal screaming. It died slowly, the echoes uneasily confirming that it was not a nightmare. Silence. And my human attempt to recognize and identify. Again the mad cacophony, this time repeated miles down the valley in an insensate fugue.

Immortalized in an absolutely accurate cliché, these were loons, uncommon in our area, on the way south for the winter.

Loons are huge birds, thirty inches or so long. They prefer lakes like ours in forested areas where they catch fish, frogs, and insects. Their size amplifies their penetrating call which carries for miles and miles on the empty October air. It is so unnerving because the quality of the call is so human, and out of a dead sleep one reacts before realizing that it is a bird.

Far and away the loon called, fainter and less disturbing. The silence was white after it had gone, the sleeping bag even colder.

🌿

This is a lake whose patterns we record in the log. The first milky fringe of ice usually appears in October, bearding the shore white. Soon it covers the lake like a shroud. The last weekend in November we skate near the south shore on ice so crystal clear that the black bottom of the lake shows through and so smooth that the skate-blade edge does not bite well. As the ice thickens it becomes milky with trapped gas bubbles. By mid-December we can skate on the whole lake before the heavy snows of January make constant snow-shoveling a prerequisite. One of the sounds of winter is that of Sara's skates scribing school figures on the ice: backwards eights, loops, and serpentines, make sibilant Spencerian calligraphy on its white page.

But snow time, even though it means the nuisance of clearing the ice, is also toboggan weather. From two-thirds of the way up the steep south slope, a toboggan ride ends in mid-lake. There is a drop where the barrow area was dug, the cause of many hair-raising launchings into space and rear-thumping landings. On a one-man wing sled the speed is less, but the ride is just as exciting because it is more unpredictable. Many adults lose their dignity somewhere between the top ponderosa and the willow bush marking the shore.

❦

Ice is not fatal to the lake community. When ice first freezes it is clear, and photosynthesis can continue if the temperature allows because the ice transmits most of the available light. Then the ice whitens, and very little light gets through. A heavy blanket of snow completely darkens the water beneath. Even when it is shoveled off the ice, the reflection from the ice exceeds the absorption; anyone shoveling snow for skating must wear sunglasses. The ice imposes a total calm on the lake surface. No wind mixes oxygen into the water as it does in the spring, summer, and fall. But the sound of water running down the standpipe indicates that there is ample inflow from the streams. Without this oxygen, decomposition would use up the summer supply and winterkill would result. But the fish survive, and those other organisms which cannot withstand the cold have long since gone to immortality in eggs and seeds.

We were curious as to the depth and safety of the ice for skating and sledding, so we cut ice plugs. In January the ice ranges from seventeen inches at the center to fourteen inches at the south shore. At the north shore, by the lake rock, it is only twelve inches thick but so extremely hard that the ice cutter requires Herman's strength to cut through.

The holes made by the ice cutter show ice with three to five inches of "milk ice" on top; the rest is "black ice," clear ice through which you can see the black bottom of the lake. The next day the holes are filled with clear new ice, portholes to the silent world below. Deep cracks boom and snap in February and Sara says she is uneasy when she skates. Warm sunny days and bitter nights cause the ice to expand and contract, and a huge ice floe covers the boat dock. It seems as if spring will never come.

❦

In some years clear water gleams around the edges in March, in other years not until April. This year a pair of mallards appeared when the lake first opened in mid-April. We would not have seen them had it not been for Folly's keen hunting nose. She had found a deckful of sunshine and was indulging in her favorite activity of sleeping. A reclining basset looks like a well-loved toy animal, with its stuffing lumpily distributed from frequent launderings. She was oblivious to all except the warmth of the sun on her upturned stomach.

She usually gives up sleep grudgingly. But this time she sat up sharply, ear muscles distended, nose quivering with new scents. I followed her eyes but could see nothing through the thicket of young aspen. I walked down to the lake, and there in the open water at the inlet of the south stream were two mallards, a hen and a drake. The male's head shone metallic green, set off by a white neck ring. He turned and his curled tail feathers were silhouetted against the snow on the hillside. Folly's heritage had not failed her. Neither had her intrinsic character; after alerting us, she flowed back to sleep.

The two ducks stayed together, moving and feeding independently, yet never farther than a few feet away from each other. The drake dipped into the lake, his wide white tail stripe showing sharp against the black water. Both were straining plant material out of the mud, and they fed almost continuously. Mallards have long grooved and serrated tongues, especially adapted for sieving food.

The drake lifted himself onto the thin ice and marched along the edge of the lake. He had the dignified purposeful mien of one who knows where he is going. The hen followed at a respectful ten paces. Going back to feed again in the open water, the drake stepped on the thin ice at the very edge. It gave way and he plumped unceremoniously into the water. The hen hesitated, and then popped neatly in with a little flick of her tail.

The two continued feeding for some time. Then the male swam around the female, somewhat disrupting her eating. He turned his head back, toward his wing, but instead of preening, merely touched it. This movement has been described as "displacement preening." It is a signal of courtship, to which the female will respond, a ritual which precedes actual mating. Such prescribed movements are characterized by being simple and conspicuous. Each species has its own system of signals so that there is no confusion which might lead to interbreeding. The female mallard will respond to this particular gesture on the part of the male and no other. In most species the signals are necessarily simple, for their performance renders the individual vulnerable; a complicated ritual would require too long to complete. Therefore the ceremony between the two is not evolved beyond that which is absolutely necessary.

The female continued feeding. By this time Herman had come with his camera, and the *sssssp* of the shutter was sharp in the windless air. With the drake leading, both ducks climbed back onto the ice and walked back along the shoreline, a little more quickly than before but still with dignity. They kept their heads straight forward, looking neither to right nor left. They walked with a certain ponderous poise, yellow bills and brilliant orange-red legs brighter than the awakening red willow twigs beyond them. They were uneasy but not frightened, like children who don't look back when they go up the dark stairs to bed for fear of really seeing the ghost behind them.

Ducks, like most flock birds, are sensitive to the slightest signs and movements of other birds, no matter how low the intensity. When one bird gives the alarm, the whole flight takes off. With the pair on the lake, since one was uneasy, so was the other. They walked a little farther and then launched themselves almost straight up with the soft *wheep wheep* of wings so characteristic of mallards.

We came one day late in July to find the hen on the lake. She didn't fly off as she had in the past. As our eyes adjusted to the shapes and shadows of the lake, we counted six tiny ducklings. They were evenly strung out behind the hen like a child's toy, all progressing at the same rate as if pulled by a string. The ducklings were as dappled as the shadows in which they swam.

The hen's soft coloring blended so exquisitely with the willow bush under which she nested that one afternoon I almost stepped on her. We both jumped with surprise, she with a loud harsh warning "Quack!" to the ducklings. Ordinarily she would have pulled a protective coverlet of down over the nest as she backed away. We avoided the willow for the rest of the summer.

In August there were four ducklings, and by September only two had survived. The adults appeared together once more, the male not totally in full dress from his summer-eclipse plumage. The young ducks were gone, old enough to fly to their own appointments.

❧

Spring comes to the lake before it comes to the land. By mid-April, black water shows around the edges. Folly walks on the thinning ice and her ponderous paws break through. She retreats, somewhat disgruntled and bewildered, finds a patch of dead leaves to roll in, and then sighs down in a heap on a sunny spot on the deck. Her mournful face says that life is too much, and that one ought to be able to walk where one wishes without unscheduled soakings. To her it is nothing but inconvenience that the lake is opening. To us, it is the beginning of spring.

A cold night, and the lake freezes to the edge again. But in the sunlight of the next day, the ice retreats even farther than before. Some years ago Herman built a raft in February and March on top of the ice in the middle of the lake. By mid-May it was floating free, restlessly tugging at anchor with the urgings of the spring flow. The lake is glossy in the spring, heavy, unawakened. The brisk breezes of May facet the surface, making it sparkle. The wind recharges the oxygen-starved winter lake by mixing the water. By June the surface of the lake is animated with fragmented sunshine. A sense of gaiety and light emanates from the surface. New shore growth glistens in the silky sunlight. And the animals of the lake appear, each to his own rhythm.

The spring runoff from the high mountains brings more oxygen of life back into the lake just as surely as sunlight brings new life to the land. I can hear the stream's swift running even over the crackling fire of the wood stove. Melting snows from the higher lands prod the streams awake and make the banks soggy with quickened water flow. Cold, full of oxygen, the streams boil into the lake. When a bottle is filled with water and held upside down, the water spurts out of the narrow neck in chunks, and this is the way the water spurts out of the runoff pipe below the dam, pulsating with the resurgence of spring.

At the edge of the lake the sun warms the water more quickly; and with the new warmth there is such a blooming and greening and burgeoning and popping of egg cases and waving of antennae and fluttering of gills that the water is colored with its intensity. Sitting on the rock by the boat dock in still-wintery March or April, I can see only black water at the edges. The lake looks ebony-empty. By June the surface is verdant with duckweeds and algae, and a glass of lake water is teeming with small creatures that dart back and forth, float up and down, and prowl in and out.

All that the eye can see is movement, for these animals are too small to be seen individually without magnification. With a microscope there appears a whole new world of precisely and exquisitely made creatures. The microscope was the joy of my summer, a gift brought by a husband who understood that some wives like microscopes better than mink. Soon I could tell the different fauna in the peanut-butter jars I used for collecting in the same way in which one recognizes a friend by his walk. Cyclops spurt as if they were doing the butterfly breaststroke. Water fleas slowly sink, then rise up swiftly to sink again. Ostracods zip in frenetic dashes like a woman in a hurry in the supermarket. Hydras hang like raveled threads or upside-down dandelion seeds.

❦

All of the animals of the lake community ultimately depend upon plants for food. The relationship between these organisms is called a "food chain," which is a way of expressing the linked dependence of one organism of the community on another.

A food chain always begins with plants since only plants are able to manufacture their own food out of water, inorganic nutritive materials which are dissolved in water, certain gases from the atmosphere, and sunlight. Through photosynthesis, chlorophyll in plant leaves and stems reacts with carbon dioxide and water. In the presence of sunlight, a basic glucose is formed from which other more complex foods are made: starches, fats, oils, waxes, and proteins. Animals need all of these for growth, for the repair of tissue, and reproduction.

A food chain may contain up to four or five links; it is sel-

dom longer. Herbivores eat the plants and are in turn eaten by
carnivores; the food chain ends with the carnivore, which is
preyed upon by no larger animal. The length of the food chain
is short because of the physical size of the animals involved and
the freshness of the food. Only man can portion his food, or
keep meat or fresh greens any length of time without spoilage.
A dragonfly must not only eat the mosquito smaller than he,
but he must catch it fresh.

To construct a series of food chains for our lake is at once
fascinating and frustrating. Fascinating because I am so over-
whelmingly impressed by the intricate interdependence of crea-
tures so small that they can only be surmised. Frustrating be-
cause the systems are so complex that my mind boggles. I can
only guess at the interwoven possibilities, for these are so many
that the most sophisticated computer could not calculate what
goes on beneath the surface of even this small bright lake.

❧

The simplest plants in our lake are the algae, of which there
are numerous species. The green algae are composed of cells
arranged in filaments which tangle across the water in colonies.
The color is almost pure chlorophyll, a beautiful, distinctive
emerald green, spread out in verdant tangles like a nereid's hair.

Desmids and diatoms are also algae, just visible under the
lens of my dissecting microscope, small geometric shapes cut
from green glass with a truffle cutter. Diatoms are golden yellow
or golden brown because a pigment masks the pure green of the
chlorophyll. They are tiny boxes, one shell fitting neatly over
the other, intricately and delicately patterned according to kind,
a box which would be coveted by a Rhinemaiden.

I think of the ordinary rooted shoreline plants—the cattails,
sedges, and rushes—as the equivalent of giant redwoods to the
microscopic animals that would have to feed on them were
there nothing else. Looking to the woods, the size of the trees
forces one to be aware of their dominance and mass, and the
fact that they provide major food and shelter. The plants in the
lake likewise provide food and protection, but in the larger
scheme of existence, far outweigh land plants in crucial impor-
tance. They are the very basis of life.

❦

The animals which feed in the meadows of algae are almost as small as the plants they eat. This is the wonderful world of the microscopic that I call Jane or Sara to see. They are quiet as they re-focus the microscope for their eyes, and then the soft wondering exclamation rewards my having disturbed their more important tasks.

As small as the algae are the protozoa. Vorticella—tiny clear drops of protoplasm on the end of a filament, minute lollipops of matter—halo the back of a tiny crustacean. Or they jewel the body of a homely insect nymph, adding a glamorous touch to an otherwise meagerly endowed creature. By their anchorage the protozoa benefit from food scraps from their host, and some protection. They are also carried about to farther horizons than they themselves could manage. They are epizoites, free hangers-on, doing no harm to their hosts.

We can more easily see the colonies of protozoa, bright green, probably either *Pleodorina* or *Uroglena,* tiny round drop-lets that turn up in various places, on the raft ladder or around the edges of the lake. Here they cling tenaciously to bits of wood and grass, half-immersed in the silt, colonies clustered together beneath a gelatinous coating which makes them look like in-finitesimal green yarn pompoms encased in glass. Those along the lake edge are spherical; those that cling to the raft ladder are hemispherical with a solid base.

We pull out the raft each year to prevent it from being frozen in the ice and having the floats damaged. Encrusted on the bottom of the steps, which extend four feet into the water, are colonies of plumatella. The colony is held to the raft by a gelatinous secretion, and I have to slip them off carefully with a thin knife. They belong to the phylum Bryozoa, or moss animalcules, so called because they resemble the Bryophyta, or moss plants. They form unattractive brownish-green traceries which belie their crystalline beauty under the microscope. They looked so unpromising, and I was so ignorant, that it was only because I didn't have anything else to do that I put them under the microscope and learned a lesson I should have known about judging books by their covers.

Under the lens they are delicately colored and beautiful of movement. The colony is made up of pale brown transparent protective tubes of varying lengths, growing in bushy clumps. When they have "settled in" on the slide dish, out of the top of each tube appears a fringe of cilia, which move as gently as shreds of chiffon. These are lophophores whose waving motion whirls food particles into the mouth within their circlet. If an itinerant copepod darts by, all the cilia retract immediately, reappearing tentatively, one by one.

Showing through the transparent tubes are tiny brown discs, some tubes containing one, others several. These are statoblasts, winter buds with which the plumatella survive the nongrowing season. The colony will die and release untold numbers of statoblasts, just as an annual releases seeds each fall. The statoblasts look like small brown buttons under the microscope, smaller than a pinhead to the naked eye. In mid-September the cove of the boat dock is peppered with thousands of these minute assurances of continuity.

❧

Plumatella are primary consumers, or herbivores, feeding on the floating algae which come their way. Another primary consumer is the little transparent bristleworm, which eats soft plant tissue. A bristleworm eats like a horse with a feed bag on, seeming to snatch up algae by the mouthful. I watch one, less than one quarter of an inch long, which constructs a floating translucent tube covered with bits of debris and plant stems. Inside the tube the worm over-ends, slips halfway out one end for a quick snack, appears at the other end for a look-see, disappears totally inside to reappear again where least expected. Bristleworms are frequent in the still waters of the lake edge, coming up, house and all, in almost every collecting jar.

❧

I am a lazy collector and it was convenient to have the little cove by the boat dock provide ripe hunting all summer. A weft of algae and duckweeds shaded the shallows enough to keep the sun from damaging the small transparent organisms which are destroyed by strong sunlight. At the same time, the shallow water

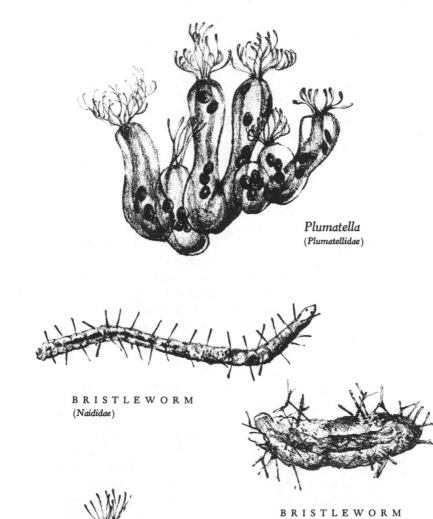

Plumatella
(*Plumatellidae*)

BRISTLEWORM
(*Naididae*)

BRISTLEWORM
(*Dero*)
IN TUBE

SEED SHRIMP
(*Cyprididae*)

Plate 2

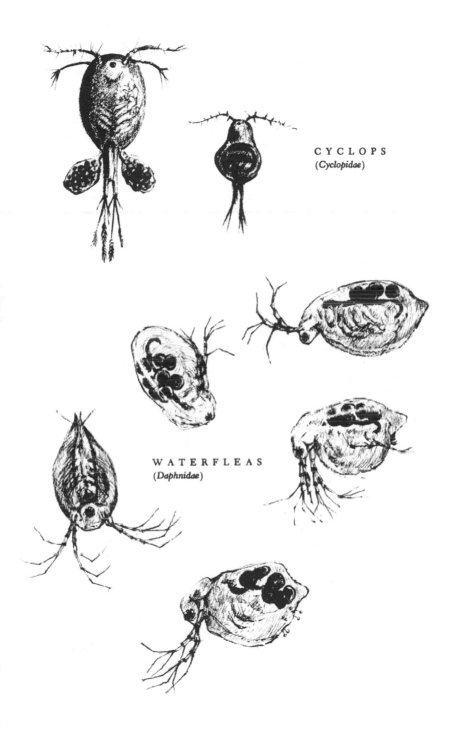

CYCLOPS
(*Cyclopidae*)

WATERFLEAS
(*Daphnidae*)

was warmer than the rest of the lake and the plankton were reproducing at top speed.

Here I found the ostracods, or "seed shrimp." Often, when working at home at night, I use a microscope lamp. Since light quickens the activity of the ostracods, they dart about in the slide dish, their frenetic dashes making them easily identifiable among the slower-moving animals. Since they live mostly near the shore, they were constant presences in any collection. The incessantly moving body is enclosed in two hinged shells, like a tiny multi-legged fat clam. The ones I watch, cross-eyed with concentration, have grayish-green shells, softly mottled with deeper color like tortoise shell. The two shells are held together by a band of elastic tissue on the top which permits the underside to be open.

Another easily recognizable swimmer is the one-eyed cyclops, a copepod. The hind legs make a jerky movement which spurts the cyclops through the water. The trailing antennae aid in equilibrium and depth adjustment. The body is the epitome of streamlined form, wide at the front, tapering to the forked tail. Even if the movements are not familiar, every female cyclops is easily recognized by the two sacs of eggs which she carries like saddle bags. She produces summer eggs which hatch immediately, succeeded by winter eggs which are sturdier and can remain dormant over the cold season. The newly hatched larvae leave the sac in about twelve hours, although some may remain for five days. New sacs are ready as soon as the old are empty. The cyclops is common in Colorado mountain lakes, most prevalent in spring and summer, but gone from our lake by the middle of September.

❧

Gone even later are the water fleas for they also are limited in both distribution and activity by low temperatures. They were omnipresent dancing motes in the jars, pale beige-pink, and I grew quite fond of them, always taking time to watch one through the microscope even when there were more important things to be done. They were named water fleas by a seventeenth-century Dutch naturalist who called them *Pulex aquaticus arborescens*, "water fleas with branching arms."

Their characteristic movement in water is a slow sinking downward, then a swift rise powered by a stroke of antennae. They have been widely studied because of the seasonal variation of head shape. During summer, when the water is warmer and less dense, they increase body surface in proportion to body volume. In this way they need expend less energy maintaining their position in the water. This adjustment to the seasonal density and viscosity of the water is incredibly precise and accurate.

If any animal of the lake, besides Mad Ludwig, has personality, it is a water flea. The single eye, bounded by a scalloped outline, almost seems capable of expression. I watched one baleful female, overloaded with eggs, that even had the injured look of Folly.

The water fleas have short bodies completely covered by a transparent shell, or carapace, open on the underside. This outer shell is delicately lined or patterned according to kind. The prevalent genus in our lake, *Simocephala*, has a shell lined with the finest of parallel ridges which reflect light in an iridescent shimmer. They have ten legs which constantly flutter, culling water from which they strain nutrients and with which they aerate their gills. Watching a water flea is like looking at the inside of a tiny watch. There are two antennae on each side of the head which somehow add to its quizzical expression, as if it had just thrown up its arms in despair. I often identify with its gesture of futility.

Our water fleas belong to a species which prefers the warm shallow weedy waters near shore. They persist all summer, in close packed flickering swarms. Although they are heavily fed on by hydra and fish, attracted by the mass of crustaceans in one place, the swarm itself protects the survival of the species, making it difficult for predators to pick out individual prey. In the water flea's world it is the species, not the individual, that is important.

Soon after their first appearance in the lake, I found a female with the dark dots of eggs caught between her back and shell. These were produced by parthenogenesis, the ability to produce offspring without fertilization. Female water fleas begin to reproduce when the temperature of the lake reaches the forties. The young are mature in eleven days, producing a new batch every four to six days. Needless to say, the reproductive rate is astronomical. A female who lives only a month is a population explosion all by herself.

The summer eggs are thin-shelled, and they produce only females. But when the water cools again, male offspring are produced which fertilize the winter eggs. These have a tougher skin and are capable of wintering over. The production of males is thought to be triggered by a lessening of the food supply, the accumulation of excretory products which are the result of overcrowding, and possibly by certain temperature conditions. When the peanut-butter jar comes up empty of water fleas, summer somehow seems over.

❧

At the beginning of the summer it is the exception rather than the rule to have a jar full of hydras. By August, in a jar taken where the light is bright, they animate every twig, curling and wafting their tentacles in a casual, lazy, deceptively innocent way. But when a tiny water flea swims within the reach of the hydra's tentacles, she is swiftly tucked into the hydra's body in a soundless snap. The tentacles are transparent and threadlike under the microscope, and the hydra throws one over its shoulder with the casual aplomb of a Ziegfeld girl with a full-length ermine.

The other end of the hydra is a "foot" by which it attaches itself to twigs, plant stems, the under-surface of the water film, or the glass of the collecting jar. It can glide sinuously across the glass, or can somersault—attaching first tentacles and then foot to the glass, cartwheeling across. Watching a hydra is better than a circus and not half so noisy.

The body is fawn-colored, lighter or darker depending upon how far it is stretched. The tan body is encased in a transparent coating which also varies in thickness as the hydra elongates or contracts. At the midsection of most hydra in the summertime are nubbins of various widths and lengths; some are tentacled, some mere bulges. These are the young, since a hydra reproduces largely by budding. The voracious offspring feed just as their parents do, swallowing food into a central cavity, casting out the useless parts by the same opening. Hydra winter over

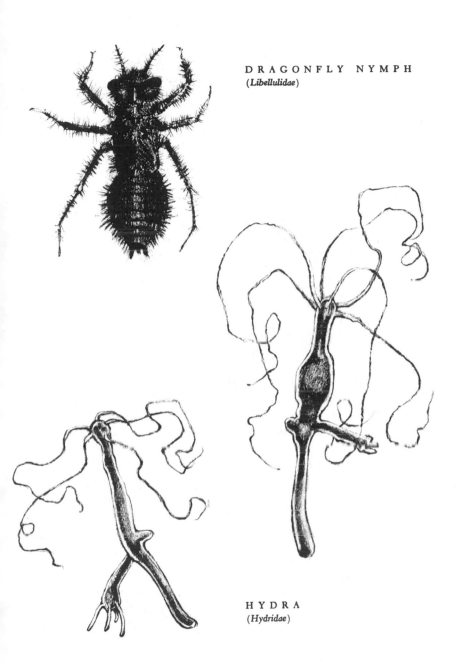

DRAGONFLY NYMPH
(*Libellulidae*)

HYDRA
(*Hydridae*)

Plate 3

by producing fertilized eggs which are impervious to tempera-
ture drop, much as water fleas and plumatella provide for winter.

❧

The monster of the underwater lake community is the dragon-
fly larva, or nymph, who fears not even the stinging tentacles
of the hydra. The first dragonfly nymph of the year came up
in a pan full of silt. The bottom of the lake is very fine clay,
sparkled with mica, a deep black-brown. I had poured a thin
layer of water and silt out into a large flat white dish. While
it settled I went inside to put wood in the stove. When I
came back I bumped the table with the dish on it, and in-
stantly three white lines, about an inch long, appeared in the
silt. Completely camouflaged, the nymphs were the exact color
of the silt. But when disturbed they had jet-propelled themselves,
the stream of water forced out of their anal openings powerful
enough to clear a path in the silt.

In mythology, nymphs were beautiful maidens inhabiting
the woods, mountains, and streams. Dragonfly nymphs do live
in the water, but otherwise the word "nymph" is a complete
misnomer. Entomologically speaking, a nymph is the young of
an insect which has incomplete metamorphosis. A butterfly, with
complete metamorphosis, goes through the stages of caterpillar,
resting pupa, and adult; dragonfly nymphs molt as they grow
larger, changing little, and with the final molt become adults.

The dragonfly nymphs which live in our lake are three-
quarters of an inch long when I find them, heavy, hairy of body,
with none of the sinuous grace of the hydras or the quizzical
one-eyed charm of the water fleas. They have a hesitant gait
across the dish, stopping, seeming to peer about, then snatching
in their prey. The dragonfly nymph epitomizes the melodrama
villain creeping up on the fair maiden. I can almost hear the
sinister laugh.

When the nymph perceives its prey, the victim is focused
at the precise point for capture. At the right distance, a large
clawlike appendage shoots out, grabs the victim, and pulls it
back into the dragonfly's maw. When retracted, the appendage
conceals the nymph's mouth; when needed, it extends and

snatches with devastating speed. The nymph's eyesight is effective only as far as the claw can grasp; when the prey is focused, it can be caught.

Being aquatic, the nymph must be able to take oxygen from the water instead of the air. This is accomplished through gills, areas of tissue richly woven with blood vessels. In a dragonfly nymph the lining of the hind intestine is pleated and fluted into gills and the nymph breathes by circulating water over these gills. When it expels internal water rapidly, the force of the ejecting water is sufficient to propel the body forward.

❧

The largest predator of the lake is the rainbow trout, and it is with them that many of the lake's food chains reach completion. Omnivorous, the trout roam the lake's perimeter, snapping up dragonfly nymphs, mouthfuls of water fleas and mosquito larvae, midges, and algae—an estimated 1000 pounds of wet algae is needed, directly or indirectly, per pound of edible fish.

Unfortunately, the word "trout" calls to many minds a corn-mealed fish sizzling and blackening in the long-handled frying pan over an open, face-blistering campfire, the picture calendar version of the "great outdoors." To us, trout are lively silvered shadows, skulking in the shallows, spurting arcs of liquid silver over the quiet evening lake as they jump at flies. Gray above and silvery white below, they blend into the background whether seen from above or beneath. If we stand quietly at the edge of the lake we can watch them poke around the shallows, their well-proportioned bodies showing that they find ample food. If we move carefully they do not "spook," more intent upon feeding than upon errant shadows.

Our little lake is ideal for rainbow trout. Because of the altitude, the water remains cool throughout the summer. Temperature is the most important single factor in maintaining a trout population. There are enough sun-warmed shallows to produce food, but not enough to warm the water beyond the tolerance limits of the trout. And, most important, there is deep water which remains cold all year. The streams provide aeration under the ice so that we have no winterkill; trout are extremely sensitive to the oxygen level of the lake and will not survive long if the water stagnates.

Their sinuous shapes weave through the summer lake. The density of the water in which they live influences the shape of those who live within it. Fish have paired limbs just as terrestrial animals do, but there is no design for support or upright posture. Because their bodies are slightly heavier than the volume of water which they displace, swim bladders have evolved for buoyancy; without them, fish would simply sink to the bottom.

Swimming near the surface, trout can see through the surface film and jump to snap an unsuspecting fly, real or artificial, out of midair. Fish have good eyesight and are also alert to disturbing shadows crossing the water, or untoward movements. Herman becomes exceedingly irritable when Sara comes gaily and vocally around the lake while he is fishing for trout for dinner, his absent-minded wife having forgotten an essential of the planned meal.

❧

When we first stocked the lake we applied to the Soil Conservation Service for fingerlings, as young trout are called. In June we received a card notifying us that fish would be available at a mountain town many miles away, at seven in the morning. We were advised to bring cans containing cold water ample to keep the fish alive for the return trip.

Herman and Susan, with Walter, a visiting cousin, got up at five thirty. In the bed of an ancient truck we used to have they carried two thirty-two-gallon cans which they filled on the way with stream water and a little ice, enough to cool the water but which would melt by the time the fish were in. City water, with its "purifying agents," could be lethal to fish used to lake water.

Herman arrived, received his two sieve-fuls of fingerlings, and dumped them into the waiting cans. On the trip back, Walter and Susan stirred the water constantly, keeping it aerated so that the fish would survive the trip in cramped quarters. As Susan tells it, there are other things a teenager would rather do than ride in the lurching bed of a pickup truck, elbow-deep in ice water and fish. But I notice that it is the unpleasant challenges which evoke the most relished memories, and she still laughs about who was wetter on arrival, she or the fish.

They arrived at the land, sloshing and splashing, almost awash. Herman backed the truck to the edge of the lake and they dumped in the fish. A few seemed momentarily stunned, but all swam off to a new life.

The humans retired for a change of clothes and a cup of coffee.

✻

One of the favored trout foods is the tiny white wormlike midge larva. The larva has a head that reminds me of a hand-puppet, and it feeds with an alternating open-snap-close gulping movement, gobbling up diatoms and desmids. A larva propels itself through the water by alternately curling up and then snapping the head and tail ends out. If you close and open your hand in rapid succession, at the same time moving it forward in a straight line, you approximate the characteristic movement of the larva. Usually less than a quarter of an inch long, it is immediately recognizable in the collecting jar, curling and flipping its way quickly through the water.

When the larva has fed sufficiently, hormones trigger the change to a resting, or pupal, stage. The pupa is a minute question mark, suspended from the undersurface of the water film. At the top of the question mark are two hornlike projections which break through the elastic surface film. Through these the changing insect inside receives oxygen.

Adult midges usually emerge early in the day, but the warmth of being in the cabin prompted one to metamorphose while I watched, late one afternoon. The pupa began to twitch. A minute two-winged creature struggled out of the pupal case which had split down the back. The black midge crawled across the water surface to the dry edge of the slide dish and rested. I looked outside of the microscope eyepiece and found it required considerable eye adjustment to see it with normal vision. What had clearly been visible under the microscope was now no bigger than a printed o. The black dot took off, probably to

MIDGE
(*Chironomidae*)

MIDGE PUPA

MIDGE LARVA

Plate 4

join the swarm of midges just beginning to form over the silt dam.

❦

While the white wormlike midge larvae are amusing to watch as they propel themselves across the water, the phantom midge larvae are beautiful. These migrate to the surface only at night, remaining deep in the water during the day, protected from the strong rays of the sun, and just by chance I caught one in an early-morning sampling. Transparent, they deserve their common name of "phantom larvae." Scarcely half an inch long, they are crystalline worm-shaped larvae, containing two pairs of air sacs, one pair at each end of the body. The effect is that of bubble-blown crystal. Intense light through their transparent bodies is fatal, so they desert the surface of the water within minutes after sunrise, not to rise again until sunset. The air sacs are thought to be concerned with buoyancy and breathing since the larvae have no outside gills and breathe entirely by absorption through body walls.

While most midge larvae are ceaselessly in motion, phantom larvae lie in wait for their food. Other midge larvae are mainly herbivorous, but phantom larvae eat minute crustaceans and other tiny animals. When a potential meal comes near, they dart at it, catching it with their antennae. Phantom larvae swim much as fish do, the moving curve of the body pressing back against the water to propel the animal forward.

The adults are mosquito-like flies, but they do not bite. By being carnivorous in the larval stage they store enough protein to last through egg-laying. On the other hand, the mosquito, being herbivorous as a larva, must have animal food as an adult to make reproduction possible. This change in feeding habit occurs often in nature: the herbivorous tadpole develops into the carnivorous frog, the insect-eating baby hummingbird matures into a largely nectar-sipping adult. And the pregnant mosquito's appetite engenders the most unpopular song of the woods.

❦

We fish only for what we can eat and to keep the population at its optimum since the trout have few natural predators. Toward the end of the summer the meat is pale salmon pink, an echo of the salmon family to which trout belong.

Herman catches just enough for dinner and cleans them. I put a sprig of fresh tarragon and a chunk of butter into the cavities, drizzle them with lemon juice, wrap each one individually in foil and steam them in the oven. We often have a baked potato, slightly charred from the heat of the wood stove, or perhaps a thick slice of homemade bread with each trout. A green salad with watercress fresh from the stream, a beautiful pale Sancerre or Riesling, raspberries picked that afternoon (if there are any left after Jane and Sara have exercised collector's rights): one of the favorite late-summer meals at Constant Friendship.

None of these animals would be here without the plant population of the lake, the basis of every food chain. The plants also profoundly affect the physical properties of the lake itself, adding oxygen to the water, changing the profile of the lake's basin. All small lakes have in common a predictable progression called succession, the inevitable change in plant population over a period of time. The succession of the lake is toward its demise; the smaller the lake, the quicker its prospective disappearance. If succession is interrupted, it will always begin again and reach the same end.

We are interfering with this succession for the moment. Normally there would be much greater plant growth extending around the edge of the lake, especially in the shallow western perimeter. But Herman has used chemicals to destroy some of the emergent and submergent plant growth, a bone of some contention between us. Numerous plants rotting under the winter ice cover use up all the available oxygen, killing the fish. The plants catch and hold soil, gradually decreasing the lake's size. Therefore, says Herman, if we want trout and a lake, the plants should be controlled.

I like their lush greenness and the habitat they make for the many small animals of the lake upon which, I point out with unassailable logic, the trout depend for food. They provide permanent cover and excellent food both in leaf and seed for larger animals. I pull out the emotional arguments of motherhood (where will the mallard nest and feed?) and conservation (we are upsetting the food chains).

But even after a dosing the lake is teeming with water fleas and midge larvae, and plenty of algae, and the trout are fat and healthy. Since there is always a frog underfoot, and the mallard raised a brood on the treated lake this summer, my logic is deflated. And for a time, at least, the lake water is crystal clear.

But we are merely holding a finger in the dike. For as soon as we stop treating the lake, succession will begin again, logically, inexorably, irrevocably.

❧

The best way to see this succession of plants in our lake is to row out to the middle of the lake and drift to shore. The best time is in early spring, after the plants have begun to sprout but before Herman has added chemicals to the water. The sun is warm and spring fever makes my apparent laziness somewhat excusable. All around, the quickening of the year delights the senses. There is a restlessness in the breeze, which yesterday was chill but today holds warmth. A trout comes to the surface to sun a little, paralleling the boat before flicking his tail and disappearing under the boat's shadow. The air smells green. The aspen grove is solid birdsong.

I put the oars in the boat and it drifts quietly. Leaning over I can see beyond my reflection to the submerged plants of a mysterious forest, undulating in unseen currents to unheard music. I dip an oar in and a plant sticks to it, hanging wet and dripping, leaves stuck together with the glue of surface tension. I separate the leaves and find them dissected and fine, thin and linear. The stems are long and slender. The whole plant is constructed to bring the majority of cells in contact with the water and to be buoyed up by the water's density.

This is chara, a common water plant. I drop it back and it opens gracefully. Last February we pulled one up through a hole cut in the ice. It was shamrock green and fresh and startling against the winter landscape, this verdant feather.

The chara has no cuticle or protective outer shell, which is needed to keep land plants from drying out. Gas exchange takes place over the whole surface of the water plant. Unlike the tree whose roots must absorb nutrients for the entire plant, the aquatic plant absorbs food over its whole surface. No energy is expended in cell differentiation for foliage, root, and stem.

As the boat drifts nearer the shore, it is slowed by the water crowfoot, Herman's nemesis. In spite of chemicals, this relative of the shore buttercup reappears each year. Its seeds have been brought from another lake, undoubtedly on the feet of a water bird. When a duck waddles in the mud, the seeds adhere to its wide flat feet, and are washed off in the next pond along the way. In this manner most water plants achieve their almost universal distribution.

The tiny white flowers of the crowfoot, with a yellow dot on each petal, seem to lie flat against the dark water like stars against a midnight sky. The submerged leaves are finely divided, like those of the chara. They carry on photosynthesis with the light which is filtered through the lake water; most aquatic plants are able to make food at lower light intensities than land plants and are undisturbed by the change in light quality. The roots of water crowfoot gain nourishment from the silt in which they anchor themselves, and have some root hairs, but the development is much less than on land plants.

On some of the plants a wider leaf, more like that of a land plant, floats on top of the water. The stomata, openings regulated by cells which control leaf water outgo and uptake of gases, are on top of the floating leaves. Here they will not become clogged with water. On rose leaves or anemone or other land plants, they are on the bottom of the leaf, protected from water loss.

At the end of the growing season water crowfoot withers and dies, just as the buttercups along the stream do. But buds will have been formed for next year's growth, just as on the aspen. To avoid desiccation, aspen leaf buds are protected by several layers of resinous coats. Submerged buds need no such protection, and so have no bud scales. Nature is nothing if not economical.

🌼

Cattails used to grow near the inflow of the south stream, where the lake is shallow and the bottom mucky. Ludwig, the Mad Muskrat, cut them all down and carried them away several years ago. One of the sights of that summer was a bundle of leaves proceeding across the lake at a steady speed with no obvious means of propulsion. Sometimes the bundle would disappear, only to emerge ten feet further on. Our laughter in no way disturbed this aquatic Frank Lloyd Wright.

The cattails grew tall and stately, a handsome vertical accent to the horizontal composition of the lake. Being slender, they cast little shade. Minerals came through roots in the silt, but photosynthesis went on only in the air leaves. Cattails are emergent plants, having the best of both worlds. They are department stores for all kinds of creatures, providing construction materials for the muskrat's house, reducing wave and wind action for the red-winged blackbirds who nested among their stems, and supplying air spaces inside the stem for a variety of insects. The stems below the water line provide anchorage for snails and tiny water beetles, hydra, egg masses, and the infinite number of microscopic creatures.

Cattails are useful to humans too. Indians used them for food all year long. The young shoots are reported to be excellent in salads, fresh or boiled. Pancakes made with cattail pollen are famous, according to H. D. Harrington in his delightful book *Edible Native Plants of the Rocky Mountains*. The roots, when peeled of the brown outer coating, are starchy and pleasant to eat, either cooked or raw. Cattails are all things to all creatures.

Since the cattails have disappeared from our shoreline, the red-winged blackbirds have gone too, and we miss them. As the plant population has changed, so too has the animal population. Now cattails grow only along the north stream, almost hidden and overshadowed by the taller shrubs and small trees.

🌼

To reach shore the boat drifts through a windrow of duckweeds. Scarcely bigger than a grain of rice, each plant is completely free-floating. They cluster in sheltered coves around the shore, swept in by the wind, and are quite as much a part of the littoral vegetation as the bulrushes and sedges. Such tiny plants have a high ratio of surface to volume to achieve maximum exposure to light. They are tiny round thin discs, paving the water with chlorophyll.

Duckweeds have neither definite stems nor leaves. Instead there is a green plant-body which resembles a small round leaf, marked with one to five simple veins. Duckweeds commonly reproduce by budding. Each green circlet produces a "daughter" from a pocket in the side; a second is produced from the other side when the first is fully grown. Budding continues until five or so have been launched, the last smaller than the first. What intrigues me is that the fourth and fifth "daughters" produce offspring of normal size. By some means, not yet understood, this tiny plant reverses the effects of physiological aging and manages rejuvenation without seed production.

By shading the water beneath, duckweeds make it possible for plants and animals to exist there which cannot endure direct sunlight. Consequently this tiny bay is one of the most opulently populated regions of the lake. Hidden beneath are the young of many land insects. Hydra suspend themselves from the thread-like roots of the duckweed, waiting for dinner to waft by. A quivering path marks the foray of a small trout who darts into the thicket and then out again.

❦

When the boat nudges the shore, pushing back the thick sedges, the land intrudes on my consciousness. The wet soil at the lake edge is cold and inhospitable to most other plants. These sedges are sun-loving plants which look like grasses. But a broken stem shows the difference: grasses are hollow and round in cross section; sedges are solid and triangular, sometimes sharply so. There are three rows of leaves on a stem, instead of the two on a grass stem. Like the cattails and other plants with narrow, grasslike leaves, sedges tend to have their leaves erect. In this way the leaves are evenly lighted on both sides and contain chlorophyll bodies throughout, not just on the upper surface, as with horizontal leaves. Reflections from the water intensify the available

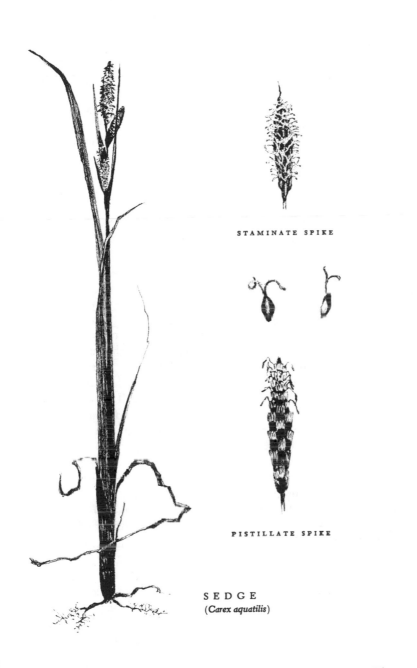

STAMINATE SPIKE

PISTILLATE SPIKE

SEDGE
(*Carex aquatilis*)

Plate 5

light so that food manufacturing goes on even without a large leaf surface.

Sedges are not affected by Herman's chemicals, which destroy the submerged plants. They remain in thick ranks, effectively holding the shore against washing. We have attempted, by deliberately deleting water plants from the lake, to interrupt the inexorable succession of the lake into land. But even as the water crowfoot defies control, so succession proceeds, with or without interference. When we are no longer petty protagonists, succession will peacefully continue. But as long as there are green and growing plants along the shoreline, the lake is fringed with doom.

The succession of our lake is developing as surely as water flows downhill; it cannot flow uphill or change the process without interference of artificial forces. As the sedges and rushes die along the edge and fall, entangled in their own stems, they mesh, holding washed-in soil and dust. Timothy and blue grasses, which could not tolerate the cold wet soil of the sedges, now push farther toward the lake. As soil formation proceeds, first emergent and then submergent plants are pushed farther toward the center. Bit by bit, water volume decreases. The water table drops. More plants have air leaves, instead of underwater leaves, and give off more water through their transpiration. The lake begins to shrink even faster. Finally plants reach from shore to shore.

And with the shift from lake to land goes the shift from trout to weasel, muskrat to porcupine, dragonfly to bumblebee, and duck to jay. Only a thick layer of peat will tell that once there was a lake here, and perhaps something more of what grew here. But it will not tell of laughter in the sunshine.

❧

But while there is still a lake, we enjoy the lake animals. Near the south shore a series of V-shaped ripples, going against the wind, stream across the lake. At the apex is a bundle of reeds propelled by an invisible motor. Mad Ludwig is castle building again.

There aren't many places around the lake he hasn't tried. One year he tunneled under a well-used path around the lake.

After each rainstorm the roof caved in, but he patiently re-excavated for the remainder of the summer with a persistence born not of intelligence but instinct. He is one of the first ones out in the spring since he more than likely has been active most of the winter. Inclement weather disturbs him not at all.

The muskrat's presence, like the trout's, indicates certain environmental conditions. He enjoys cattails, bur reed, and bulrushes when they are succulent and green, and digs for roots and submerged tubers in the winter. He is a fine swimmer, using his naked scaly tail as a rudder. He uses his forepaws as hands as well as feet, as a raccoon does. The hindfeet are partially webbed paddles, so that he swims somewhat like a duck. He weighs only a couple of pounds dripping wet, which is what he usually is. Without water, he would long since have migrated elsewhere.

He burrows into the sides of the banks or into the dam, leaving his entrance hidden underwater for safety. We have to watch him swim to the doorway in order to find it, and although we often think there are young inside, we have yet to see them. Despite the fact that muskrats are largely nocturnal in habit, Ludwig moonlights in the daytime, and the furrow of his path across the lake is one of the familiar sights of our summers.

❦

Summer seems really on its way when the first leopard frog explodes underfoot in a green arc of surprise. The leopard frog is the only frog able to withstand the temperatures of the Montane Zone. It has an optimum temperature range lower than that of other frogs, allowing survival and reproduction at high altitude. Lowland frogs are able to reproduce from February to April; our mountain frog reproduces only in June. Tadpoles grow to adulthood within the year in the lowlands, and need up to three years in the mountains. The shorter duration of vegetation and insect life, the modification of light and temperature, combine to slow down the life cycle. Since periodical activities are slowed three or four days for each higher degree of latitude, this amounts to about a thirty-day delay at our altitude.

Late in May I found a string of eggs near the shore. Each

egg was a quarter of an inch in diameter; they were strung together in a sticky necklace. Inside, the black dots had already begun to imitate tadpoles, but must have been several weeks from hatching. Later in the summer the free-swimming tadpoles are so camouflaged against the black-brown silt bottom that it is only by chance movement that the eye can discern them.

The tadpoles are primarily herbivorous, feeding on green algae, diatoms, and desmids, and decaying plants and detritus. Their long coiled intestine is typical of plant eaters. The adult, sitting on his haunches among the sedges, is carnivorous. Like other meat eaters, he has a short, compact intestine, since there need be no provision for the difficult digestion of plant cellulose. He snaps and gulps flies, mosquitoes, beetles, caterpillars, worms, snails, and small crustaceans. He is largely a day hunter with a quick tongue keyed to a keen eye. A third eyelid, which is transparent, sweeps across each eye from the inside corner outward and cleans the surface so that a frog does not have to close his eyes to blink and perhaps miss a meal.

The older frogs, which grow to be about three inches, are wary. But the young ones sit under an inch of water and feel themselves secure, ostrich fashion. They are handsomely patterned. Their prominent dark spots, rimmed with white, overlay the bright olive green of the back. In the brilliance of the summer day and the clear water they gleam as if enameled. They are summer incarnate.

❦

Every summer afternoon at about five o'clock a sharp cold breeze through the aspen grove announces the end of the day. The last frog slips into the sedges; the water striders disappear for the night. After that, quiet.

Trout come to the surface to feed, as they did in the morning. Swifts winnow the air, catching mosquitoes on the wing. The lake mimics the darkening sky until they are both the same color, separated only by the darker line of the dam. A night hawk dives, unseen, cupping his wings just as he reaches the earth. The soft hollow sound echoes across the evening. The darkness becomes total.

Stars and planets, seemingly more plentiful with no competition from city lights, sparkle in the clear high-altitude atmosphere. They appear in pairs, one in the sky and one in the lake. Cassiopeia wheels up over the eastern horizon. Another world glimmers coldly down upon this one. Something splashes in the lake with a delicate neat liquid sound. Looking upward, I wonder if any of those other worlds can possibly match this one.

3 ❧ ❧ The Streams

There are two sounds that will forever remind me of Constant Friendship. One is the intermittent rhythm of wind through the pines and aspen, sometimes sibilant, sometimes sonorous. The other sound is the persistent perpetual purling of the streams. Even in the depths of winter, under a foot of snow, I can hear the quiet murmuring. The wind may or may not blow, the sun may or may not shine, but the streams speak as long as there is water.

Some years the streams thin to a trickle in August and September. Some springs their waters scour the banks with the impetus of melting mountain snows. But always the water goes down: down to the lake, down to far meadows, down to other streams and rivers, down to the sea, a continuum against which birdsong is lute and wind is recorder.

Each of the streams has its own personality. The south stream is clear and bright, flowing purposefully to the lake. The north stream is devious and often hidden, seeming to flow along because it has nothing better to do. The runoff stream below the dam is usually full and chortling, larking through protected grassy banks to the lower limits of the land.

❧

I often walk the length of the south stream as it crosses our land, a pleasant walk in woods stocked with wildflowers. The stream enters the land just a few feet from the southwest corner and runs diagonally across the aspen grove to the lake, dropping about thirty feet on the way. It is a swift clean-flowing stream, wetting the soil along the edges of its banks, but never stagnating. Its banks are grassed to the edge and high enough above the stream to be stable on one side or the other. The stream's flow, except in the desperate days of drought, is continuous and consistent. But even when the weather is dry, the bottom flickers with running water.

Most of the time the chatter of the stream describes the obstacles it must pass on its way from above to below. The current makes riffles, twinkling around boulders and trapped logs. Its sounds tell of a different world for plants and animals than the stiller waters of the lake. The south stream is cooler than the lake because it is continuously flowing, preventing the accumulation of heat soaked up from the sun. The lake is open to the sun; the stream is shaded for almost its entire length. Its current mixes the water, maintaining a constant temperature throughout. When I plant watercress in the stream each spring, my hands get cold so fast that I can only do a few sprigs at a time and eventually resort to using an iced-tea spoon to keep my hands from numbing.

The lake is dependent upon the spring freshets to recharge its water with oxygen. The stream is permanent, whereas the lake is temporary. As long as there is water, the stream will run downhill, for it was there before the lake and it will be there after.

❧

I could walk down the middle of the stream, were I so courageous, and never step on a plant other than the watercress I have planted. The south stream has few of the aquatic plants which form the basis of the lake's food chains. No skeins of algae thread its surface. No water striders hyphenate the stream from bank to bank. A jar of water from it looks empty and absolutely clear. I set it beside a jar of lake water which is slightly cloudy and pale brown and animated with all kinds of movement. The stream water looks sterile. It contains none of the miniature shamrock clusters of duckweed, no bobbing water fleas or darting ostracods. The current of the stream is too swift for the plankton of the lake.

But the occupants are there. Every mossy stick I pick up is well attended. Stonefly larvae and snails lurk inside the moss's protection. Clinging tightly to stones are flat planarian worms and tan-pink leeches. From every rock crevice tiny antennae sample the stream, well anchored against springtime rushes which can clean out the banks. If I hold a fine mesh screen from bank to bank downstream and Jane does some vigorous gravel-stirring and rock-turning upstream, an amazing number of surprised and undone inhabitants are snared, bucketing down into the screen.

🌼

One day in February, when it was much too cold to work out-doors, I brought indoors a plastic bag full of moss from the streamside. On the side of the bag, imprisoned in a tiny drop of water, no more than an eighth of an inch across, was a stone-fly nymph. It was pushing and poking at the edges of the drop in an irritable way, imprisoned by the surface tension. A larger nymph appeared in the moss itself. The nymphs are almost impossible to find unless they venture out on their own, for they are the same dark brown as the dead sticks and debris in the stream, and can slither into hiding in a second. They are active even in winter when the temperature is zero and the stream is running ice water, and any sensible creature should be hibernating or sitting feet up in front of a warm Franklin stove.

Stonefly larvae are never found in stagnant or polluted waters with a low oxygen content, or where the water is still. Since swift current provides good aeration, the nymphs seek shelter along the bank or flatten themselves out on rocks, clinging by the double claws on each foot. In this bottom sixteenth inch of the stream the current is perceptibly less. The nymphs

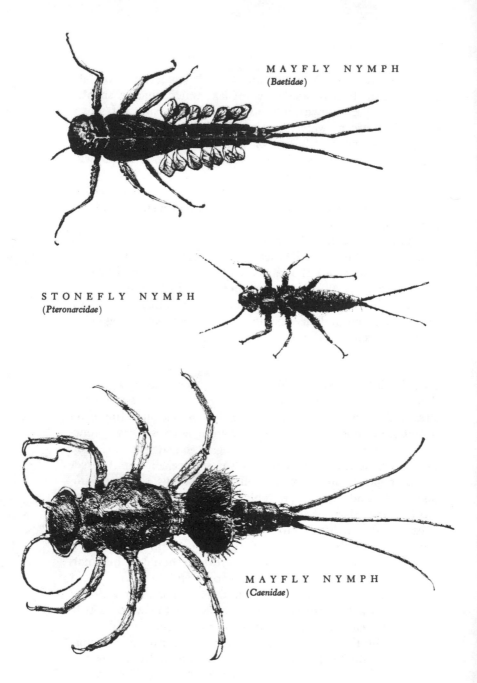

MAYFLY NYMPH
(*Baetidae*)

STONEFLY NYMPH
(*Pteronarcidae*)

MAYFLY NYMPH
(*Caenidae*)

Plate 6

feed mainly on the detritus swept along the stream bottom or caught in the moss and liverworts of the stream border; as they grow larger, they also eat other smaller nymphs.

Another wriggling body likely to turn up in my collecting bag is that of a mayfly nymph, easily recognized by the seven pairs of gills extending from the abdomen and looking like fourteen small paddles. A long period of feeding and growth is necessary to store enough energy for molting and reproduction, since mayflies do not feed as adults and they may remain nymphs for several years.

The mayfly's three long cerci—tail-like projections that stream out behind like a train—act as balancers. (Stonefly larvae have two.) Mayfly larvae swim little, however, preferring to lurk in the dark corners of the stream bed. They survive because of their agility and high reproductive rate, for they are sought out for supper by the larger nymphs of the stream. Mayfly larvae themselves are primary consumers, living on tiny particles of vegetation.

Nymphs of another mayfly species live in the silt, burrowing to eat the riches of the diatom ooze. They have only a few single abdominal gills; the remainder are reduced in number and are tucked under a protecting flap on the back. The last pair of gills is transformed into a peplum-like cover which protects the functioning gills; a fringe of hairs on the cover interlocks to sift out the silt and prevent gill damage.

Mayflies are the only insects to molt again after reaching adult form. They live only long enough to mate and for the female to lay eggs. Ephemeroptera, the order of mayflies, is derived from the Greek *ephemeros,* meaning lasting but a day and from which our word "ephemeral" comes. The females swarm in lacy clouds, always against the light where they can be easily seen by the males. After mating, the female quickly lays her fertilized eggs near or in the water where the young will be properly housed and fed. Then she flies toward the lights, to which she never was attracted as a photo-negative nymph. We find dozens dead on the ground around the night lanterns, their short lives ended in a swift singe of wings.

Lake life fills the collecting jars; stream life has to be looked for. I find that I have to examine a stream rock for some time before my eye can discover a planarian worm. Its flat ribbon-like body adheres so closely to the rock that only a glint of water shows movement. The current flows over and around it as if it were indeed part of the rock.

A planarian in the slide dish is an animated ribbon, folding back on itself, winding and unwinding, spiraling through the water. Thousands of cilia, or tiny hairs, pulsing in succession, give planarians their flowing gliding movement which would be the envy of any water ballet team. Two slight points, called auricles, differentiate head from tail and give direction to the planarian's gyrations. To feed, it swings out a pharynx tube from its underside through which it sucks up films of algae. Planarians are also carnivorous, and a good way to catch them is to dangle a piece of fresh liver in the water.

Planarians reproduce by simple division and through eggs. Cut a planarian in half in either direction, and each portion grows what it lacks. Even more intriguing, some researchers suggest that the new side takes advantage of the "intelligence" of the older side and learns more quickly than a totally new all-of-one-piece planarian.

Leeches, in spite of their bad reputation, are quite delicate and as sinuously beautiful as the planarians. A pale pink-beige, they are segmented and the segments are further creased with deep wrinkles. They can expand like an accordion, stretching until their bodies are almost translucent. They can make themselves flat and are able to paste their bodies to stones or to slither into a crevice. Our leeches, although bloodsuckers, are not especially fond of humans and feed on the smaller animals of the stream.

When they feed, they insert the same kind of noncoagulating substance into the wound that a mosquito does. It is said that if one waits until a leech finishes feeding there will be no itching from the bite. I have found no one who can verify this and have chosen not to experiment myself.

❧

PLANARIAN WORM
(*Planariidae*)

LEECHES
(*Glossiphoniidae*)

Plate 7

When we first came to Constant Friendship, Herman built a small log dam, about a foot high, across this stream, the beginning of all our building projects. He wedged a runoff pipe into the dam so that water dropped about a foot and a half. Children can find as many excuses to avoid washing hands in the wilderness as at home, and we intended that lack of "running water" would not be one of them. The pipe also made it possible to fill a cooking pot without dipping stream water by the cupful, and I am all in favor of these civilized conveniences.

Ostensibly, practicality was the reason for the dam. But having observed many friends over the years, I suspect that there is something of the water-child in us all. Actually, it is impossible to dam the stream. The water escapes through tree roots and rocks and flows almost as quickly around the dam as under it and through the runoff pipe. But making a dam is mudpie-making raised to respectability and I enjoy watching the utter contentment with which our guests go about patting and chocking the dam's crevices. It happily fulfills both the childhood enjoyment of squishing mud between the toes and the adult's interest in a more efficient way of life.

The small dam still exists, even though we are now so civilized as to have an indoor pump. The runoff pipe spurts water in an icy silver plait, splashing on a cement splashboard beneath in a constant melodious pattern. It freezes into a huge icicle in December, not to run again until April or May. By summer the ideal place to cool a bottle of wine is under the pipe's cold spray. At the edge of the splashboard is the best place to plant our watercress. Sprigs of a native plant, water springbeauty, sway in the current, firmly anchored to the bank. Liverworts have begun to grow on the cement steps, covering the sharp angles of man's invasion. A scrap of wood is flowered with scarlet elf caps, tiny vivid red-orange fungi not much bigger than ground pepper grains. Snail eggs glisten and gleam on the rocks and the board. Cases of caddisfly larvae, made out of the small stones of the streambed, give themselves away by facing precisely upstream.

❧

CADDISFLY CASE
(*Limnephilidae*)

CADDISFLY CASE AND LARVA
(*Hydroptilidae*)

TADPOLE SNAIL
(*Physidae*)

WHEEL SNAIL
(*Planorbiidae*)

SNAIL EGGS

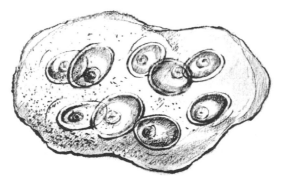

Plate 8

I can seldom persuade the caddisfly larvae in the collecting dish to leave their tubes. They cling tenaciously to the bottom of the tube with two drag hooks which are really modified feet. They poke their heads and front legs out to snatch food from the current. The cases are impeccably constructed from whatever material happens to be at hand. Each species adheres to a different architectural style, some square, some round, some rococo, some Renaissance. The current coming off the splashboard is swift and keeps the bottom clear of silt, exposing tiny chips of granite, and from these this particular caddisfly makes its case, cementing it with saliva. Each sliver of stone is as neatly joined as if laid by a skilled stonemason, and no one case is larger than the single joint of my little finger.

There is another caddisfly larva that occupies the quiet corners of the lake, and it builds its tubes out of tiny snail and mussel shells, sometimes with the occupants still inside. These are anchored to dead sticks, and when I first found one and was absolutely delighted with the discovery, Jane informed me that she had known about them for years and proceeded to bring me dozens to draw. They are like miniature Victorian treasure boxes, pavéed with shells. A third larva makes little quarter-inch packets which are attached by the hundreds to the steps of the raft and the raft chain, each one holding a tiny green bulbous larva.

Caddisfly adults are small winged creatures that often rest on branches near the stream, fluttering in my face when I go to pick the watercress. They have long antennae pointing forward, giving them a rather inquisitive look. They are soft netted grays and browns, blending into the shadows of the stream, modest and insignificant in the scheme of things perhaps, distinguished only by their offspring's masonry.

❦

Two species of water snails scrape the splashboard, frequently slipping across the cool green or brown of the wine bottles. The damp air and green bloom of algae on the splashboard make it ideal hunting ground.

A tadpole snail is a left-handed snail; that is, when you hold the opening toward you, it appears on the left side of the shell. The lower coil is very large, the upper coils very small, ending in a short sharp spire. Two tentacles, characteristic of water snails, sample the water world. Strong transverse muscles in the foot, working in succession, propel a snail at a snail's pace, which, on a good day, may be as much as a foot an hour. This is about the same rate that Jane or Sara produces when it is either's turn to set the table. Tadpole snails are the first to disappear in the fall, burrowing into the safe silt of the stream or lake edge to hibernate.

Wheel snails do not disappear until ice covers the pond, and are the first to appear in the spring. Some are no bigger than a capital o and others reach the size of a dime.

All snails feed by rasping algae from stones or leaves. On the floor of a snail's mouth is a ribbon-like tongue with a row of teeth which file off the soft surface of the plants. A snail's mouth is as tiny as a pinprick, but there are over twenty-five thousand teeth, patterned distinctively according to species.

🌿

The pool formed behind the little dam is the only quiet place of the south stream. Herman calls it a silt-collecting pool since it helps to keep silt from being carried into the lake. Against the background of the dark-brown velvet bottom, cabochons of light make kaleidoscopic patterns, reflections of the dimples made in the water surface film by the feet of the water striders. The striders drift quietly on the surface until I drop a pebble into the water, and then they rearrange themselves in a swift skittering quadrille. Dark brown on top, silvery white beneath, a strider is difficult to see from a trout's angle of view or a human's, but the reflections give it away.

The striders remain on the surface film because of the water's surface tension and their own body adaptations. Water molecules are attracted equally to each other throughout the water, but where water meets air, the attraction of air molecules and water molecules is not as strong. Water molecules cling to each other more tightly, forming an elastic surface film of such strength that snails can glide on its underside, hydras can hang from it, springtails can jump from it, and water striders can traverse it, holding their forelegs up off the water in mincing

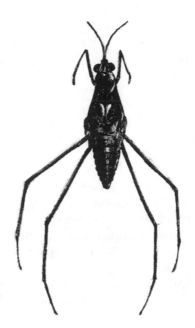

WATER STRIDER
(*Gerridae*)

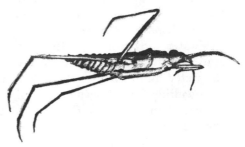

Plate 9

fashion as if they preferred not to wet them. In addition, the strider has a waxy coating which repels water and helps to keep it dry.

The strider has tactile hairs on its legs, helping the insect to maintain its proper position in the water and to perceive other movements on the surface film. These hairs are set into sockets well supplied with nerve endings. Minute vibrations set up by an insect falling on the water film send the striders over to investigate; my pebble, which makes waves, sends them all to the shore for shelter.

Striders are still active late in the fall, maneuvering among the yellow aspen leaves that clot the surface of the pool. When other insects are silenced and gone, I can still watch their kinetic patterns. They are still skating when the leaves have become water-soaked and tannic brown and have drifted to the bottom. When the pool freezes, the striders hibernate in the dead grasses around the edge, popping out as soon as there is free water, spurting here and there like tiny toy boats containing pieces of camphor.

I seldom go by the pool or the lake edge without stopping to watch the striders' gyrations. Once I saw one, thinking itself unseen behind the sedges, cleaning itself like a cat, shifting weight from one leg to another, cleaning each upraised leg in turn with thoroughness and care.

❧

A pan full of silt from the little pool is generally full of the red threads of chironomid larvae, commonly called bloodworms. They are also plentiful in the silt of the lake. They move with the same open-close-snap progression as the other midge larvae of the lake, looping into alphas and omegas across the collecting dish. They are brilliant red from the haemoglobin in their blood which enables them to extract oxygen from the silt where the oxygen supply is meager. The whole body works like a gill. The haemoglobin is distributed just under the thin permeable cuticle, making the little worms look like a snip of coiling and uncoiling red thread.

The adults spend most of the summer dancing over this same pool. They flicker like a cloud of pepper sneezed into the late summer afternoon warmth. Even the eddies of air around the trees and the convection currents coming down the slope are sufficient to bring them to wing.

The swarms are predominantly male, a huge stag party which attracts the females. One of the problems of creatures so small is that in the vastness of the air it is difficult to find a mate, especially one of the same species. The swarms are more easily seen and the chances of a female's finding a mate are greatly abetted. Midges emerge from the pupal state in the morning, swarm and mate by evening, and die within a day or two. The female lives only long enough to lay her eggs—she lays the largest number of eggs of any of the aquatic flies, thus making up for the tremendous mortality rate of the larvae and the adults.

❧

The swarming midges attract the dragonflies. These hawks of the insect world regularly patrol the lake shore, but one afternoon I watched a particularly adventurous one define its hunting ground over the silt pool, darting after any would-be dragonfly intruder with a clatter of wings. The dragonfly cuts through the midges like a scythe, using his basket legs to scoop them up, eating his own weight every half hour in mosquitoes, midges, and assorted other small flying insects. The hole in the swarm closes after the marauder passes through and the midges continue in their slow rising and falling. The swarm protects the species, but it also attracts the predator.

The dragonfly's abdomen flashes brilliant blue cloisonné in the afternoon sunlight, almost as if he had just come alive from a jeweler's display. The blue color comes not from pigmentation but the scattering of light from particles just under the surface of the cuticle. Beneath these particles is a dark background. As the light strikes, the particles reflect back a blue more brilliant than pigmented colors can achieve.

Strong pliant wings propel the dragonfly forward and backward, or hold him hovering in space. One who puts on a burst of speed can outrun Jane or Sara chasing it with a butterfly net. The dragonfly's maneuverability is phenomenal; the panting human cannot match either its ability to corner or reverse field. It darts out over the water to its pursuer's cries of "No fair!!"

This energetic activity on the part of all three participants had been engendered by my offer of a quarter to the first one to bring in a dragonfly specimen for me to draw. I had long since given in to being outrun.

The eyesight of a dragonfly is astonishing, unmatched by that of any other insect in the myopic six-legged world. This remarkable creature can see twelve to fifteen feet; and the eyes, which are so large that they meet on top of the head, contain as many as 28,000 facets, each one six-sided. With no means of focusing, each separate facet presents a slightly different angle to the view. In addition, a dragonfly has a ball-and-socket-type joint between head and thorax, allowing great rotation of the head so that it can see in several directions at once—the proverbial attribute of schoolteachers.

I often sit on the flat rock by the boat dock to watch the children swimming and still be near the stove. A wood stove needs lots of tender attention; maintaining even heat in the oven requires constant surveillance. While sitting on the rock, I am always very aware of the dragonflies, for they are not shy if I sit still, and they sweep close by, coming back to hover and investigate this strange rock that moves.

Their activities pace the summer. At the end of June they first appear, clinging to grass stems, wings shiny and wrinkled, newly varnished, freshly hatched. They hover hesitantly on new wings while the wings harden, tails slightly raised like miniature helicopters.

By July there are always several pairs mating. The male, flying in front, clasps the head of the female with two claws at the end of his abdomen. Thus held, she curls the tip end of her abdomen under and up to a pocket near the middle of the male's body. There she retrieves a spermatophore, a packet of sperm which provides intact transferral and avoids desiccation of individual sperm. One male, weary with the weight of the female, clings to a branch of the willow growing out of the rock. Several times she attempts to reach the abdominal pocket before they finally separate.

The pair are completely vulnerable; I could easily have reached out and caught them in my hand. Many a frog has made a healthy meal from an absorbed pair. Egg laying is also

SEEDS

FRAGRANT BEDSTRAW
(*Galium triflorum*)

WATER SPRINGBEAUTY
(*Montia chamissoi*)

Plate 10

hazardous. From this same rock I watched a female laying eggs in the shallows. Each time she dipped the tip of her abdomen into the water, an egg dropped. A small trout angled by, saw the movement, and snapped her up for lunch.

🌑

Many of the flowers that we have in common with Eastern woodlands are likely to grow along the south stream. Water makes the difference, mitigating the short dry growing season. Many of these plants are less typical of a montane environment, which tends to demand the extreme in tolerance from most plants.

Water springbeauty is a constant presence. It grows throughout the stream, sprigs of green raised above the water or sometimes totally submerged. The long white roots absorb minerals from the soil of the banks and help to hold the stream bank steady against the current. The flowers are tiny pale stars, almost unseen. I looked at this plant for years, wondering what it was, and not until last summer did I find a bloom and finally identify it.

Two mustards also prefer the wetness of the streamside. Brookcress is characteristic of cold running streams and grows at the very edge where the sunlight brightens the water. Its roots sometimes extend into the water in a wide white thatching. About ten inches tall, it has bright dark leaves, shiny and ivy-shaped, which set off the four-petaled white flowers.

The Latin name of the mustards is *Cruciferae*, describing the cross made by the four white petals. Some mustards are hardy weeds in many areas, spreading feverishly over the countryside. Brookcress is just the opposite: orderly, neat in growth, its white flowers gleam bright against the darks of the stream's shadows. To me it symbolizes a mountain stream's clarity and crispness.

Our other stream mustard is edible watercress, which I buy at the grocer's each spring, root at home, bring up and plant. So far none has wintered over, probably because the stream beneath the runoff pipe eventually closes with heavy snow. Fine white roots anchor the thick-ribbed buoyant hollow stems. In the chill temperatures of the stream water the watercress mul-

SWEET CICELY
(*Osmorhiza depauperata*)
IN FRUIT

SEEDS

Plate 11

tiplies. By the end of summer it is in such profusion that every salad has a crisp peppery bunch in it and I can indulge in my favorite lunch of watercress sandwiches. The characteristic bite of the leaf comes from an oil which permeates the whole plant.

At the edge of the stream's bank, plant roots are constantly dampened by stream water and their leaves freshened by stream atmosphere. Sweet-smelling bedstraw, which looks very much like my garden woodruff, grows overhanging the bank. Whorls of simple leaves surround the square stem. The flowers are tiny and pale green, a part of the cool shadows, giving way to tiny seeds haloed with minute hooks.

Sweet cicely grows taller, but its flowers are so pale and insignificant that I usually forget to look for them. By the time I remember to notice the plant the long barbed seed pods are hanging, continually catching on my sweater. This is a green world with a way of its own, thin-leafed and flickering, a place where one might fall asleep with enchanted eyelids.

❧

Marsh marigolds are in bud in late April, when the streamside is still black with water-soaked leaves glued to the bank. Bright green heart-shaped leaves coming right up through the snowbank, this plant is able to flower even when the temperature is below zero at night. The flowers, although smaller, resemble the early blooming Pasque flowers of the meadow. lavender-tinged on the outside, white inside, with a bright gold ring of stamens. Like the brookcress, they epitomize this stream to me.

Instead of being richly furred to retain heat, as the Pasque flowers are, marsh marigolds are waxy and thick-petaled. In spite of the name, both Pasque flowers and marsh marigolds belong to the buttercup family. *Ranunculus*, the Latin name of the genus, means "little frog" and refers to the penchant of many members of the family for damp places and wet feet. The buttercup family contains many irregular and incomplete flowers: delphinium, monkshood, anemone, columbine. In marsh marigolds, Pasque flowers, and anemones, the sepals (the tiny green leaves which form immediately beneath the petals of other flowers) are colored like, and take the place of, petals.

HOMELY BUTTERCUP
(Ranunculus inamoenus)

MARSH MARIGOLD
(Caltha leptosepala)

SAGEBRUSH BUTTERCUP
(Ranunculus glaberrimus)

Plate 12

FRUIT

LARGE-LEAVED, OR
BUR, AVENS
(*Geum macrophyllum*)

ACHENES

SHORE BUTTERCUP
(*Ranunculus cymbalaria*)

The first yellow buttercups are sagebrush buttercups, low-growing, tucked away in the corners of the streamside, and it was some years before I discovered them. Like the marsh marigolds, they seem more brilliant by blooming against a background of unredeemed brown. The first leaves are heart-shaped but succeeding stem leaves are divided into linear lobes. The yellow blossom is the familiar shiny, waxy, five-petaled cup, framed by five green sepals and buttoned with a green center—a sprig of molten sunshine. Another buttercup with small heart-shaped leaves, shore buttercup, creeps in the dampness of the path to the boat dock, sending out runners to conquer new worlds.

Tall yellow avens, looking much like buttercups, bloom by the streamside, too, almost waist high. These large-leaved avens bear thimble-sized seedheads made up of achenes, tiny dry one-seeded fruits. Each one is hooked like a crochet needle. They snag in my clothing with such tenacity that they often don't wash out in the laundry. Behind the avens, from where I sit to draw, is a screen of Canadian reed-grass, growing at the very edge and into the stream. As tall as my head, their stems form a screen of green lines that unite the foreground flower patterns into a glowing Matisse.

❦

At the south edge of the little dam grows a large clump of chiming bells, or mertensia. Like a well-loved child, chiming bells has many other names: Virginia bluebells, cowslip, languid lady, lungwort. Pendent clusters of blue corollas quiver in the air currents rising from the stream. In our plants the buds are pink, suffusing to cobalt blue in full bloom. The stamens hang outside the corolla as the flower matures, like the clappers of small bells.

The mertensia's leaves are heart-shaped and thin. By comparison, the same mertensia growing in full sun below the dam bears thicker, darker leaves. A thicker layering of cells allows for more photosynthesis in sun leaves; a heavier cuticle on top prevents excessive transpiration and leaf burn. Shade leaves need not be as protected, and do not receive as much light for food production. What gentle light reaches the shade leaves can penetrate clear through the thin leaf, activating the bottom cells

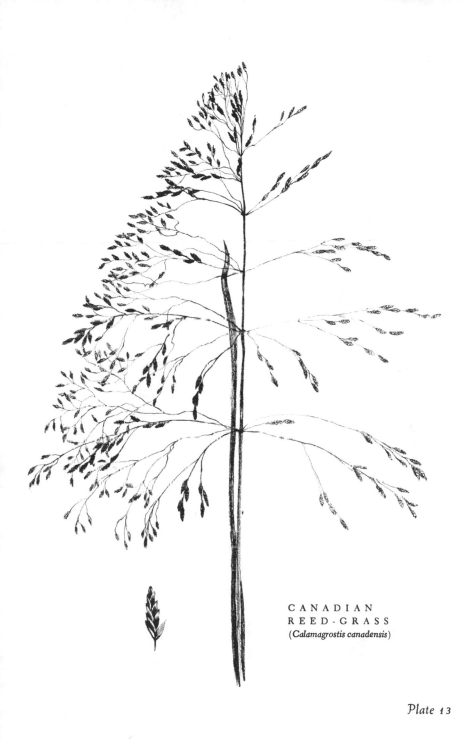

CANADIAN
REED · GRASS
(*Calamagrostis canadensis*)

Plate 13

MERTENSIA
(*Mertensia ciliata*)

BUSH HONEYSUCKLE
(*Lonicera involucrata*)

HONEYSUCKLE BERRIES

Plate 14

as well as the top ones. In July I find the mertensia plants further leafed with small white moths, waiting with folded wings for the day to end.

Across the little dam, opposite the mertensia in both placement and aspect, is a bush honeysuckle, or twinberry. It looks ill-kempt and shaggy, with shredded bark and angular stem joints. Paired green shoots, charged with chlorophyll and not yet covered with the winter-protecting cork, poke out in ungainly fashion at the ends of the twigs like an adolescent's wrists poking out of last year's sweater. Paired yellow flowers, growing from four close-cupped green bracts, appear early in June. (A bract is a modified leaf, usually at the base of the flower cluster.) When the bract is brightly colored it can be mistaken for the flower itself, like the brilliant red bracts of the Indian paintbrush or the poinsettia.

One afternoon I surprised a portly bumblebee on the then unopened flowers. He would alight on the top of a flower, slip down until he was upside-down, hanging on the very tip. In this precarious position he worked busily, his weight giving him an advantage over the featherweight moth who would have to wait until the flower opened to probe for its nectar. Many flowers pollinated by moths and bees attract them by sweet aromas. Those especially attractive to moths are often pale and luminous in the dark, such as the yellow or white evening-primroses. These pale-bright bush honeysuckle flowers are surprisingly visible in the evening dimness.

The flowers are succeeded by a pair of shiny black berries, held within the bracts which have turned carmine red. Whereas the mertensia looks somewhat in disarray in seed, the bush honeysuckle is truly handsome. The mertensia is as feminine as a Botticelli painting; the honeysuckle is as rugged as a Remington portrait of the West, reflecting the beauty of a pioneer spirit.

❦

Close by grow the primitive horsetails. When their ancestors grew some four hundred and twenty million years ago, they were trees with trunks a foot in diameter. Now the horsetail is twelve or so inches high, merely another tenant of the streamside community.

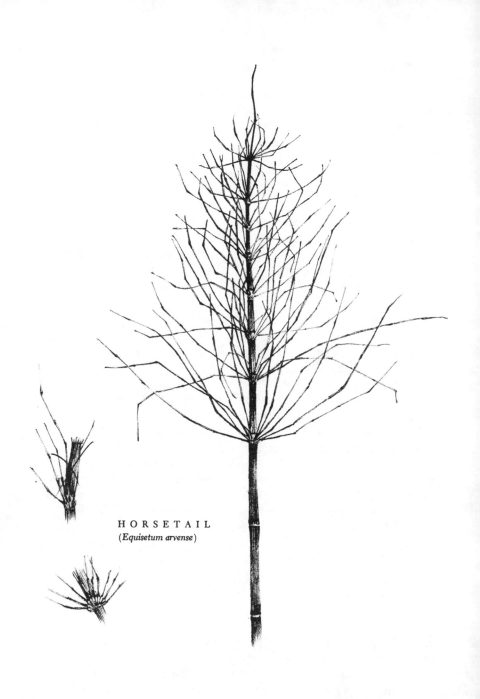

H O R S E T A I L
(*Equisetum arvense*)

Plate 15

Leafless fertile stalks arise from an underground stem in late spring, looking like some peculiar leggy, spindly mushrooms, leafless and brown. At the top is an oval cone filled with spores. As soon as the spores are shed, the stalk dies away. These fruits produce spores of a single kind which grow into minute plants bearing male and female organs. The male's sperm requires moisture to reach the egg, so the plant must grow where water is present. The fertilized egg sprouts into the green horsetail which is familiar to us. Horsetails also spread by underground rhizomes; when I try to dislodge one choice specimen to draw I find it connected in every different direction.

Instead of the familiar alternate or opposite pairing of familiar leaf shapes, horsetails have linear and jointed branch stems, arranged in whorls on the main grooved stem. The plant feels scratchy in my hand from the high amount of silica the plant has taken from the soil. Many a pioneer and camper has used them for scouring pans.

❧

When I stoop down to pick watercress I am always entranced by the patternings of liverworts on the rocks. They are a lovely clear lucid green, always glistening with the spray from the pipe. The name comes from the liver shape of the thallus, a vegetative body without stems, leaves, or roots in the usual sense; "wort" is derived from the old Anglo-Saxon word *wyrt* for plant. The scientific name *Marchantia polymorpha* credits Nicholas Marchant, a seventeenth-century French botanist. *Polymorpha* refers to the plant's many sizes and forms.

The thalli are attached by cottony rhizomes which shred when I try to pull one off. The cell pattern of the thallus is clearly visible, as impeccably laid as a mosaic. The cells are crowded, pushed into hexagonal shapes like the facets of an insect's compound eye. In the middle of each of the cells is a dark-green pore through which minerals and water pass.

The liverworts fruit in July. The leafy thallus is either male or female. The female produces daisy-like umbrellas which grow on a quarter-inch stalk above the thallus. The eggs are folded within the spokes of the umbrella and can be seen, neatly packed, with a hand-lens. Similarly the male structures arise

L I V E R W O R T
(*Marchantia polymorpha*)

GEMMAE CUP

FEMALE PLANT

THALLI

THALLUS CELLS

Plate 16

above the leaf. *Marchantias* also produce "gemmae," tiny green bird's-nestlike structures that bud off to form new plants. These begin to form in late April. I never see them growing over the splashboard without admiring them; they do much with very little.

❧

A few feet to the south of the stream a ridge rises sharply, precipitous enough to require a scramble to get to the top. I find it almost impossible to scale when the fall carpet of aspen leaves is slippery and wet. It requires an undignified ascent, which I am inclined to do only when there is no one around to watch.

Several tall boulders ballast the base of this hill. Similar boulders extend across the width of this valley, one in the middle providing a corner support for the cabin. On the far side of the valley these boulders are assaulted by full sun and are weathering constantly; they fragment easily into gravel. Only crusted lichen can survive the severity of conditions on the rocks' surface.

But here in the shade it is always cool and damp, snow remaining knee-high even in June, protected from sun and drying wind. Weathering is slower and the rock surface is rounded and smooth. One ten-foot-high boulder is split vertically with centuries of prying frost fingers. Lichens are elaborated into curls and sheets. Thin brown tissue-paper lichen ruffles out along the vertical crevices. Fingerprints of grays and browns, apricots and yellows, encrust the granite's smooth face. Ferns and mosses and liverworts festoon the rock with delicate green garlands and pad it with soft cushions. Baneberry and wild larkspur grow at the base. There is a green brown smell of good damp earth.

The moss flora grows on the vertical faces and the dark undersides of the rock. Some grow above my head; others I have to lie flat on my stomach to see. Mosses are an acquired taste. Susan teases me about my hands-and-knees botanizing, but I notice that even she (who paints on ten-foot canvases) sometimes enjoys this myopic world of mine.

Mosses have a soft green magic that gives the south stream much of its charm. They can be green when the rest of the world is brown and gray. Mosses are commonly found growing

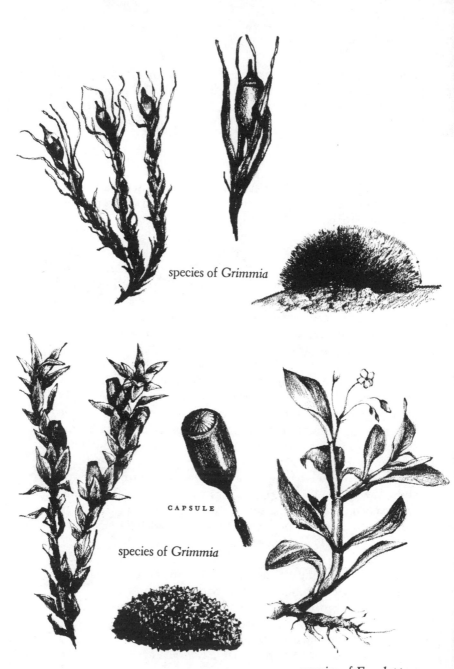

species of *Grimmia*

CAPSULE

species of *Grimmia*

species of *Encalypta*

CAPSULES

Plate 17

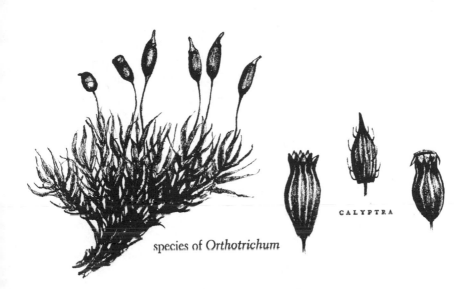

species of *Orthotrichum*

CALYPTRA

ACROCARPOUS MOSSES

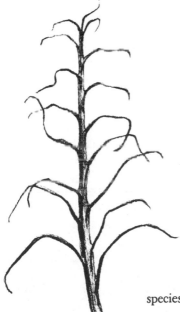

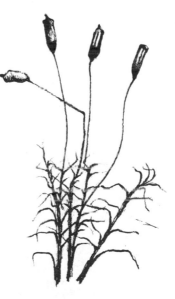

species of *Distichium*

with liverworts, but unlike them, have stems and often midribs on the leaves. *Mnium* (there is no common name) is pure bright green in drifts on the rock in February while the species *Grimmia* are beginning to fruit.

Sometimes the plants form a patch no larger than a bean, only an eighth of an inch high. Some are emerald, some olive, some black-green. In other spots they are luxuriantly thick, overlying large areas of rock or matting the ground. They produce spores at various times of the year, the capsules first pale translucent green, sometimes on hairlike yellow or red stalks, sometimes immersed in a cluster of leaves. Topping each capsule is a "calyptra," a miniscule cap which falls off when the capsule ripens. The capsule is shaped like its name, a tiny deep narrow bowl, rimmed by in-pointing teeth. Sometimes the capsule is plain, sometimes ribbed, sometimes missing, according to the species. When weather conditions are suitable for spore dispersal and sprouting, the teeth open and the spores are freed. Many of these mosses grow on bark at lower altitudes, but in our dry climate they grow in sheltered rock crevices and crannies.

Both types of mosses grow here: acrocarpous and pleurocarpous. Acrocarpous mosses are usually unbranched and erect in habit, forming neat rounded cushions. The leaves nearly always have a strong central nerve, and the capsules arise from the tip ends of the branches. Pleurocarpous mosses are branched, generally prostrate, often mat-forming, webbing the ground with intricately interwoven branches. The capsules rise from the sides of the branches instead of the end.

They can look entirely different when dusty and dry than when damp. I skinned my knees trying to get a sample of one moss which grew in a very high horizontal crack. Under the dissecting microscope, the leaves were held tight against the stem and were a dusty gray. I put a drop of water on the sprig and felt the same wonder I used to feel as a child when someone gave me one of the tiny Japanese gardens pressed into two tiny clam shells—if you dropped it into a glass of water, it slowly unfolded into unsuspected delights, always culminating with an American flag. One by one the moss leaves under my lens opened, in the halting movement of a stop-motion movie. The dry gray leaves were transformed into brilliant fresh green by the

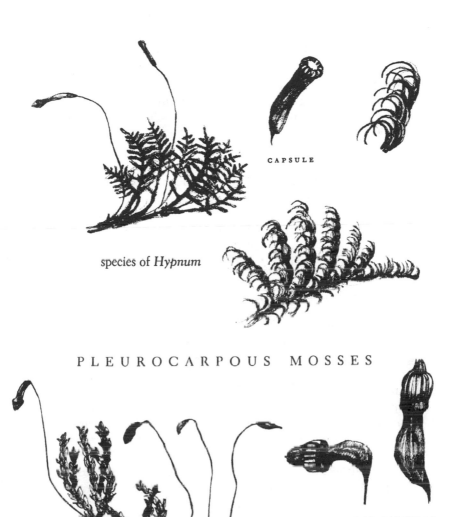

CAPSULE

species of *Hypnum*

PLEUROCARPOUS MOSSES

OLD CAPSULES

species of *Hypnum*

NEW CAPSULE
WITH CALYPTRA

Plate 18

water, ending in a pure-white pointed tip, delicately notched. This was *Hedwigia ciliata*, growing in green profusion near the base of the rock, right under my nose, where it could be easily collected.

🌿

Baneberries grow in the boulder's shelter, producing berries as red as the drops of blood on a *santo* or as white as porcelain. Their tiny inconspicuous flowers are submerged in the larger patterns of the setting. The petals drop almost as soon as they are open. The berries swell to tiny green beads by the middle of July, ripening through August, falling in September. I can calendar the summer by their progress.

Either white or red, baneberry is a baleful plant. Like larkspur and monkshood of the same family, it is poisonous. Apparently the poison acts upon the heart. The rootstock is a violent emetic. Although the seeds seem to be eaten by some birds with impunity, they are avoided by most animals.

Larkspur and monkshood both grow five and six feet tall in the shades near the baneberries. Both are regal purple. Larkspur contains poisonous alkaloids; if an animal eats only a small amount it may be fatal. The plants are most toxic in early spring when they are most likely to be eaten by winter-starved animals; they lose their potency after blooming. Monkshood also contains poisonous alkaloids although the drug "aconite" is used medicinally. These are stately plants, and it is hard to believe them guilty of evil.

🌿

I have walked this south stream when to believe in spring was an act of faith. It was spitting snow and blowing, and within two days of being May. The thirty-degree air had enough wind in it to numb the hands. Snow totally covered the ground and clung in blotches to the aspen. Where the stream entered the land, deadfall striped the ground. Ancient willows and alders had split, bridging the stream with a solid cross-hatching of shredded limbs. But as if to assert the triumph of climate over weather, one ancient willow managed a few gray pussy willows, soft and barely visible against the snow-blurred gray background.

MONKSHOOD
(*Aconitum columbianum*)

LARKSPUR
(*Delphinium ramosum*)

Plate *19*

Mosses festooned the stream edge, beneath the snow, just beginning to fruit. Lichens on the rocks were full-ruffled with the fresh moisture, and glistened with the wetness, but the moss kept its snow cover in coin-sized drifts. Under a blackened branch, soaked for many springs past, was a green grove of moss and liverwort. Caught in the microscopic green forest was a snail shell, less than an eighth of an inch long, a mere speck. But under the hand-lens it was as opalescent as mother-of-pearl. A stonefly nymph wriggled for cover and dropped into the stream. Beneath a dollop of snow a rosette of dandelion grew, green as summer. An exposed cushion of moss held a tiny drop of ice on each capsule.

The stream was running 35 degrees, literally running ice water. Every watersoaked log in the stream, black as a stove pipe, had a garden of moss tipped with pale yellow-green growth. The sun slid out for a moment. The snow sparkled and the bottom of the stream glinted with mica dust. It lasted but a moment and the snow set in again. Temperature and moisture combined to form granules of snow, halfway between pellet and flake, and when they hit the cold black branches they held in thick, six-petaled flower shapes—the flora of a mountain spring.

❧

The north stream is a hesitant stream, perking along only in the springtime. I seldom walk it as I do the south stream. It is not only that it is marshy and I am liable to have feet full of smelly mud and wet socks—it is its whole way of going. Where the south stream chatters, the north stream is largely silent. Where the south stream runs clear over a graveled bottom, the north stream goes furtively, sometimes invisibly, often known only when it spurts up over my boot top. Yet it has many treasures to offer. Perhaps it is like the difficult child, seemingly sullen and unresponsive, but with a wealth of awareness which is a wondrous reward for those with patience.

The difference in the two streams lies in the terrain. The south stream enters the land where there is enough downward slope to make it quicken and run. The north stream enters on the flat. Moreover, terracing was done in the 1950's to conserve its flow. Its entrance onto our land is marshy, about thirty feet across. The overlaid dry rushes and sedges twitch and crinkle underfoot, hiding the pockets of water beneath. Wherever I step, tiny black spiders shoot out, like drops of black water splashing.

There is almost no green here in May, only the dried stems of the rushes and sedges. The boggy ground makes my feet cold, for it is colder here than in the meadows or the aspen grove. Growth is slow to begin in such a cold soil. Bog soils are formed by a combination of standing water and the remains of semi-decayed plant. They tend to be acid, and since bacteria do not work efficiently in acid soils, decomposition is slow. The top layer of muck is black or very dark brown. The lower layers are more solid and usually peat, several feet down. Below are mineral sands, kept constantly wet by the high water table. Waterlogging and a lack of oxygen form soils of a neutral gray which are called "gley." Partially decomposed vegetation or undissolved minerals cause gleys to be mottled with browns and rusts and gold.

The only plants that can grow here must be able to withstand the lack of oxygen. Rushes have air spaces in their roots and stems, and where they grow in profusion, as they do here, they indicate a poorly drained soil. Perennial rootstocks creep just under the surface, forming a mat from which the smooth dark-green stems rise, as fine and delicate as a Japanese brush drawing.

Sedges also are able to grow in waterlogged soils, here as well as around the lake edge, and are often found in cold alpine and montane situations, growing where it is too wet for grasses to grow. Sedges are peat-forming plants, and leave acid remains to such an extent that grasses often cannot grow where sedges have once been plentiful.

They reproduce both by seed and tough creeping rhizomes which net the soil. In pulling up one stem to draw, I frequently find myself with a handful, all attached and dripping muck. The seeds are plentiful and adapted to remain viable after long immersion. The bract enclosing the fruit forms a tiny air space which keeps the seeds afloat. They form a valuable food source

SEDGE
(*Carex heliophila*)

SEDGE
(*Carex microptera*)

SEDGE
(*Carex utriculata*)

Plate 20

RUSH
(*Juncus filliformis*)

BALTIC RUSH
(*Juncus arcticus*)

for wildlife because they are high in carbohydrates, more so than grasses, and plentiful. They are relished by ducks, grouse, chipmunks and porcupine, and even mule deer.

❧

There are relatively few wildflowers in this cold marsh, but those that are here are spectacular. Most of them are flowers which are also at home in the Subalpine Zone, and they grow here because the marshy soil is so cold.

The sparsity of other colors makes the brilliant lavender-pink of the shooting stars visible clear across the marsh. The stems disappear in the reiterated green, and the lightly poised magenta blooms truly look as if they were falling stars. The five stamens are dark, growing to a point at the tip, with the bright pink petals reflexed above. As soon as the flower fades it begins to turn upward, and the seed pods form a brown broom. Even in October the structural purity of the pods evokes memories of the primrose-spattered marsh.

A tall star gentian grows in the shadows at the very edge of the stream. Cool greenish-lavender, the starlike flowers have the gentian's fringed corolla. Some flowers have four, some five petals, in a willful variation. There are so few here that I choose not to pick any, and instead sit on the wet and cold ground to draw them where they grow.

A few grass-of-Parnassus are scattered nearby, coolly white-flowered with petals streaked with green. These glistening green lines which converge toward the center like the spokes of a wheel advertise the rewards of nectar to the short-tongued flies who feed on it. At the base of each petal is a fringe of stamen clusters against which the fly brushes while feeding, carrying the pollen of one flower to another.

When I sit to draw the grass-of-Parnassus it is almost impossible to avoid sitting on the field mint or the lavender woundwort. The pungent odor scents my hands when I pick a few sprigs to put in tea. Mint contains an oil which permeates the whole plant, and volatilizes immediately upon touch. According to Greek legend, Menthe was a nymph, changed into a fragrant plant by Proserpine. When I pick it I can feel the squareness of the stem, each corner formed by a strand of

SEED PODS

SHOOTING STAR
(*Dodecatheon pulchellum*)

Plate 21

GRASS-OF-PARNASSUS
(*Parnassia fimbriata*)

STAR GENTIAN
(*Swertia perennis*)

Plate 22

FIELD MINT
(*Mentha arvensis*)

WOUNDWORT
(*Stachys palustris*)

PINEAPPLE WEED
(*Matricaria matricarioides*)

Plate 23

strengthening plant tissue. The flowers grow crowded in whorls, small pale lavender corollas a quarter of an inch long. But a closer look shows color subtly deepening toward the lip, a corolla tube doubly and triply lobed, daintily opening outward to show feathered stamens. Small flowers like these convince me that it is a hand-lens, not a silver spoon, that a child ought to be born with.

Equally modest is the wild blue-eyed grass, taking advantage of the damp soil and full sunlight. It blooms later than those in my city garden, waiting for warm temperatures before opening. Although bright lapis-lazuli blue, they are so small as to be missed if I am in a hurry. Many flowers fade by noon—a good excuse for a morning walk. All the small blooms, turned upward to the morning sun, have an appealing childlike quality. And adding to the pleasantness of the walk is the aroma arising from the pineapple weed matting the road beside the blue-eyed grass colony. An insignificant plain little plant, once believed to help in childbirth, it releases its fresh fruity smell at a touch.

❧

The second sign of spring for me, after the meadow Pasque flowers, is the willows. Here in this north stream marsh is a crop of new young willows, none yet waist high. Near the end of April the first gray tufted catkins appear. Held tight against the branch within a shiny brown scale, they open one fine warm spring day. As each shrub blooms a weft of gray softens the severe pen strokes of winter. I remember a pussy willow tree that was "my tree" in our yard; these smaller hardier editions evoke a childhood which looked for spring and always found it at the end of the garden.

The first blooms to appear are the staminate male catkins— soft-packed mouse-gray—which begin to set pollen from the top downward. As the pollen ripens, the catkins become haloed with yellow. The early bees cluster around them, frantically competing for the first taste of spring. Catkins are compact spikes of flowers, often with bracts and scales instead of sepals and petals. They are the common flowers of the trees and shrubs of the poplar family, familiar on cottonwoods and aspen as well.

The male flowers are fading as the pistillate, female flow-

YELLOW-TWIGGED
WILLOW
(*Salix monticola*)
PISTILLATE CATKINS

STAMINATE CATKINS

Plate 24

ers come into bloom. These are green, becoming white and cottony as seeds develop. The seeds are tiny and brown, supported by a tuft of white down. The fallen catkins look like woolly worms on the ground. If the seeds do not sprout within a week or two they will lose viability. Judging by the many that catch in spider webs around the deck and float downstream, few do sprout. But once established they grow rapidly. Some of these bushes that I knew as sprigs only a few years ago are now small shrubs.

Most of the callow willows here have gall swellings. There are two kinds on our willow, one forming on the stem below the leaf, and the other at the growing tip, the so-called pine-cone galls. The overlapping growth is green during the summer, but browns in the fall and looks like a very small straight-up pine cone. The galls are commonly caused by the larva of a small fly, laid as an egg in the growing tissue of the plant. An enzyme, produced by the mother when the egg is laid, changes the starch of the plant cells to sugar, stimulating the tissue to abnormal growth. The larva literally eats itself out of house and home, tunneling to the outside when ready to become winged and fly away.

Sawfly eggs cause the willow stem gall, which is bright rosy apple-red. I find that cutting open the gall is difficult; the shell is surprisingly tough and needs a sharp razor blade; its smallness and roundness make it hard to hold steady. The larva is thus well encapsulated, silently sucking nourishment from the spongy plant tissue, safe from all except curious humans.

❦

To the south of the marsh there is an older thicket of alders, birches, willows and dogwood, tangled and impenetrable. I walked through it once, when we were fencing, and came out wet of foot, scratched of face, and short of temper.

Alders and birches, like the willows, indicate the presence of surface moisture year-round. With their cluster of many stems they often form screens, the patterns of overlaying branches fragmenting the sky. Since these trees often grow in poorly aerated soil, the branches are marked with prominent specks on

STEM GALL LARVA

CROSS SECTION
OF GALL

"PINE CONE" GALL

STEM GALL
ON CINQUEFOIL

WILLOW STEM GALL

Plate 25

the bark called lenticels, tiny openings through which air can get to the tissues beneath.

The flowers of both open before the leaves—tiny individual florets scarcely a quarter of an inch long. The river birch fruits are small cones which hang like miniature Japanese lanterns at the ends of the twigs. They persist from year to year, and in the winter the slightest breeze brings a shower of tiny nuts onto the snow, each circled with a thin wing which aids its flight. In the summer, the leaves are shiny above and dull beneath, alternately brightening and sobering with the wind. In the early spring these river birches are often stuffed full of pine siskins, chittering and nibbling, an incessant accompaniment to the expanding of the season.

Another shrub of the streamside community is one of our most distinctive. Wild dogwood's bright rosy-red branches are unmistakable against the snow. The foliage appears in May and forms a proper background for the red stems and clusters of tiny white flowers which begin blooming at the end of June. The flowers turn into green berries which change to china white. Drawing one day, sitting at the picnic table, I watched a rabble of robins on a dogwood near the cabin. The berries were ripe and a dozen birds sat and gorged, all talking with their mouths full.

The wood of dogwood is strong and resilient and was used by the Indians to make bows. *Cornus*, the genus name, is from the Greek word for horn, referring to its tough tensile strength. The bark of another dogwood species was once used in a solution to wash mangy dogs, hence the common name.

❧

The north stream's overflow in early spring forms small pools beside the stream, slightly bubbling with gases from decaying leaves and grasses beneath, and beginning in early May to smell just a little unpleasant. Graf, who walks with me, finds a pool just big enough to stand in and drink, disturbing the silted bottom with his big paws. Graf is definitely not the companion for a collecting walk. The water striders skitter out of the way, the water boatmen take shelter. Herman calls him and the dry rushes creak like an old wicker porch swing as he bounds away.

RIVER BIRCH
(*Betula occidentalis*)

DOGWOOD
(*Cornus stolonifera*)

DOGWOOD BERRIES

Plate 26

After Graf leaves I watch the tiny pool come back to life again. The bottom, about ten inches below the surface, is black muck. The first to venture out are the water striders, skimming and darting. A tiny bright red mite, big as a pinhead, goes gliding through the water. Water boatmen appear all at once, shooting from surface to bottom and back up again. And the water film begins jumping with springtails. Intermission is over and the dance is in full swing.

I spent the better part of ten minutes trying to dip a water mite into a jar. They are so fast and so tiny that they slip away even in the current caused by the lowered jar. They have eight legs and a one-piece body, first cousins once removed of spiders. Although they breathe air on the surface, they are capable of staying underwater for long periods. They are carnivorous, clutching their prey and sucking out the juices.

Water boatmen are also difficult to catch and I get my sleeves wet before I finally snag one. The boatman rows underwater as the strider rows on the surface, using its very long middle legs. At first I mistook them for bubbles moving through the water, for the insect takes a blanket of air down with it. Its body is dark, dark gray and invisible against the dark background, but the bubble maneuvers in the water and its rapid diagonal spurts are a contrast to the slow vertical bubbles of decomposition which float to the top.

When disturbed, as almost anyone might be by Graf's feet, a boatman catches the claw of its middle leg in a submerged stem. Since they are very light they must have means of anchoring in order to stay down. When they need to replenish their air supply they rise and break through the surface for a fraction of a second and dive down again immediately, so fast that my eye cannot follow them.

Graf's curiosity is too much for him and he returns to see what I'm doing. He is mystified by the specks of black which pop off the surface beneath his nose. After snapping and getting nothing but air, he gives up and goes in search of Herman. Herman is using the chain saw which wildly irritates Graf. He hates the sound and he tugs at the quivering log that is being cut, binding the saw. I can hear Herman yelling at him over the snarl of the saw.

The tiny black dots that intrigued Graf are aptly named springtails. They bounce off the surface of the water like minute black ping-pong balls dropped by the handful on a mirror. They need this quiet surface water from which to operate, for they are so tiny that they can find no purchase on moving water. They spring by means of a fork-shaped "furcula" attached to the fourth abdominal segment. When at rest, the furcula is kept tightly horizontal against the abdomen, held under tension by a catch on the third segment. When the furcula slips out of its catch it flips downward and presses on the water surface, propelling the springtail several inches up and forward, somewhat like a tiddly-wink.

Springtails are primitive unwinged insects, which are found all over the world, living on water surfaces, in the soil, or in the debris on top of the soil, even in Antarctica or on top of Mt. Everest, ready to jump as soon as the warmth of their bodies melts the snow around their feet enough to release them. They can feed upon decayed and decaying organic matter which is found universally. Springtails are the lowest possible denominators: insect life reduced to its simplest form. They have no metamorphosis, no change in food habit or environment during their life span.

The eggs of the springtail are among the tiniest laid. The male deposits sperm in tiny packets, each on a stalk. The female collects the spermatophore at the tip of her abdomen, where it opens to release sperm and fertilize her eggs. Being tiny, springtails need infinitesimal amounts of food to reach maturity. The price paid for such miniaturization has been the restriction of more complex development of other body functions; nevertheless, no one can dispute the success of springtails in populating the earth. And there they are every spring, bouncing and bounding in every little pool and puddle.

❧

I find myself unconsciously holding my breath when I watch the goings-on in this little pool. The smell is hardly pleasant, indicating the necessary decomposition of organic matter. Organic and vegetative matter must be returned to simple elements which can be reused by plants for growth in the endless cycle of production-consumption-decomposition.

The process by which organic matter is broken down into elemental forms for plant use is decomposition. When the three processes of production, consumption, and decomposition are taken into account, a continuing cycle is apparent, a cycle characteristic of any and every animal and plant community. Decomposition changes matter from organic to inorganic; compounds, from complex to simple. Decomposition is carried on by both fungi and bacteria, each to its own specific area: bacteria are more important in the breakdown of animal remains, fungi of wood.

Temperature and water are necessary to decomposition processes. This little pool is cold, far below the optimum for rapid bacterial action. But being small, the pool warms quickly in the sunshine and decomposition can occur sporadically. Both water bacteria and aquatic fungi are active here, but the lack of thorough decomposition can be seen in the pieces of identifiable vegetable material still intact in the muck. When the oxygen supply of the pool is exhausted, aerobic bacteria cannot work. Anaerobic decomposition, occurring in conditions of very low or no oxygen, produces hydrogen sulfide, the perfume of rotten eggs. It also creates the acid conditions in which few plants can live.

One of the commonest water fungi is *Saprolegnia*, apparently present in water everywhere. I scooped up a dead fly floating on top of the pool, which was completely encysted in a white fuzz. Under the microscope the fuzz separated visually into threads, radiating outward. These fungal threads are hyphae, the needle-like tips of which penetrate the fly's body and feed upon the dead organism. On the outer tip of each hypha a spore case develops, loosing millions of spores into the water.

❧

A month later, at the beginning of June, the little pool is beginning to disappear, and in July it is gone. By summer the water of the north stream is confined to the stream bed itself. The water meanders, the tilt of the land steepening for a few feet, just enough to channel its width into a narrower, more confined pattern. Logs have been piled across the stream in years past to further retard its progress, and for the first time it speaks, whispering its way around, over, and under.

The water catches the light as it passes through handker-chief-sized patches of open grass interspersed with thickets. The stream insinuates itself under a tangled patch of raspberry brambles, which produce berries that alone make August worthwhile. I'm quite willing to stumble through the thicket and do unaccustomed gymnastics for wild raspberries; no amount of bruised shins or scratched hands deter me. If I can keep from eating them before dinner, we may have them for dessert, sprinkled with a little raw sugar and kirschwasser.

The stream brings moisture to the raspberry bushes in these miniature hidden meadows. Rosy three-flowered avens, head-high monkshood and delphinium, buttercups and mertensia abound. Perhaps it is well that the raspberries are so tucked away in inaccessible corners; the struggle makes me appreciate the rewards of berry and wildflower all the more.

❧

As the stream reaches the lake, it spreads and slows again, stagnating pockets which can be cleaned out only with a good rain. Sometimes a summer guest who has nothing else to do becomes an amateur sanitation engineer. He attempts to create enough straight flow to flood out the tangle of brown decomposing algae and to eliminate the stagnation which offends him. Ankle-deep in muck, he channels and reroutes and excavates. But the plan is doomed to failure. There is not enough water, the slimy swarms of algae refuse to be relocated, the land is too flat to promote swifter flow, and tussocks of bulrushes have made a maze through which the water can only work slowly. We have simply learned to hold our breath when we cross on a late hot summer's afternoon.

Herman built a footbridge over the stream here, and the uprights of the railings are almost hidden in the profusion of bulrush stems. When the water is running clear the little stream is at its most pleasant. White brookcress grows upstream, bush

WILD RASPBERRY
(*Rubus idæus*)

THREE-FLOWERED
AVENS
(*Geum triflorum*)

Plate 27

PHANTOM CRANEFLY
(*Bittacomorpha clavipes*)

LARVA

Plate 28

honeysuckles and alders cast a pleasant shade. The little stream is all dark shadows brightened with green and white.

Last summer, when I was crossing the bridge, what looked to be a salsify seed wafted over the bridge railing. I automatically caught it in my hand and it turned out to be not seed but insect, a phantom cranefly floating almost vertically on the soft breeze of the streamside. The gangling legs were banded smartly in black and white; the lower leg joints were pillowed out with air sacs which provide extra buoyancy. When I first saw it, the black sections of the legs faded into the background, leaving only the white specks which seemed to float by like seed. In addition, their flight attitude is vertical rather than horizontal, contributing to my impression of un-insectlike behavior.

Cranefly larvae live in the shallow waters of the stream where they feed upon decayed vegetation. They breathe air and are able to remain submerged for a short time. There are posterior passage entrances into the larva's body called spiracles through which air is pulled; the spiracles of a cranefly larva are surrounded by six lobes, each fringed with filaments, making a cranefly larva's backside look like some exotic underwater flower.

The adults of most insects live where food is most available for their larvae, as parents choose a neighborhood with good schools. But the quiet stream community may offer other advantages to the cranefly. The dangling hind legs are very noticeable in the bright light, and here in the shadows they are less likely to be snatched by a keen-eyed dragonfly or frog. Compared to the horribly efficient housefly, craneflies are primitive and perhaps on their way out, evolutionarily speaking. I for one will be sorry to see them go; they make an all too sad parallel to the frequent sacrifice of romance to efficiency.

🌿

The bridge is the point beyond which water-seeking shrubs cannot go. The water table is so high that all air passages in the soil are permanently blocked. Mountain water is "soft" and contains little lime to counteract and neutralize the acids of the muck. Only bulrushes—with special aerating systems in their stems—sedges, and some dock grow here. The softly triangular

B U L R U S H
(*Scirpus pallidus*)

Plate 29

bulrush stems support a big loose head of miniscule brown flowers which turn to a skyrocket of brown hard-coated seeds in late summer.

Late one September, just before the aspen grove turned, a bittern flushed out of this marsh as Herman walked down to the lake. Pale-green legs extending behind the dappled body, it circled the lake and landed again in the tall sedges and rushes. It held its head stiffly upward, mimicking the plant growth around it. Mottled feathers dissolved in the wavering light and shade of the drying stems. Immobility, posture, and concealing coloration provide defense against sharp-eyed enemies. The bird had thought the marsh was safe, the glint of light on water telling of food, protection, rest, and now it was disturbed.

It flew, leaving no empty spot in the vision, so much had the bird been a part of the marsh and the sedges, the sunlight and the shadow.

❦

The third stream, formed by lake runoff and fed by many springs, flows from the base of the dam to the northeast corner of the property. It blurts gutturally out of the runoff pipe. By the time it reaches the boundary fence it has achieved an Eliza Doolittle charm and grace which it shares with anyone who walks its course. If I have only a short time to take a guest for a walk, I always go here, for I am drawn to this peaceful place and I find that others are too. This is where a friend of mine sat, back against a spruce-tree trunk, and said, "I never want to go back to the city!"

From the dam the stream runs about twenty feet through very high grassy banks carrying moisture-loving plants in lush profusion: mertensia, bush honeysuckle, cow parsnip and angelica. Then the stream is blocked by huge boulders, dropped as if by a careless giant hand. The water percolates through in tiny murmuring falls, cooling the air. Ferns and mosses and liverworts emboss the rocks. Water springbeauty and forget-me-not-blue speedwell dangle languidly in the current.

Years ago Jane named this place the Whale's Mouth. Footsteps make no sound inside the cavern. The floor under the rocks is soft black humus, sifted down from the forest above. The

BERRY

TWISTED-STALK LILY
(*Streptopus amplexifolius*)

Plate 30

water is so clear as it runs over its gravel bed that only sparks of light tell where it slips away. It makes no noise as it goes; only the far hidden sounds of its falling in the recesses of the rocks announce its coming. All the small green plants of moist places ice the rosy-gray granite surfaces; lichen of the same color crust the vertical faces. It is a still, lovely place, just big enough for one or two, sheltered and hidden. I find myself consciously lowering my voice.

The little valley through which the stream runs is narrow and steep here. Over the centuries the spring-fed and lake-fed stream has incised it deeper and has undercut some of the boulders in place on its flanks; a few have thundered down into the valley. The roof of the Whale's Mouth was formed by one which fell and balanced on top of a smaller boulder already in place. Water ran over the roof rock's rounded edge, slipping down the undersurface until pulled into drops by gravity. Beneath, there are corresponding concavities in the lower rock, each the size of a soup bowl, hollowed by centuries of melting snow and spring rain.

From within the Whale's Mouth the vast, brisk tree-and-wind-and-rock world of Constant Friendship is hidden from view. Inside, the accidental architecture has created another world. The back of the cavern is dark, full of mysterious crevices where no light falls to show their depth. Only tiny midges animate this stillness, swarming around my head, then returning to the warmth outside, rising and falling on the drafts of air.

My view out through the entrance is of the stream's world only, framed by sentinel boulders. A tall, pale twisted-stalk lily is stationed at the entrance. It is perfectly named; the stem gives a sharp quirk at each node, which is marked with a broad pleated leaf, looking as if it had been folded fanlike before being attached to the stem. Beneath each leaf hangs a corkscrew stem from which dangles a pale-green lily. Three petals plus three petal-like sepals form a flower smaller than a dime. The flowers at the bottom bloom first, ripening into bright red berries.

Brittle ferns, characteristic of high altitudes and rocky situations, tuft out of a crack on the entrance boulder on the right. They grow far up, so that I have to stretch to reach a frond. On the back of each fertile frond, late in summer, I find black

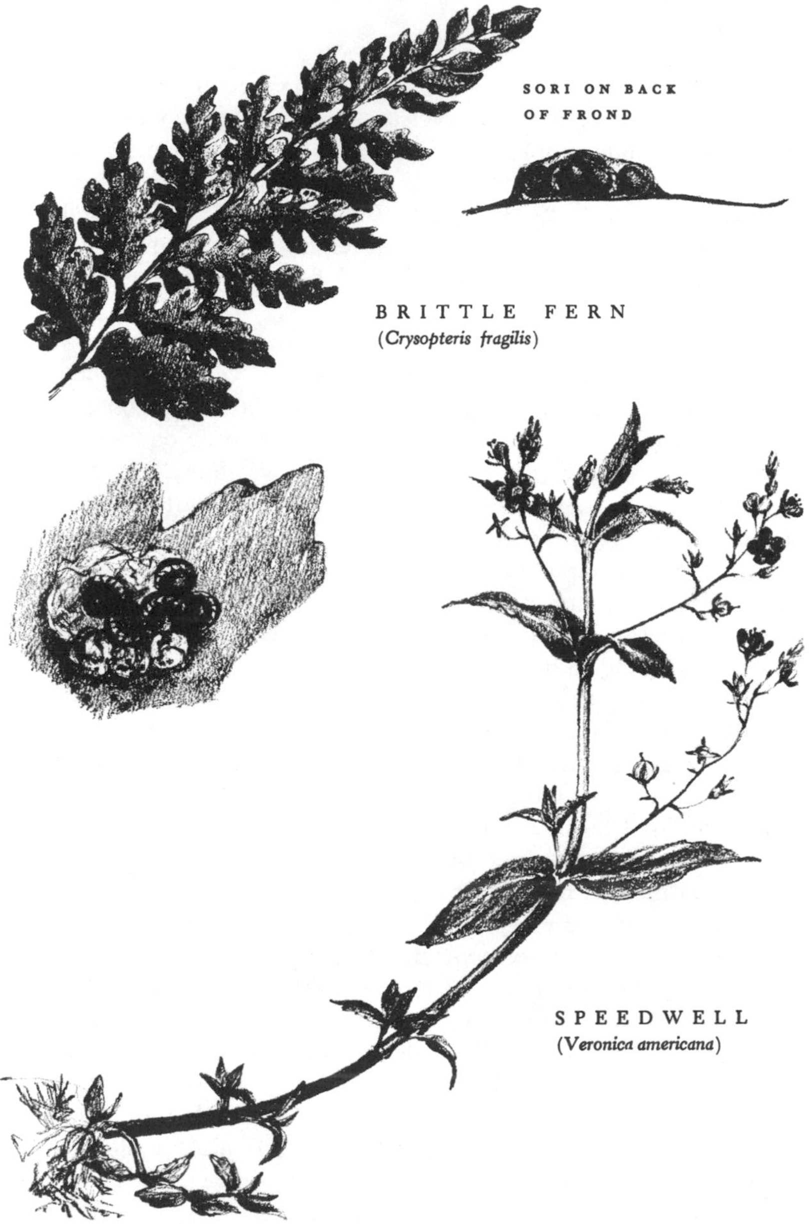

SORI ON BACK OF FROND

BRITTLE FERN
(*Crysopteris fragilis*)

SPEEDWELL
(*Veronica americana*)

Plate 31

dots. These are sori. Under the microscope they are visible as cases holding smaller sacs dark with spores. The sori are held to the frond by a thin transparent film which contracts as it dries, splitting open to allow spore dispersal. Brittle fern, despite its delicate appearance, is green late into fall, finally blackened by persistent frosts. The fresh curled fronds of early spring are curled as tightly as a snail's shell, unfurling into new growth.

❧

Just above the Whale's Mouth entrance a spring bubbles out from beneath a rock, keeping damp a patch of grass. In the middle, almost lost in the lushness, is a small colony of bog-orchids. The colony is not here every year; there is another unpredictable colony at the mouth of the south stream, also hard to find in the grasses. Their scientific name, *hyperborea,* characterizes their place of growth "beyond the north," a poetic description of our high-altitude climate. The tiny flowers are clustered so solidly that the thick stalk is hidden; only in intricacy of outline do they deviate from the column. In color they are identical.

A yellow lady's slipper blooms above the Whale's Mouth. Its generic name, *Cypripedium,* comes from two Latinized Greek words which mean "Aphrodite's sandal." During the Middle Ages such pagan terminology was made respectable by changing the Greek goddess to "Our Lady." The flowers are worthy of either. They are solitary, borne at the top of a thick stem. Three of the twisted sepals are brownish-green, traced with brown; the similar fourth one is a petal which rises like an open hood. The other two petals fuse to form the lip, a slipper of brilliant translucent yellow, shading to chrome.

Besides the obvious fact that loutish people have picked them almost to extinction, the rarity of orchids is due to their problems of reproduction. None can grow beyond seedling stage without the help of a special fungus. The fungus invades the orchid roots; the relationship is called a mycorrhiza. It is mutualistic, the same as that of the algae and fungi which form lichens—each plant contributes to the welfare of the other without being parasitic.

NORTHERN BOG-ORCHID
(*Habenaria hyperborea*)

YELLOW LADY'S SLIPPER
(*Cypripedium calceolus*)
SEED POD

←1MM→

Plate 32

Mycorrhizal relationships exist in many plant families, being especially prevalent between trees and mushrooms, and aiding in growth to a greater or lesser extent. The orchid cannot survive unless the hyphae of the fungus grow into the intercellular spaces of the root; it is thought that this enables the young plant to extract from the ground, via the fungus, food which it cannot obtain alone. Uninfected at sprouting, the orchid must find its fungal partner to survive.

To compensate for such risky odds, seed output is tremendous, up to a million per bloom. The number of ovules may be ten thousand or more, and the plant makes efficient use of pollen grains to produce astronomical numbers of seeds. The seeds are minuscule. In drawing them I had to be careful not to breathe on the page lest they blow away. The seeds are transported en masse in a pod about the size of a wren's egg—a peculiarity of orchids. Either the pod drops nearby, releasing seeds when it dies, to sprout there or be windblown elsewhere, or rolls intact to a new area.

The seed embryo is not completely formed when it separates from the parent plant; development proceeds over autumn and winter, in time for spring germination. Since the food supply is inadequate, the seed must germinate quickly in order to establish its own food supply. Its best place to germinate is where its fungal partner is already established, so orchids tend to form colonies. I have taken seeds from the bog-orchids, as well as the lady's slipper, and planted them in a variety of places nearby; so far none have grown.

❦

Farther downstream are the cow parsnips and angelica. They look Victorian, growing prim and straight, up to six feet or more, although most of them are my height of five feet. They are topped with what at a distance looks to be a large white lace doily. This is an umbel of white flowers. Like an umbrella, all the spokes emanate from one point on a center stem, the characteristic flower arrangement of all the flowers of the parsley family.

Size alone is distinctive, but the cow parsnip is further identified by the large bulbous sheaths at the base of each leaf

GIANT ANGELICA
(*Angelica ampla*)

Plate 33

COW PARSNIP
(*Heracleum lanatum*)
WINTER STALK

SEEDS

stem; these sheaths cover the leaf until it unfolds to grow out-
ward. The individual flowers in the umbel are tiny, perhaps one-
quarter inch across, with varied and irregular petals. The seed
head is as attractive as the flowers. Then pairs of flat oval ribbed
pods form the flat top, each the size of a watermelon seed. When
the seeds are gone, the empty ribs remain like dead umbrellas,
their fabric covering swept away by the wind. The big hollow
stems persist all winter, rattling in the chill sharp wind, bearing
white tufts of snow like winter blooms.

Angelica is just about as large but blooms somewhat later.
The umbels have stems of equal length, so that the flower head
forms a ball. Tiny green bracts, missing on the cow parsnip,
form at the base of each umbel. The stems are hollow and
ribbed with strengthening fibers. But they have no ability to
curve and bend, so they break into an angle as a drinking straw
does.

❧

When I leave the Whale's Mouth I walk along the streamside
which is grassy to the edge, sun-speckled and mushroom-laden.
A giant puffball that takes both hands to carry home lurches out
of the ground. Steinpilz (the boletus mushrooms called *cèpes*
by the French), are prizes for the hungry collector. Unfortu-
nately those I find have already been invaded by hungrier mush-
room-fly larvae.

Sticks and branches, ensnared by the banks, form steps
over which the water gossips and warbles. It drops a foot into
a tiny pool, then runs hidden under a bridge of logs and sod.
It never runs straight, but pokes its way around the boulders
and banks like a little girl on her circuitous way home from
school. The stream's sound is three-dimensional: behind, ahead,
and beneath. There is a hypnotic continuousness in its mur-
mur, a comforting rhythm just slower than the heartbeat. The
soft padded greenness of moss and grass is softer and greener
here than elsewhere on the land. The trees and thickets mute
the light and the shadows are blurred. A tiny burst of violets
grows beneath a drift of leaves, and I think of my mother, who
loved them.

Nosegays of cow parsnip, growing as high as my head, give me an odd sense of scale and proportion, and I feel a little like Alice. This stream might well have been drawn by Tenniel or painted by Arthur Rackham. I catch myself looking for a Rat with a picnic basket full of hamandchickenandpicklesandsandwiches. When a rabbit flushes out of the brush, does he have a pocket watch or was that merely the golden glint of a buttercup in the breath of his passing?

When I sit down on a patch of grass, full of heavy-headed clematis, I am eye-high with a thick clump of mertensia, a plant which grows in the East and perhaps by a Maryland streamside. I wonder if the mistress of the other Constant Friendship ever sat by a stream, remembering another fanciful world of her childhood, hoping that her children too would find peace in this quiet place, and for herself, being glad for the now.

4 ❧ ❧ The Meadows

The wind plays the high gate meadow, scraping and bowing against its curve. As I walk up its slope I instinctively button my sweater against its sharpness. At the crest of the meadow is the highest spot on the land, and I turn to a view which opens to the east and north, across valleys and ridges so far away that the tree tops seem to be just another meadow of darker green grass. To the southeast the summit of Pikes Peak gleams pristinely. The light in the meadow, unfiltered by tree branches, is of pure eye-squinting intensity; the thin mountain air does not filter out as much of the sun's ultraviolet rays. If I have forgotten my sunglasses I might as well go back down to the cabin and get them, for work is impossible here without them. Even color film registers this sharpness: Herman uses a warm filter to compensate for the cool, hard brilliance of the light.

I watch the birds performing chandelles and Immelman turns overhead. They seem to enjoy the unencumbered freedom of the sky as much as I enjoy the windy freedom of the meadow. But when the wind gusts we both seek shelter in the ponderosa grove that outlines the meadow. Cabbage butterflies and mountain blues flutter like scraps of paper near the ground. A large yellow swallowtail wings high over my head with slow dignified wingbeats.

On the ground the multicolored medieval tapestry of montane grasses and flowers catches and gentles the ground breeze. The whole meadow shimmers with each gust. The flowers and grasses bend to the breeze, then straighten up to await the next breath. Red gilia, magenta locoweed, yellow cinquefoil, and white thistle appear and disappear among the flickering grasses. A crackling grasshopper soars and lands on a rock, disappearing into the background. An iridescent blue beetle climbs to the top of a grass stalk, then down the underside of another. A spittle bug blows a white froth on a dogbane stem. This is where I walk when I want wide-open spaces and lots of sky, and a mountain wind to blow away the cobwebs of my mind.

Another high meadow near the southwest corner of the land covers the steep hill between the two streams. It differs from the gate meadow only in having a steeper slope, and therefore I am less inclined to enjoy its high view. It too is raked by winds, any time of the year. When the aspen grove, low on its flank, merely whispers with the breeze, the meadow bears a wind that makes my eyes water.

There are other meadows at Constant Friendship, more sheltered, moister, more protected, like the lake meadow. In them the wind is tempered by surrounding trees or good ground cover. The dryness is alleviated by more available ground water. They are quiet, lacking the wind's bluster and rough humors. They are tame meadows, for reading books or playing games.

The gate meadow is for hollering.

❦

The big gate meadow slopes to the northeast, draining into the ponderosa woods below. The surface is bone dry for most of the year. But I have counted some forty plant species here, almost all perennials, which seems to me a generous count for a meadow which, in all its outer aspects, seems incapable of producing anything at all.

One of the ways of discovering exactly what grows where is to select, mark, and map small segments of ground. These are called quadrats. Just as countries can be mapped, showing rivers and ranges, so vegetation can be plotted. I mapped square quadrats because they were easier for me to set up and the equal-length bars easier to carry. Herman cut me four pieces of strap iron and drilled holes in them so that they can be locked into a square by metal eye-loop stakes at each corner. They are cali-brated on the sides for ease of mapping. I have left permanent labeled wood stakes in the ground so I can compare the changes over the years, and this, I trust, will keep me busy in my old age. After setting up a quadrat, one simply sits and carefully notes where and what the plants are. Many conceptions I had about this meadow turned out to be wrong, and I learned much more than I anticipated when I started out with springtime optimism and a heavy jacket.

I set down the first quadrats in the meadow in mid-April, on a day barely warm enough to work without gloves. I worked here in the meadow many days, glad to be outdoors, often so coming so absorbed that I forgot to go back to the cabin for lunch, and Herman enjoyed the bounty of an extra sandwich.

There were brief hand-chilling snow showers while I worked; spring comes late at 8400 feet. A Western mountain spring is brown and spare. Still, it is one of my favorite times of the year, for the first flower comes more unexpectedly and the first light breeze is more welcome than when spring has been winding up for weeks. Out of brown nothingness the first Pasque flower blooms; out of bleak nowhereness the first wild candytuft opens. And winter is not yet over; there are still snows and frosts to come.

Pasque flowers were about four inches high one day when I sat in the meadow; most bloomed singly but sometimes there were two or three to a cluster. Their stems are covered with a coat of soft gray hairs well over a quarter of an inch long, making the whole stem look three times thicker than it is. Even the petal-like sepals have a soft pile, tufting at the tips like the fur on the tip of our Manx cat's ears. The hairs trap in the precious air and deflect re-radiation; they also absorb much of the harsh meadow light, diffusing it for the tender green tissues so that they do not overproduce for the amount of warmth and moisture available.

In the foothills, Pasque flowers bloom in March; in the

mountains I have noted in the log their first appearance as being anywhere between March 26 and May 1. They bloom early and avoid the rush, for they have no competition at this cold end of the season. They respond to warming day temperatures and are equipped to withstand the cold nights, closing as tightly as a bud. Their limiting factor is not cold but the amount and persistence of warm temperatures during the day and the amount of moisture in the soil.

As the flower nears the end of its bloom, the stem elongates. A cluster of linear leaves which are just above ground, furl close about the stem. When the blossom begins to brown, the leaves are about halfway up the stem, developing and opening. They crisp and curl at the end of the summer, often lasting through following seasons. As the petal-like sepals drop, the styles, part of the plant's ovary, elongate to form feathery plumes almost as distinctive as the flowers. This ordered sequence of growth is triggered by the different temperature requirements of each phase. By the time it is warm enough to have our first outdoor party of the summer, the Pasque flowers have bloomed and left.

❧

The same orderly pattern of growth appears in the succession of the meadow. As the lake's succession is toward its disappearance, the meadow's is toward becoming a ponderosa woods, a progression from the lowest and simplest plant forms to the highest and most complex forms that the environment can support.

It is hard for me to imagine this bright meadow as once barren. No grasses caught the wind. No wildflowers alleviated the monotony of the granite surface. The unhindered scourging winds of altitude abraded the bare rock surface.

The only plants which can grow on bare rock surface (as distinct from rock cracks) at the beginning of a succession are mosses and lichens. On almost any piece of gravel I pick up, lichens still scab the surface. The fungal partner of the lichen is able to hold fast by threadlike hyphae to rock or soil or bark, and its leathery cover resists drying. But it has no chlorophyll and so cannot manufacture its own food. Algae, which are free-

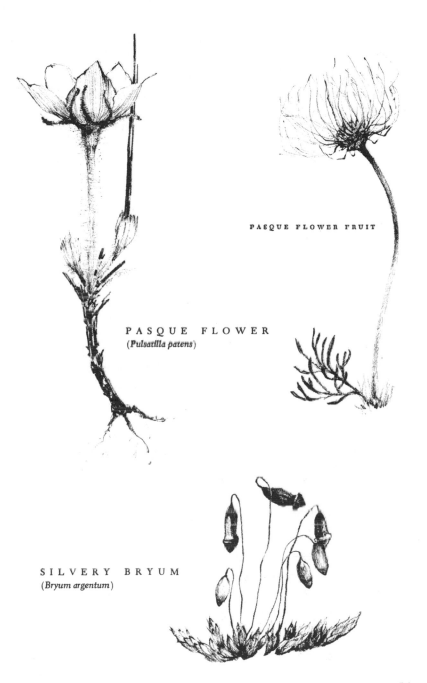

PASQUE FLOWER FRUIT

PASQUE FLOWER
(*Pulsatilla patens*)

SILVERY BRYUM
(*Bryum argentum*)

Plate 34

growing and could survive in most instances without the fungal partner, nevertheless are able to extend their range because of the protection of the fungus.

These simple lichens are crustose, almost inseparable from the rock surface. I cannot remove them with my fingers or fingernails; if I forget to bring a sharp knife I cannot get them off at all. The hyphae probe into the granite, lichenic acids hastening decomposition, nibbling away at eternity, creating fissures into which water seeps, freezing and thawing to further break down the rock surface. Lichens are long-lived, and possibly the encrusted pebble in my hand bears a plant hundreds of years old.

❦

I can find moss here in this bright meadow only if I look in the lee of the grass clumps. Only there are the tiny dried mounds which look even drier because the leaves are grayed: *Bryum argentium*, so named for the silvery tips of the leaves. When the moss dies, it not only returns to the earth the elements it took from it but also those it created. Moss seems fragile in comparison to the tough lichen, but it makes up in persistence what it lacks in imperviousness.

As soon as the first soil was formed, perhaps no more than a thimbleful of sand or clay, sturdy, hardy vascular plants appeared. Only seeds of drought-resistant plants with shallow roots could first take hold. Seeds are not as light as spores, but their dispersal is ingenious and efficient: windblown, hooked to the coat of an animal, or passing unharmed through the digestive tract of another. Seeds are able to carry a food supply to help in sprouting.

Annual seeds are generally small seeds, and produced in profusion, just as midges and waterfleas produce, to be able to withstand a high mortality rate. When the seed leaves the parent plant it dries out; very little moisture remains which can freeze and destroy plant cells. It has a coat which is resistant to almost everything: heat, cold, water, pressure, abrasion, bacteria, and desiccation. Green plants blacken the meadow at the first frost but the seeds of many can withstand temperatures many degrees below zero; some can withstand minus 200 degrees.

If the seed is not eaten by animals, if it alights where it can sprout, if the weather is not freezing, if there is sufficient moisture, if the seed is viable—perhaps germination will take place. Then the stored proteins, fats, and starches of the seed are converted into growing compounds which flow into sprouting areas. A ·tiny venturesome green shoot appears, countered by a white thread which augers into the earth.

Hardy annuals, such as shepherd's-purse and penny-cress, are likely to appear in any new situation, be it a mountain meadow or a New York roof garden. The success of pioneering annuals depends upon their widespread germination under adverse conditions, and the ability to flower and set enough seed to provide next year's growth. As soon as the flowering phase is reached, all food is channeled into flower production. Older leaves are not replaced and drop off; the plant loses its capacity for manufacturing food for anything other than the developing ovary. After seed production is finished, the annual has spent its capital and lost its income.

But it has very likely populated the earth.

❧

Next in line are the biennials and perennials. Biennials produce only a green plant with a short taproot the first year of growth, often in a rosette form. The leaves are arranged in a flat spiral on the stem which provides maximum exposure for each leaf plus the protection of a low-growth form; this is a form often found also in perennials in the high mountains. Possibly rosettes are the result of high ultraviolet-light intensities which restrict the length of the leaf stem, holding the leaf close to the main stalk.

In the second year, biennials send up flowering and fruiting stalks on which seed is produced. Then the plant dies. Acres of mullein all over the United States, an Asian native introduced from Europe, testify to the colonizing efficiency and size attainable by this method. The montane green gentian, scarlet gilia, the tall common evening-primrose, and the familiar bull thistle are other plants which utilize a two-year growth period to grow above the rest of the meadow flora.

❦

Invading perennials also begin with seed germination but may require several years to reach maturity. Their patience is rewarded by longevity and survival not keyed solely to seed production. Generally a perennial will produce seed only when the basic growth needs have been realized; it does not need to produce seed to survive. The annual produces seed at the expense of the rest of the plant; the perennial continues to make food after seed production and up until frost.

Little is known about the germination of native perennial species, other than that the habitats which are most favorable to the quick germination of annuals are least likely to be favorable to dormancy. Dormancy, accompanied by cold, is necessary for some seeds before they can grow. Many wildflowers have a cold-storage period, and the same is true of some garden plants: crocuses and tulips must be planted in the fall in order to undergo a period of low temperature before growth in spring.

Dormancy insures that perennial seeds will not sprout until the environment is favorable. Annual seeds are impatient; perennials bide their time. Dormancy also provides for intermittent germination so that the whole crop of seeds does not sprout at once. An area of annuals will sprig the ground with uniform green. But dormant perennial seeds respond to more specific inducements which will vary locally. The first seedling may not survive, but the second one may.

Rising temperatures of spring accelerate all metabolic processes, both for plants and animals. In humans this is known as "spring fever." Seasonal and daily temperature changes are stimulating to plant growth—fortuitous, indeed, considering mountain weather. This presumes that the fluctuations keep close to the optimum range of the plant; a June snow-and-sleet storm does not. Mountain natives seem better able than city plants to endure these inclement Colorado changes. I have tearfully watched my city garden disintegrate in a hail storm, not to recover fully that season. Mountain flowers may look a little bewildered, but will keep on growing as if the storm had never happened.

❦

The perennial extends its root system each year, tapping more of the soil's moisture and resources. Because the plant remains living over the winter, it is ready to grow and leaf out at the first signs of warmth, stretching its growing season. It avoids the hazards of yearly germination. Even if a freeze nips the new growth, it can continue to produce leaves and survive because it already has a root system; many mountain perennials have small cells filled with fluids heavy with dissolved nutrients which work like antifreeze. A bad frost does the annual in, then and there.

As perennials become established, annuals largely disappear. Perennial root systems, going many feet deep, take priority on soil nourishment and moisture. Perennial roots can survive with less soil moisture than tender-rooted annuals. The short growing period at mountain altitudes shuts out common weeds like tumbleweed; so few survive above 6000 feet that they are not serious nuisances. The presence of so many native perennials in the meadow suggests that the meadow probably holds all the plants it can hold under present conditions of climate and soil; succession has gone as far as perennials.

And it means that each year we can look forward to the first Pasque flowers to brighten the same spot of ground.

❦

I had always thought that the gate meadow was full of plants, but the quadrats say otherwise. The effect of density is from last year's stems, still persisting in the dry sunshine. Underneath, there is bare graveled soil; in many quadrats over eighty percent of the surface is empty.

The backbone of the gate meadow is Pikes Peak granite, so coarse that I can break it loose with my fingers. It lies inches below the soil surface in many places and its loose gravel sprinkles the top of the ground. Every time I pounded in a survey stake it broke. Some laths still lean crazily for lack of deep support. The soil is a sandy loam with a large amount of coarse sand particles, creating a very porous soil which drains quickly. In some areas there are veins of heavier clay loam, carrying large pieces of gravel. Clay particles, the result of the weathering of

Pikes Peak granite, are much finer than those of sand and tend to compact when wet. If I add water to a handful of this soil I can work it into a firm mass. Where the meadow cracks with alternate rains and droughts there is a large proportion of clay in the soil.

The meadow soil that is bare beneath the overhanging grasses receives its color from the granite. If I rub it between my fingers they are stained reddish-pink from the feldspar, and sparkle from minute fragments of biotite, a kind of mica. Biotite turns golden when exposed to air and is one of the many minerals called fool's gold. Black specks in the rock are hornblende. Large pieces of quartz lie scattered about—glossy white or sometimes pinkish, fractured, semi-opaque and milky with impurities. The soil's coarse texture is largely the result of the hardness of the granite materials.

In this coarse graveled soil the percolation is so swift that the meadow seems scarcely damp after a light rain. If the rain continues, it is absorbed for about half an hour until the interstices of the soil begin to fill with water. Then the ground is unable to contain any more and the water runs off the surface. The meadow must depend upon frequent showers since it can store so little water, and these come in summer, just heavy enough to send us inside, just wet enough to soak sneakers if a walk is taken too soon after. But the rest of the year the meadow lies dry and dusty.

❦

A soil is known, like a movie star, by its profile. In the late nineteenth century Russian scientists noted that each soil type had a unique series of horizons. These horizons ran parallel to the surface, were of varying depth and composition, depending upon the parent soil material, the length of time the soil had been forming, what grew there, what the climate was, and so on. All the horizons taken together describe the soil profile.

To take a soil sample in this meadow requires a sturdy shovel and a strong right arm. The top layer or "A horizon" is coarse, finer particles having been washed down into a lower layer. It is often high in organic matter and low in bedrock material, and generally the most productive. The meadow soil is not especially fertile, lacking the dark brown particles that indicate the presence of humus. Humus is produced by the decay of organic matter, both plant and animal. It not only adds fertility, it makes the soil lighter in texture, more friable, better able to retain water and permanent moisture. Only the sturdy native plants that have survived over the centuries can withstand the paucity of food and water here.

I look for a gopher digging where the soil has already been loosened for me to dig down to the "B horizon." Here would be a layer that has accumulated soluble salts and fine particles from the A horizon. But at Constant Friendship it is largely missing; it is not only time but the coolness of a high-altitude mountain climate which has limited soil formation here.

The shovel grates on the decomposing granite just a few inches below the surface. This is the "C horizon," the underlying parent material, unaffected and unweathered. I am thankful we don't have to farm here.

🌱

When I sit in this meadow I am subject to the kind of difficult world in which these plants exist and understand why the ground is so sparsely covered. The sun is hotter here, the light is bright enough to hurt the eyes and I always have to sit with my back to the sun in order to cast a shadow on the glaring white of the drawing paper. The wind is fretful and drying, and after a morning in the meadow I am dehydrated. It chills quickly when the clouds come over. But unlike the plants, I can pack up pencil and paper and go back to the cabin where it is warm and peaceful.

The light and wind increase plant transpiration beyond the ability of the soil to replace the lost water. Although the meadow is on its way to becoming a moderate plant habitat, its lack of cover warns of a struggle for existence in a stage of succession still dominated by the environment. Temperature limits soil formation. And here, at this stage of succession, the meadow may remain for centuries.

The harshness of the open meadow is indexed in the vigor of the plants that endure it. The Pasque flowers are smaller and less robust than those in the deeper-soiled woods. The dandelions are shorter, with threadbare seedheads, compared with the luxuriance of those in the lake meadow. The lavender love gentians are tiny and die each year before they produce much seed; at the sunny lake edge they produce well-branched thick plants. There are a few rose twigs, stems totally coated with large thorns, all under a foot tall, barely leafing. Since flowering and fruiting have higher requirements than the simpler vegetative processes, these twigs produce neither.

Still there are those plants that thrive here, especially in the early spring, and they are one of the many pleasures of a mountain year.

🌸

The wild candytuft are so minute as to go unnoticed until they are in full bloom. I get stiff sitting on the cold ground, trying to get low enough to draw them. There is no solution; getting nose to nose with a one-inch plant is just simply difficult. Candytuft is named after its place of origin, Candia, the ancient name of Crete.

A good reserve of stored food gives impetus to growth, made rapid by a large intake of water supplied by runoff and spring rain. Growing in warmth-holding rosettes, the lower leaves often have a deep reddish-purple cast, enabling the leaf to absorb more heat than pure green can.

Most plants are an inch high; robust ones are all of two inches. Wild candytuft appears straight out of the gravel, for it blooms best where it has no competition from other plants. Root growth begins, as with many native species, at temperatures below that which is conducive to cultivated species; the candytuft in my city garden is just greening.

In the road or along its graveled edge, they checker the bank every eight inches or so. In the meadow, where the wind sweeps, they often grow in the lee of a grass clump—tiny, tiny sprigs with flowers so small that I have to look twice to tell one from a snow pellet caught in the dried grass stems.

Even tinier are the rock-primrose blossoms, each bloom less than a quarter of an inch across when fully open. Sometimes blooming while the whole plant is half an inch tall, they are one of the rewards for dirty knees and stiff joints and undignified

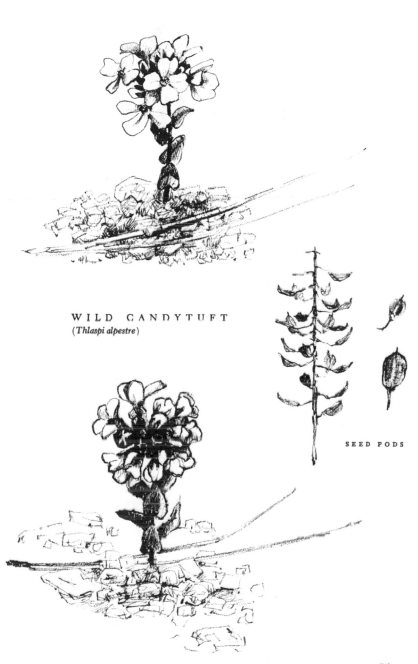

WILD CANDYTUFT
(*Thlaspi alpestre*)

SEED PODS

Plate 35

ROCK-PRIMROSE
(*Adrosace septentrionalis*)

FRUIT

Plate 36

postures which provoke one's family to laughter. Often there are a dozen within a few square inches, hidden beneath the screening stems of last year's grasses. On the road cut near the gate they too rise out of the gravel, a harbinger of spring.

The leaves have a deep mahogany tinge. The stems, as fine as wire, are deep brilliant alizarin red, as are the tiny pointed buds. As the flower opens it is bright pink, fading to white. Rock-primrose is everywhere, blooming even into late summer on three- or four-inch-high plants. If it is true that the meek shall inherit the earth, one hopes it will be rock-primrose.

Two small daisies are just beginning to flower as the Pasque flowers fade. Cut-leaf daisies form a low gray-green cushion made up of finely divided leaves, lightly furred. Set into the cushion are shirtbutton-size daisies, centers big and yellow against the tiny white petals. As spring encourages them, the stems will elongate, but for now they are nestled in the protection of the leaves. The other early daisy has simple leaves and the ray flowers shade from white to lavender. It too seldom grows over five inches.

Daisies belong to the composite family, "composed" of two types of flowers on the same bloom. Those in the center are disc flowers and the petals contain the ray flowers. In all the variations of this form there are many composites blooming all summer in the meadow: early daisies, pussytoes, blue lettuce and dandelions, followed by thistles, asters, goldenrod, salsity, yarrow and ragwort, to name only some.

❧

Sitting down to draw these small flowers in the spring has one serious disadvantage: April, May, and June are tick months with open season on humans and dogs. One can only admire the hopefulness of this small beast, clinging to a blade of grass, waiting for a warm body to happen along. Since the odds are against the tick, the number of eggs laid by each female is astronomical in order to insure survival of the species.

Some Rocky Mountain spotted ticks harbor tick fever from one generation to the next; our ticks are common ticks but no less unpleasant, and some of these may carry a less virulent form of tick fever. The tick is a small gray watermelon-seed of a crea-

CUT-LEAF DAISY
(*Erigeron compositus*)

WHIPLASH DAISY
(*Erigeron flagellaris*)

Plate 37

ture. Its legs, which the tick no longer needs for walking, are atrophied into hooks for hanging.

It takes about three hours for the tick to burrow into the skin, and then it is hard to dislodge. We have a "tick kit" containing acetone, cotton and tweezers. When the tick is gassed with acetone, it reluctantly loosens its grip and can be removed *in toto* with tweezers. This is important since the head detaches easily and remains embedded. The wound can become infected and quite sore.

In simple justice, ticks are parasitized by protozoa who have carried parasitism to its logical conclusion of transforming their environment into their food. Ticks are part of the springtime in the mountains, part of the food chains of the land, and adverse as I am to harboring them I wouldn't, because of that, miss seeing the first Pasque flower or wild candytuft.

🌿

There is quite another unexpected reward in mapping quadrats and drawing outdoors in early spring: while lifting up last year's grass stems which are lying on the ground and obscuring the accurate outline of existing plants, I surprise a great many insects as they scuttle to safety. The meadow seems devoid of activity on a windy day, but only because sensible small souls take refuge in a clump of grass or an old locoweed patch.

One day the meadow seems empty. Less than a week later it is whirring and hopping with a crop of insects. A grasshopper perks out of every footstep, always landing just another footstep in front of me where I nearly step on it again. Small black spiders run everywhere. Ladybug beetles forage among the dried grass stems. Tiny bugs of all shapes and markings, all about a quarter of an inch long and all almost impossible to catch, putter about the dried leaves and stems. Like the plants that needed only moisture and warmth, the eggs laid the previous fall feel the touch of sun and a great hatching and popping and emerging take place, seemingly overnight.

I found the first grasshopper nymph in February when Herman and I were walking in the meadow, marveling at the amount of green that one could find by poking under the dried thatch of grasses. The nymph was a small brown wingless thing, scarcely navigating. The young have no wings and need many molts before they scatter across the meadow, spurting out from every leaf and twig, snapping and crackling.

The grasshopper that objects to my passage always lands in a sunny spot, its body oriented to the best sun exposure. On cold mornings a grasshopper sits at right angles to the sun's rays in order to receive the most warmth. On hot afternoons it sits lengthwise to absorb the least. These short-horned grasshoppers are found on barren rocky areas almost everywhere. One is airborne in a thirtieth of a second, usually before I can see it on the rock. Jules Renard's description of a grasshopper in his *Natural Histories* is most apt: "He is afraid of nothing, because he has seven-league boots, the neck of a bull, the brow of a genius, the belly of a ship, celluloid wings, devil's horns, and a big sword on his backside."

❧

It is seldom that a human being can look ahead to what will be after his own life span. But if this meadow is allowed to be, I can know that someday it will be a ponderosa woods, for the quadrats show not only what the meadow is today, but what it is becoming.

Sprigs of shrubs, rose and mountain mahogany, have rooted. And there are also young trees. Beginning about midway up the slope are young aspen, none more than two feet high, most less. Their trunks are as big around as a man's finger. Although they have not been browsed, they show little branching or extension. There are buds of the branches, but few; the dried leaves on the ground are barely an inch across—those of the mature aspen grove are two inches or more.

Their severest competition comes from the root systems of the grasses. Some grasses form clumps of sod which can prevent a tree seedling from becoming established. Grass roots spread and efficiently consume available soil and moisture, overwhelming the tree seedling. Once established, however, a tree will eventually shade out and usurp water from the herbs. In spite of impoverishment, the trees are there, and that is what is important. They are the pioneers of the future, just as lichens were the pioneers of the past. Scattered here and there are a few ponderosa seedlings, nothing more than branched bottle brushes. One, only eighteen inches high, has a trunk as thick as a broom handle, and is doing nicely, perhaps more at home than the aspen in the dry soil. Ponderosa have exceptionally efficient root systems, able to find and extract water in the most unpromising situations.

The trees and shrubs forecast the far future of the meadow: mixed ponderosa and aspen woodland with an underlayer of rose shrub, with the aspen gradually giving way to a stand of pure ponderosa. When mature trees cast overlapping shadows, the ground will be closed to grasses. The soil surface will no longer be seared by direct sun. Tree roots will reach deep for water. Intervening decades of grasses will have grown and flowered and rotted into humus to enrich the soil, a process of time. The wind will be trapped in the needles of the pine, no longer pervasive enough to spread the pollen of the grasses. The meadow will be gone.

❦

I sit in the roadway to draw the little ponderosa tree. The road is cut, on the meadow side, about eighteen inches below the surface, and it is a convenient dry place to sit. From here I can see the vertical layering of the meadow. Tall, medium and short, each plant has its own place of growing. Layering makes it pos-sible for more plants to grow in the meadow, just as growing at different seasons does. A green gentian stalk towers over the other plants; below it, but still high enough to catch the wind necessary for pollination, are the grasses; lower perennials such as cinquefoils and harebells grow about ten to twelve inches high. On the ground are the wild candytuft, rock-primrose, moss, and all the rosettes of the new biennials.

Layering provides protection for lower plants, ample light for higher. The tallest plants compete most successfully for light and consequently develop a broader and deeper root system. For what goes on above ground is reiterated below, especially in the meadow. The roots achieve different levels, absorbing nourish-ment and water without infringing upon the needs of their neighbors. The roots of the little trees reach most deeply, while those of rock-primrose penetrate only an inch or two. Roots of grasses are deep and fine, a mirror image of the growth above. Kinnikinnik scrambles along under the surface as it does on top of the ground.

There are fewer layers in the meadow than along the stream edge. From tall tree to ground moss, the streamside layers attest to a rich and fertile soil, comparatively speaking, capable of supporting a great deal of vegetation. In the meadows there are only a few layers, the visual diagram of a soil that can support no more.

🌿

While we were surveying I was sitting in almost this same place in the road, resting. A golden-mantled ground squirrel, evidently taking me for part of the landscape, scrambled out of his burrow a few inches away, from an entrance so hidden beneath a crumbling log that I had not seen it although I had been looking at it for several minutes. He sat on his haunches, surveying his domain, before venturing out. He found some seed upon which he nibbled, tail flicking constantly. The white stripe on his flank was very bright, and the throat and shoulders were a lovely warm golden brown, hence the common name. There are no stripes on the head, as with a chipmunk, and the eyes, which are outlined with white, seem larger.

Some friends of ours have trained ground squirrels near their mountain house to be hand-fed, but ours are much too wild. I moved, and the ground squirrel simply vanished as if I had only imagined him there.

🌿

There is, in this dry meadow, food and cover for small animals only, and the most abundant of these are rodents: ground squirrels, chipmunks, and gophers. Chipmunks build well-hidden underground chambers, tunneling in from one end to dig out about a square foot of soil. They remove the soil and tunnel out the other side of the cavern. The first entrance is then filled with excavated dirt, concealing it from view, and the second more inconspicuous entrance is used for comings and goings. Chipmunks have no protection other than their ability to dig themselves out of reach, their swiftness of foot, or nearness to home. Their cheek pouches help conserve the number of trips they must make between source and storage, making them look like a small child with a mouth stuffed full of forbidden candy. I see them most often sitting in their dark doorways, ready to slip inside at the first unfamiliar noise.

Chipmunks are very destructive of seedlings, especially tree seedlings. Foresters have found it necessary to have some sort of control when trying to reforest an area. Chipmunks may hide away as much as twenty bushels of food although they will utilize only a tiny fraction of it. But the remainder are seeds that will never sprout. Chipmunks are fond of sedge, brome grass, gooseberries, fireweed seeds, wild geranium; the presence of all these plants on the land makes possible the chipmunk's existence. The chipmunks are in turn fed upon by hawks, for whom they are easy prey.

As I watch for the ground squirrel to come out of his hole again a swift shadow passes across the road, and I look up to see a hawk circling, alert for movement or shadow patterns. He rises and flies on to other meadows where small creatures may be less wary.

❧

Fan-shaped and circular mounds of soil tell of pocket gophers at work below ground. The meadow surface is usually dry and hard; once in a while there is a soft spot that gives way beneath my foot when I inadvertently step on a gopher's tunnelings. Pocket gophers are a nuisance to farmers because they feed on young green plants, often pulling them down into their tunnels from below. But in the wilderness and in this hard-packed soil of the meadow, perhaps they are an influence for the good. They turn the soil, aerate it, bury dried top grasses and bring subsoil to the surface, aiding in soil formation. When his environment was changed by man from open meadow to cultivated field, the pocket gopher maintained his role. That he was no longer welcome to man was hardly his fault.

They are named "pocket gophers" for the fur-lined pouches on the outside of their cheeks. Their most familiar feature is their large yellow grooved teeth which show even when the mouth is closed. The front paws have long powerful claws, which they certainly need in this meadow. They are burrowers who seldom come above ground. As long as I have worked in this meadow, I have never had even a brief glimpse of one.

❦

At the end of June and the beginning of July it is hard to believe that winter ever touched the meadow. It can be dry and hot here now. When Folly follows me, her tongue hangs out. She is determined not to be left behind. She drags up the hill, her short legs making slow passage on the rough terrain, and is often hidden behind a screen of grasses.

The wind that plays with the grasses silvers the lake surface. Blue flax flowers top stems so tough that I can hardly break them. Fetid marigolds and harebells are in full bloom, along with purple skullcap and yellow wallflower. Grasses shake thousands of seeds, guaranteeing their continuance. Their narrow leaves are unresistant to the wind. Or, like the scarlet gilia and Canadian sage, the leaves are finely divided and the wind passes through them without breaking them. When the wind stills, the butterflies flower.

A white thistle is topped with a mountain blue butterfly. Yellow puccoon holds a yellow butterfly so close in color that for a moment I am surprised to see the flower take off. Another white thistle holds three western painted ladies, their long coiled proboscises bending up and down into the individual flowers of the head.

Summer is the time of the thistles. The tough spines discourage insect climbers, but the butterflies come in by air. The thistle head is a compound mass of tiny white trumpets and it is here that the butterflies probe for nectar.

A western painted lady is orange and dark brown in a varying pattern on top of the wings and more subtly shaded beneath. Its jerky erratic flight is low, making it an easy catch, not at all like the mountain blues which are quick and darting, or the tiger swallowtails which put on a burst of speed just above and beyond the net.

When feeding, the painted lady folds its wings vertically, making a knife edge which casts the least shadow and which easily disappears in the busy movements of a wind-swept

CANADIAN SAGE
(*Artemisia canadensis*)

SCARLET GILIA
(*Ipomopsis aggregata*)

Plate 38

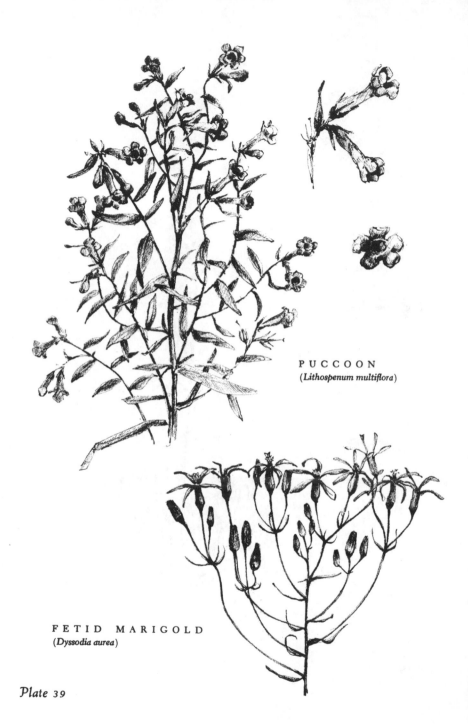

PUCCOON
(*Lithospenum multiflora*)

FETID MARIGOLD
(*Dyssodia aurea*)

Plate 39

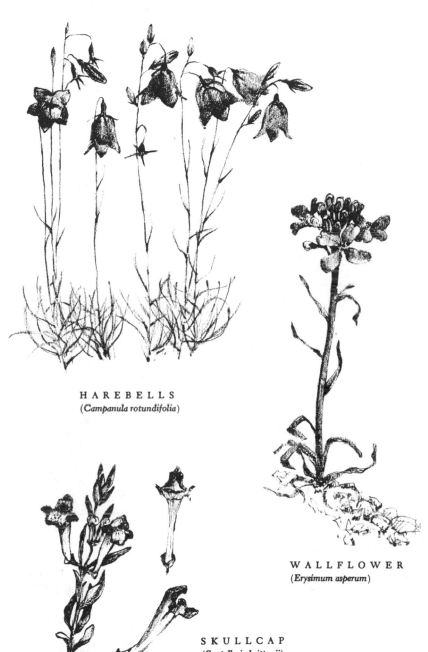

HAREBELLS
(*Campanula rotundifolia*)

WALLFLOWER
(*Erysimum asperum*)

SKULLCAP
(*Scutellaria brittonii*)

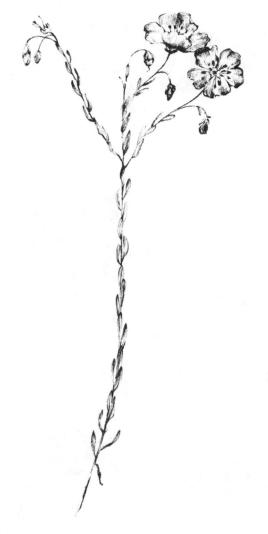

BLUE FLAX
(*Linum lewisii*)

Plate 40

WHITE THISTLE
(*Cirsium canascens*)

meadow. The underwing has opalescent spots along the back edge, set against a soft tan-and-gray-spattered background. The mottling and contrasting mother-of-pearl dots take attention away from other details, especially the distinctive outline. The blacks and browns of the wings are accidental colors produced by melanins, the same substances which pigment human skin. But the whites are structural. The "eyes" on the underwing achieve their silver sheen by being smooth and reflecting the light; the whiteness comes from air bubbles trapped between translucent scales, just as the weasel's white coat derives from air bubbles trapped between hair cells.

Western painted ladies are ubiquitous. They feed not only on the thistles but in great numbers on dandelions and chokecherry. There are some chokecherry bushes below the dam that release a cloud of butterflies when I walk through on a summer's morning. They are attracted to sunlight, appearing in the bright of the morning, flower-hopping. Taste organs in their feet enable all butterflies to pre-taste the flower and decide whether to stay or not; the registering of enticing taste triggers the uncoiling of the proboscis.

The proboscis is a slender tubular coiled tongue, formed by highly modified mouth parts. It is flattened to roll back up again, like a steel measuring tape or a New Year's Eve noisemaker. The proboscis consists of two tubes which are interlocked by both hooks and spines, the original Velcro tape. About one-third of the way down, there are muscles which oppose the curving of the upper surface, making a "knee"; this kink in the tongue makes it possible for the butterfly to insert its tongue at any angle. Herman took movies of the butterflies in the thistle, constantly coiling and uncoiling as they sampled floret after floret in the thistle head, like a cluster of youngsters around one ice-cream soda.

❧

All the small mountain blue butterflies fly low across the lake meadow, specks of blue sky avoiding the higher windier levels patrolled by more robust species. Sometimes I feel as if I were walking through a meadow of butterflies. Their beautiful iridescent blue is caused structurally, just as the dragonfly's blue, or the blue of the sky. But two mating, wings closed, clinging to a dead aster stalk, looked more like dead leaves on the stem, the soft brown-gray of the underwings matching the curled dried leaves of the plant.

A large tiger swallowtail seems to float just over my head, tantalizingly close, putting on a burst of speed if I made a dash for it. It has hatched from a voracious larva which spent its young life riddling the leaves of many of the parsley family's plants. A swallowtail's flight is insolently slow, as if it knew it was safe and need not hurry. And in a sense it is, for its black-and-yellow coloration is a signal to sharp-eyed birds that eating is unpleasant. A bird need eat only one or two yellowjackets to be wary of all yellow-and-black flying creatures, a color pattern that gives warning just as clearly as a human's traffic signal. The big swallowtail, whether it tastes bad or not, profits from this interpretation of its blatant coloring. Such cryptic coloration is most frequent among day-active insects, such as wasps and bees and some flies, and helpful only when the chief predator hunts by sight.

A dozen white cabbage butterflies flit and zigzag in their low flight, busy in late spring and summer. The eggs laid in summer produce fall pupae which remain dormant until spring. The pupae have the same built-in dormancy that many perennial seeds do: the length of day determines whether the pupa will open or remain sealed. Less than thirteen hours of daylight keeps them closed.

The male cabbage butterfly investigates all small white flower heads, being able to discern at about twelve inches whether the object is female butterfly or flower. I follow him down to the lake meadow. His path is a tangled trail of white yarn lacing the meadows together in an eternal springtime quest, as Jules Renard wrote, "a billet-doux folded in half and hunting for the address of a flower."

✿

Where the high gate meadow focuses on the sky and the distance, the lake meadow is lower and points like an arrow to the lake. When the gate meadow is bone-dry, the lake meadow is receiving drainage from above. The top of its slope is dry and graveled, but by the time the meadow reaches the lake, its soil has deepened and the plant cover is thick and lush.

Many of the plants of the gate meadow are here, plus others which the gate meadow does not have: several clovers, a thick cover of bluegrass, and timothy. Missing are those plants which demand dryness or cannot compete with the dense root systems of the grasses: kinnikinnik, cactus, Pasque flower, candytuft.

The mountain winds have greater velocity in the exposed gate meadow. In the lake meadow the friction of the denser plant cover reduces the pressure of the wind and its drying effects on the soil. The lower edge of the lake meadow has trees on both sides, further tempering the wind. The water supply of the gate meadow is dependent entirely upon the amount of rainfall and the soil's capacity to retain it. The lake meadow has the added advantage of underground water, making possible clover and bluegrass and plants which have a greater demand for water. The added moisture makes it easier for seeds to germinate, although the many seeds which roll downhill to moister pastures now find the competition already well established. Just as in animal territoriality, the invader is likely to lose out to the home team.

A handful of soil is damper and darker in my hand than that of the gate meadow. Like the gate meadow soil, more than ninety percent is derived from granite, one of the poorer soil parents. But even a slight accumulation of humus raises the soil's fertility and lightness of texture. Dry weather does not cause the soil to crack as it does in the gate meadow.

❧

The lake meadow is a grassy meadow, green and glossy with summer. Grasses have little of the glamour of a Pasque flower or a wild rose, yet their usefulness outweighs that of any other mountain plant. There are more species of wildflowers than grasses here, and the flowers are brighter and showier, but there are many, many more grass plants numerically.

Just as pollinating insects and flowering plants developed at the same time in prehistory, so did grasses and mammals. Grasses have been widely studied just because of their importance as food. They are equally important in soil building. Many grasses have short life cycles, coming to flower each year and contributing their dried leaves and stems as litter to hold the soil surface from washing and to decompose into humus. Although decomposition proceeds more slowly in high-altitude climates, humus is added to the soil by grasses ten times faster than by forest trees. Each succeeding generation of grasses grows deeper roots, and traps dust and dirt to heighten the existing surface.

The grasses of the gate meadow grow in tight clumps, a growth pattern indicative of a limited water supply. The grasses of the lake meadow are spreading, and irregular, their open growth showing clearly on the quadrat maps. The edges of blue grass clusters are sprigged with new growth. Brome grass tuftings escape inches beyond the periphery of the thickest growth. Here in the full sunlight they flourish and extend.

There are all heights of grasses at Constant Friendship: head-high reed-grass, medium-high wheat-grass, and low grama-grass. In the meadow, grasses of medium height form a preponderance of the cover. They flower just as a rose flowers even though there are no showy petals and no fragrance and much of their structure goes unappreciated without a hand-lens. Grass flowers need no color to attract insects since they are wind-pollinated. The flowers have evolved a structure that aids such pollination: extruding stamens and feathery female stigmas, held high on tall stems; and round, smooth pollen grains, easily lifted by a breeze. Many of the resulting seeds have small tufts of hair or surfaces extending into miniscule wings which give them added lift.

Grass stems are hollow between the solid nodes. Most other plants grow only at the tip of a stem, but grasses can grow at every node so they can survive mowing and grazing where other species cannot. Herman mows a swath down the middle of the lake meadow each year so that guests making the long trek to the latrine do not get dampened by rain-soaked leaves. The clovers and the grasses thrive in the open path because their growth pattern permits continuing extension. The taller herbs are damaged by being cut down and do not recover.

Grass leaves are arranged around the stem in two rows. They have parallel veins as any child who has ever whistled through a leaf has seen—these veins give stiffness to the long narrow leaf to make a good whistle. They are sap channels which bring moisture from the root hairs up through the roots and stems. The leaf lengthens all summer, instead of achieving maximum growth and stopping. The narrow leaves do not shade out those below, so that light is received directly throughout the day and there is no slowing of photosynthesis. The grass is literally making hay while the sun shines.

❧

The most prevalent grass of the meadow is nodding brome, a native grass growing throughout the West. "Brome" is derived from the Greek word for food. The graceful nodding stems remain through the winter, forming exquisite patterned shadows on the snow. The empty seedheads have dropped food for birds and chipmunks, ground squirrels, and mice. Chipmunk holes dot the meadow, near the source of supply. Vigorous, rapid-growing, with a deep root system, mountain brome flourishes at high altitude.

There are some native bluegrasses, but *Poa pratensis* that grows here in profusion is the sturdy omnipresent favorite of lawns, an introduced mountain resident and one of the most prevalent grasses all over Constant Friendship's pleasant acres. It does not begin to form tight sod until low in the lake meadow, where it grows with great vigor, eighteen inches tall with wide, graceful panicles. Bluegrass often has abundant underground stems which form a very close interwoven sod. It starts to grow when the temperature of the soil reaches 36 degrees, long before humans are out and about. The stems lengthen with increasing daylight. New shoots and underground rhizomes are produced with declining daylight and descending temperature. If one could watch a bluegrass plant grow, it would be possible to know precisely what time of year it was, how long the days were, and the soil temperature and conditions.

The stems of western wheat-grass stand four feet high, stiff and unyielding, like a man with a stiff collar. It was one of the first grasses I learned, as the spikes are easily identified by their plaited appearance and by the alternate nubs which the empty florets leave when they fall from the stalk. The leaves roll during dry weather, protecting the plant from desiccation and enabling

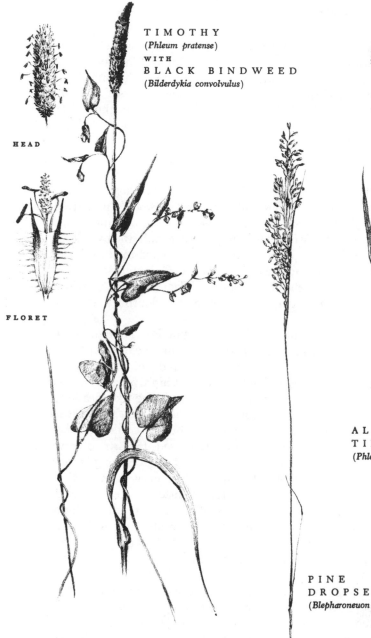

TIMOTHY
(*Phleum pratense*)
WITH
BLACK BINDWEED
(*Bilderdykia convolvulus*)

HEAD

FLORET

ALPINE
TIMOTHY
(*Phleum alpinum*)

PINE
DROPSEED
(*Blepharoneuon tricholepsis*)

Plate 41

ORCHARD GRASS
(*Dactylis glomerata*)

BLUEGRASS
(*Poa pratensis*)

SMOOTH BROME
(*Bromus inermis*)

WESTERN
WHEAT-GRASS
(*Agropyron smithii*)

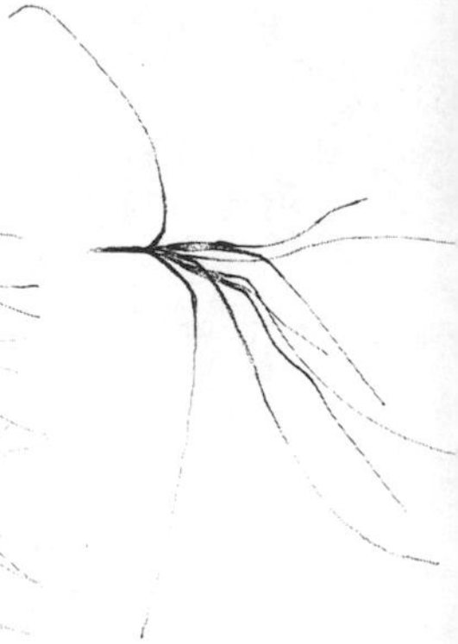

SQUIRRELTAIL
GRASS
(*Sitanion longifolium*)

CRESTED
WHEAT-GRASS
(*Agropyron desertorum*)

SLENDER
WHEAT-GRASS
(*Agropyron trachycaulum*)

Plate 42

it to survive long dry spells in late mountain summers. Most of the stomata are on the top of the leaf while the lower surface is cutinized. The leaf rolls inward, leaving the tougher surface outside.

The color of the plant varies so widely that I sometimes have to hold the stalks together to be sure they are the same plant. Some plants are a silvery gray-green, others purer green, and others are a definite reddish-pink.

Another variety of wheat-grass, crested wheat-grass, was introduced from Russia in 1898 and is well adapted to montane regions. It is drought-resistant, tolerant of a wide range of temperatures, and high in protein for grazing animals. Because crested wheat-grass prefers a soil where runoff water accumulates, it grows toward the bottom of the lake meadow.

❧

The grasses tame the wind to a light breeze, and on these days the sound of bees in the lake meadow is almost soporific. The deep purple-blue stalks of penstemons are frequently centered not by their own stamens but by the yellow-striped rear of a bumblebee. Blue is the favored color of bees, and they respond to larger fields of color, a bunch rather than a single flower, and to motion. The light breeze that flickers the flowers brings them out.

I watched one portentous-looking bee and counted his timing: three seconds in each flower, then on to the next, visiting only one species of penstemon and no other. The penstemons, named for their five stamens, only four of which are fertile, grow on a stalk from a cluster of green leaves and come to flower in June. The open lip of the corolla is a handy bee footrest.

Flowers pollinated by insects often have a relatively large number of ovules per flower, each ovule requiring one grain of pollen to develop it into a seed. The plant tends to adapt to attract the insect upon which it depends for pollination, as the heavy white blossom of yucca attracts the yucca moth, or the deep blue of the penstemon attracts the bee. The advantage to the flower lies in more efficient cross fertilization, allowing a greater variety within the species so that selection may be made of the finest and fittest, a necessity for the rigors of mountain

TALL PENSTEMON
(*Penstemon unilateralis*)

Plate 43

growth. Insect pollination is more precise than wind pollination, and much less pollen needs to be produced—another one of nature's economies.

The bees which forage the penstemons are not hive bees but solitary bees which live in the soil. Their burrowings can be almost as efficient as an earthworm's in aerating and mixing the soil. They collect pollen which they store in the ground as food for their larvae, laying eggs on a mass of honey-moistened pollen.

The bees lumbering around the penstemons were heavy-legged with pollen, fertilizing the penstemons as neatly as Old Herbaceous. One of the bees hit the penstemon stalk with such velocity that it knocked off a ladybug beetle that had wandered up the stem in search of aphids or mealybugs. The helpfulness of ladybugs was recognized in the Middle Ages when they were dedicated to the Virgin and known as Beetles of Our Lady. A medieval remedy for toothache was to smash several beetles and stuff them into the cavity of the ailing tooth. No doubt the taste was bad enough to obliterate the other pain, for ladybugs are so bitter that even a starving bird won't eat one.

The ladybug waddled off across the ground, and then, finding this slow going, opened her wings. The shiny orange outer shards parted to reveal the gossamer flight wings beneath. The orange is the same red-orange found in carrots and tomatoes, a pigment composed solely of carbon and hydrogen. For their meager demands upon the environment—a pittance of food, a drop of dew—ladybug beetles save many green plants from severe damage and so protect the food supply at the very beginning of the food chain.

❦

When I poke among the dried thatch of grasses in May, I find a clover leaf hardly as big as a dime, each of the three leaflets smaller than my little fingernail. Hidden underneath the roofing of old grasses, the clover clings and covers the ground, its bright green patches becoming more and more prominent as the meadow dampens and warms. They vastly enhance the efficiency of the grasses in creating soil.

Legume roots have an ability to attract nitrogen-fixing bacteria. A secretion from the root hairs advertises the presence of the plant; the bacteria respond by clustering around the root, forming a nodule. When the legume dies, the nitrogen-rich roots add one of the most important nutrient elements to the soil where it can be readily used by other plants.

The clovers begin to bloom in late June with fifteen- and sixteen-hour days, just when we are beginning to enjoy spending days and days at a time here for the very same reason. Sweet clover grows a rangy five feet tall, full of tiny fragrant yellow flowers. Sometimes the plants are so thick along the road coming into Constant Friendship that the fragrance can be caught from the car. Sweet clover is a biennial which produces both hard and soft seeds; the latter germinate quickly while the former lie dormant. It is well adapted to our clay-loam soils, and the roots decay rapidly after the plant dies, an advantage to mountain meadows.

Smaller heavy-headed plants of red clover are few, but common white clover is plentiful. Each flower head is formed by many tiny sweet-pea flowers, closely packed. Clovers are widely eaten by many small animals, especially grouse, for their high crude protein content. Having flowers and seeds in a compact head makes eating easier.

Alfalfa is also a legume and the plants that grow on our land are escapees from cultivated meadows many miles away. The deep-purple flowers bloom late in the summer, the lower flowers and early sprigs ripening into seed while the later flowers begin. The seed pods are tiny helices, like a pea pod twisted into a spiral. As they dry and open, they spit the seeds outward to wider horizons.

Alfalfa butterflies busy themselves in the purple flowers and are largely responsible for their fertilization. Bright yellow, they are the complementary hue which intensifies the color of both flower and insect. But when the butterfly feeds, the wings close, and muted random pattern markings join to form a camouflage of mottled dull greens and yellow—just dry leaves quivering on a flowering stalk.

❧

Colorado locoweed grows profusely at the top of the lake meadow but toward the lower edge is shut out by the grasses.

SEED PODS

COLORADO LOCOWEED
(*Oxytropis lambertii*)

Plate 44

Locoweed blossoms shade from brown brick-red to pale pink, with magenta dominating, a white species and a magenta species hybridizing to the various shades between. Locoweed is able to extract a poisonous chemical, selenium, from the soil; when eaten in sufficient quantity, the plant is poisonous. Continuous feeding causes the animal to go "loco" and eventually causes death. The silver-leaved plants are distinctive without the bloom, sometimes frosting whole meadows. Silky hairs provide the sheen. Many other dry meadow plants are also silvery: pussytoes, yarrow, sage, thistle; it is thought that this may protect the leaves from strong light damage. The overall aspect of our meadows is grays and muted greens, never the verdant greens of New England.

This year another loco, showy loco, appeared in the meadow, blooming much later in the summer. It is so woolly that the flowers are almost lost in the coating of stiff white hairs. Colorado locoweed marks the beginning of the summer, showy loco its end. They grow side by side but cooperate by making their demands upon the habitat at different times of the growing season.

The change in water content of the meadow from top to bottom is colorfully illustrated by the magenta loco at the top of the slope and the wild iris at the bottom, neither being able to grow where the other does. Irises are largely bee-pollinated plants, the sepals forming the floor of a passageway leading to the nectar. Wild iris resembles garden iris but is more finely drawn, belying the vigor of the robust rootstocks which can grow in a wet area which other flowers shun, and compete with grasses on their own terms.

❦

There are no "garden weeds" at Constant Friendship. Because we cultivate nothing, we welcome all green and growing things. The first spring dandelion which makes the lowland gardener run for his knife is a welcome spot of concentrated sunshine here, golden among the still-dry grasses matting the ground.

Dandelions belong to the successful composite family even though they have but one type of flower in the flower head. The scourge of gardeners is the long taproot, which stores food for next year's growth. Above 6500 feet, dandelions tend to dwarf, but they make up in number what they lack in vigor in this meadow. Their notched leaf gives them their name *dent-de-lion*, or lion's tooth.

The dandelion's propensity for making the most of any situation—rooting in poor soil, tolerating excessive light, withstanding poor surface drainage and still producing full seedheads—makes it obnoxious at lower elevations. The seeds of most members of the composite family are windblown. They are composed mainly of oil, and this large proportion of nourishment contained in the seed gives twice the food value to the sprouting plant and provides impetus to an early start. They do not flower in profusion, however, until the days are at least twelve hours long. After flowering is complete the stalk elongates, raising the familiar diaphanous white ball above the ground where it can take advantage of the lightest draft. Only a one-mile-per-hour breeze is enough to keep a dandelion seed aloft.

Nearby grow taller plants with huge dandelion-like seedheads, the size of a baseball and larger. These are salsifies, with the composite seedhead carried to the ultimate. The flowers are lemon yellow and modest in size, but the seedheads are magnificent. Both dandelion and salsify have a hairy pappus which acts as a parachute, holding the seed at the bottom. The parachute "ribs" are furred with horizontal hairs which interlock and catch the air, keeping the seed buoyant—nature's shuttlecock. This is the most efficient seed-dispersal system in the plant kingdom, as every gardener knows to his sorrow.

❧

The seed pods, fragmenting with the wind, tell of the shattering of summer. The aspect of these meadows in autumn is much like that of spring: some plants now bloom late, avoiding competition with the summer grasses. As the spring seems eager, so the fall seems to me glorious but sad, a last defiant splash of bloom, brighter because of what tomorrow is to be. This is a pensive time of year in the meadows and I find my walk slows to match.

There are only a few late flowers able to endure shortening

YELLOW EVENING-PRIMROSE
(*Oenothera strigosa*)

SEED PODS

Plate 45

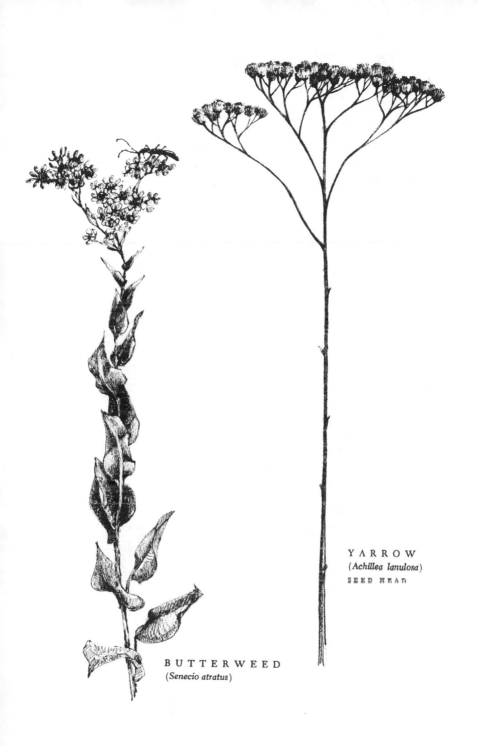

YARROW
(*Achillea lanulosa*)
SEED HEAD

BUTTERWEED
(*Senecio atratus*)

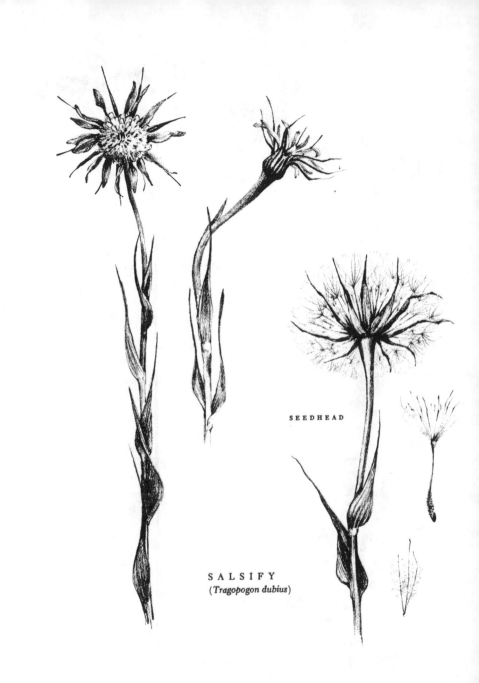

SEEDHEAD

SALSIFY
(*Tragopogon dubius*)

Plate 46

days and cold nights. All are composites. The purple of the asters deepens in color and brilliance, intensified by the chill nights. Porter's asters are just fading. Golden asters, low to the ground, are in bloom as late as October, weeks after the first frost, catching the long rays of the sun in their yellow petals. A stand of butterweed hosts dozens of small black beetles. It will take a hard frost to blacken the stems and finally blur the flowers.

The grasses are drying and the autumn winds make them whisper among themselves about the late-stayers. The heads of timothy, the drooping panicles of brome, the austere formal heads of wheat-grass, rustle and whisk in the winter wind. This is when I enjoy the grasses most, for they have the severe and impeccable beauty of a form which epitomizes its function. Yarrow is even more handsome in seed than in flower.

I spend as much time as possible in the sunshine drawing. All the drawing that I was going to do "tomorrow" suddenly must be done today. Time has run out. And after a few hours sitting on the ground drawing, I grow aware that fall is also "chigger" time.

Actually these tiny pests are not chiggers but harvest-mites, tiny red parasites that live in the soil. To me they might as well be the chiggers of my Indiana childhood. While in the first of two larval stages, chiggers attack animals. They lie in wait as a tick does, on a sprig of grass, hopping off onto a likely meal. They crawl to a belt line or wherever tight clothing causes an area of warmth. There they burrow in. They feed by inserting their mouth parts into the skin, at the same time releasing a digestive fluid that liquefies cells and tissues and causes itching and swelling.

As I itch and scratch and grumble I pay the price for drawing the late yellow evening-primroses which are blooming in a last burst of summer. These are plants which need long hours of daylight and begin to bloom in July. The tall stalks open only one flower at a time so that a visiting bee or moth will not be distracted by numbers and be sure to pollinate each single flower. The square flowers are formed by four brilliant yellow petals which open during late afternoon or evening, bright enough to attract the evening moths.

By the end of summer the evening-primroses are no longer

SEEDHEAD

SMOOTH ASTER
(*Aster laevis*)

Plate 47

SEEDHEAD

PORTER'S ASTER
(*Aster porteri*)

GOLDEN ASTER
(*Heterotheca villosa*)

so miserly. Like a traveler who has carefully saved money the whole trip and goes on a shopping spree when he suddenly discovers that it is time to go home, the evening-primrose now opens many blossoms at once.

🌿

The meadow becomes evenly colored, the brightness of the summer lingering only in a few errant asters. Leaves and stalks have withered into a golden bronze. The thistles and clovers have become shaggy and unkempt with seed. The flax carries small spherical pleated boxes full of next year's blue.

I walk up the gate meadow to the crest of the slope on a last inspection tour. The sun is bright but the wind is sharp, and the warmth fools no one. There is snow behind this wind.

But somehow, to me, this is a spring and summer meadow. I see this meadow as I saw it early one June morning, so early that the daisies were not yet open. It was as if the meadow had been surprised asleep. No wind stirred. The opposite of its usual boisterous self, the meadow seemed as vulnerable as a sleeping child. I remember the painted lady butterflies languishing on the dandelions, the mourning-cloaks with their dark dusky wings rimmed with cream flirting along the meadow's edge, the monarchs who sampled our meadows on the way to greener ones. I see the first Pasque flowers brought to bloom by the early sun. I am reluctant to let summer go.

5 ❧ ❧ The Aspen

I count the spring year well begun when the aspen dangle their three-inch catkins, fuzzy earrings which dust the cabin deck with pollen. The buds spill them out anywhere from late March to the end of April. The catkins appear before the leaves do, open to the pollinating spring breezes. The amount of pollen is prodigious. When I cut a bouquet of spring branches, the table on which they sit is deep in pale sulphur-yellow pollen the next day.

Our log notes the appearance of the first leaves between May 14 and May 20, the third week in May consistent over the years. The leaves are a pale lucid green, circles cut out of green tissue paper and overlaid in shifting patterns. Now is the time to hang out the hammock and feel, in the chill warmth, intimations of summer. A week ago the light was too bright for reading comfortably in the grove; now the leaves make kaleidoscopic shadows on the book page.

Lying in the hammock, looking up at the leaves, I can see the gall swellings which appear almost as soon as the leaves open, opaque against the translucent leaf. Galls usually appear in the early leaves, looking like green peppercorns. Leaf miners make meandering mines in the thin galleries between the upper and lower leaf surface when the leaves are larger.

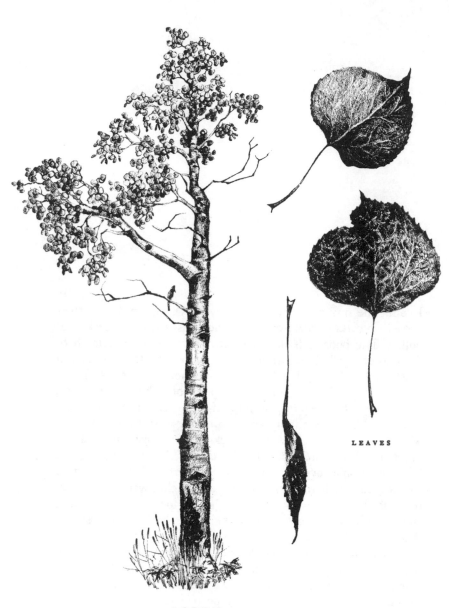

LEAVES

ASPEN
(*Populus tremuloides*)

Plate 48

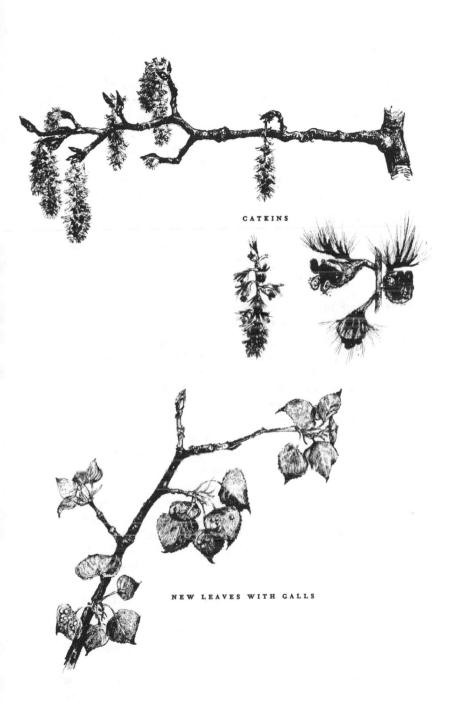

CATKINS

NEW LEAVES WITH GALLS

The deep-green topside of new leaves contrasts with the paler underside. The leaf stalks are longer than the leaf itself, and are flattened at right angles to the leaf, acting like pivots. The leaves quiver and catch the light in a nervous rhythm which explains their familiar name of Quakies. Father de Smet, an early missionary to the north country, recorded that the superstitious north woodsmen believed that the Cross was made of aspen wood and that the tree had never stopped quaking since the Crucifixion. The sound of aspen leaves is distinctive: a soft permeating gossiping of the goings-on of breeze and bird. Any whisper of air sets them sibilating, telling all they know over the back fences of the pine ridges.

🌿

The change between spring and summer in the aspen grove is not gradual. One day the wind is brisk and chill. The sun is warm on my back if I sit in a sheltered place, but the wind is sharp enough to mute the warmth and make my nose red. The ground is cold, still mostly brown with a few tiny sprouts of green seeking sun. The only plant in bloom around the cabin is a gray-green mound of golden smoke. It is cool, crisp weather, a little like fall, a time to work, to paint the raft, to scrape the road, a restless time of becoming when we feel the need to do something constructive. A mourning-cloak butterfly tilts over my head and is gone, the first one of the year.

Then one day, not until the end of May, there is a perceptible change. There is scarcely more green on the ground, and the wind is just as capricious. But from the earth arises a warmth that envelops like a cocoon. The sun has finally heated the soil enough so that it is able to give back its radiation.

The breeze is softer, more like cotton, soft over the face, first from one direction, then another. The sun is warm on the back, now a reinforced warmth, not intermittent. The smell of pine rises from the ponderosa grove. Butterflies are more numerous, western painted lady and Butler's alpine and mountain blue. There is a humming and buzzing and clicking sewed together by the whirr of the hummingbird. He begins before the daisies are even open in the morning and is the last to settle in at night.

What there was the day before summer is still the same,

still here, but there is just more of it, all molded together by the warmth that rises like a mist from the soil. Yesterday was spring, the chill spring of the mountains where night temperatures are still in the twenties and thirties, and the pump must be drained to prevent freezing. But one day it is all of a piece, and that day it is summer.

❦

The first day I can work outdoors, on the deck, is a little like trying to balance a checkbook in the midst of a three-ring circus. In a dish of silt brought from the south stream there are red bloodworms and clams. The bloodworms are frenetically active, looping and unlooping. The clams write their own private messages in white lines on the thin layer of brown silt. I set out pencil and paper for notetaking, clean the glass in the hand-lens, set up the microscope, and prepare to work.

A movement in the brush below is distracting. After watching for a minute I can see nothing, so I return to the microscope. The restless rustling resumes. Finally I give up and move to the edge of the deck where I can see into the brush. The rustlings resume and take on a pattern, and by watching very carefully I finally discover the cause. So well is the tiny body camouflaged that the mountain vole comes out to feed several times before it is possible to make out what sort of an animal it is. About four inches, a grayed tan, ears flat against the head, it is indistinguishable from the over-layer of dried vegetation. It runs along beneath the winter grasses, making a sound but entirely hidden from sight. Out of the end of the runway it dashes, a foot or so, snatches a geranium leaf, nibbles it, and then ducks back into the runway. The timing is precise, each cycle lasting thirty seconds by my watch. He appears again, running at an even gait, pulls another sprig, and softly disappears into the grass.

This vole, like his cousins by the dozens, prefers high grasses near streams where he can be both well hidden and well fed. Voles feed on grasses, sedges, bark, seeds, and probably some insects. They in turn are prime food for both day-hunting hawks and night-hunting owls, since they are active throughout the twenty-four hours. Many a weasel's nest is lined with vole fur.

I often hear a vole when crossing the north-stream bridge, shuffling in one of its seemingly endless runways. Voles are ready to breed when three weeks old and able to produce a dozen or so litters a year; the thought makes one thankful for weasels.

I am so intrigued by the vole's systematic feeding that I go down to see his run in the alder thicket. While looking at the geranium whose new growth the vole had completely discouraged, I find a small plant that I hadn't seen before, and for good reason. It is a peculiar small flower, about three inches tall, all pale green, well hidden under larger plants. It is muskroot, or moschatel, also called town clock because there are four quarter-inch flowers facing outward just like an old town clock. The fifth flower caps the other four, facing upward. After finding one, I now find them in many shady places on the land. It is, after all, only a matter of knowing what to look for.

This was an intriguing spot that I kept watch on all summer. Another tiny plant next to the muskroot turned out to be, six weeks later, a five-foot-tall sow-thistle. And another, innocent-looking and smooth, turned out to be a well-armed stinging nettle.

❧

I return to the silt dish and the microscope, but there is such a chattering and scolding that in spite of good intentions I look up; two black-capped chickadees are househunting in the crook of an old aspen tree. Finally they settle down to one choice on the outside angle of the branch, and proceed to bring construction materials. They are two marshmallow birds with cloves stuck in at a rakish angle for beaks.

More small sounds in the brush again destroy my concentration. A househunting male house wren is investigating the birdhouse outside the kitchen window. He inspects it, goes in and out, flying away and returning. Eventually he decides that it suits his fancy and he begins decorating it for his intended. He does not sing, he just flits from ground to perch and back again. He brings up a Y-shaped twig, which catches in the doorway; after much futile tugging he drops it.

He flies off and comes back with another twig, about six inches long. This one slips out of his beak and he has to fly down to pick it up. Patient poking finally gets it partially in the hole. He slips inside and takes the other end of the recalcitrant twig; all but the last inch disappears inside. He pulls until it finally snaps in the middle and then impatiently tucks it all the way inside as if he were tired of the bother and wants to get on with it. I can hear his feet scuffling on the empty wood floor. It is obviously his first day on the job. He eventually stuffs the whole house with dry twigs, leaving only a small hole for the nest. Herman remarks unkindly that it looks like my studio. But unlike the studio, this nest was never occupied.

The wren also built another nest in another birdhouse on a nearby aspen, near the dogwood thicket. And there he sat and sang, his labors finished, making a statement of availability to arriving females and a statement of territorial rights to other males. The lengthening of daylight hours had triggered changes in the pituitary gland that had pushed him north before the female, and now the same impetus would bring her. The wrens at lower elevations were already nesting; the lateness of the time of the mountain wrens correlates with the rule of thumb that events are slowed down four days per 400 feet of altitude and each degree of latitude. As with the breeding of other animals, the narrowing of the season would limit our wren to producing only one brood while lowland wrens will lay two.

The male's establishment of territory assured him sufficient food for a family. There he sat on the aspen branch, bubbling with a song which rose and fell in pitch as rapidly as his nervous tail bobbled up and down. In the ensuing days the interruption of his song was a signal for us to look out the window, for it invariably meant that he had unwanted company. He flew, with a great show of ferocity, at any other male wren happening by. His tiny body darted here and there, feathers puffed up to make him look more formidable. Territorial fighting is mostly bluff and the possessor is nearly always the winner. The male needs only to protect and preserve his area, not to kill, which would endanger the species.

One day the female arrived, decided that she preferred a propertied mate, chose the dogwood nest, added a few twigs to the nest in wifely prerogative, and laid one egg a day until four were laid. Two weeks later we came to the land to hear the

TALL BLUE LETTUCE
(*Lactuca biennis*)

MUSKROOT
(*Adoxa moschatellina*)

Plate 49

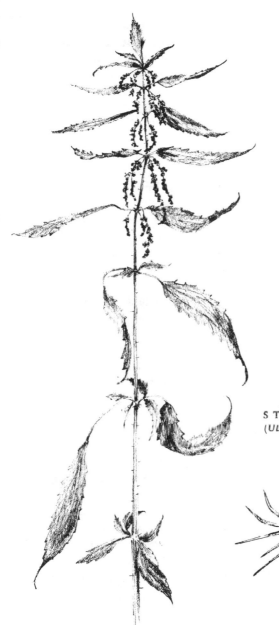

FLOWERS

STINGING NETTLE
(*Urtica dioica ssp. gracilis*)

STINGING SPINES

squawking of the newly hatched. By this time the male had stopped singing, not because of the oppression of domestic duties, as Herman claimed, but because singing made him noticeable and might attract predators to the nest. When the mating urges are stronger than caution, at summer's beginning, he sings loud and long, deserving his Chippewa Indian name which means "big noise for its size."

Our family watched the care and feeding of their family. The quivering of the dogwood bushes often betrayed their food searching even when we couldn't see the birds themselves. The young are heavy eaters, with seemingly bottomless stomachs. Their diet is almost totally insects: spiders, beetles, caterpillars, and grasshoppers that must have scratched on the way down. Wrens, unlike most birds, will eat ladybugs. Since the young completely digest their food in an hour and a half, the parents must hunt all day long.

As soon as a parent returned to the nest, the unmusical squawking of the young began, as melodious as a squeaky hinge. Without this noise, the parent will not feed the nestling. A quiet bird will starve to death. There is a precise pattern of signal and response highly developed in most birds. The parent brings food, the young beg and open their mouths, the parent feeds. If the young do not beg at the sight of a parent, the parent ignores them. Usually these are weak birds to begin with, and this is nature's way for assuring the survival of the strongest. Begging is restricted to the period when the adult is at the nest with food; constant noise, again, would attract the attention of enemies. Begging gradually becomes less effective as the season progresses. Parental drives wane, disappearing about the time the young can feed themselves.

After feeding, the parent waits at the doorway of the house. In a moment he pokes his head in and removes a small white packet of uric acid solids, keeping the nest clean. One or the other parent waits patiently each time and will not leave until the whole feeding pattern is complete.

❦

The day before summer is also the time of year for the most brightly colored of all western birds, the western tanager. The first time I saw one I was out sketching and thought someone had planted a brightly painted wooden bird on a ponderosa trunk, an avian salting of the woods. The male has an enamel-red head, black back, and brilliant yellow breast. The female is pale—dappled, cool, yellow-green—colored to blend into the foliage where she nests.

At midday the male comes and alights on the aspen trunk nearest the deck, about head height, and lunches with us, looking like a refugee from a tropical rain forest, brilliant and handsome and a little out of place. We eat lunch with a sandwich in one hand and binoculars in the other.

❧

Night in the early summer grove is quiet, with the smell of coolness. It is good to have a fire in the Franklin stove. Jane puts the day's butterfly catch, pinned on a stretcher, in the wood-stove warming oven so that the mice won't find them. I write myself a note to remove them before lighting the stove to cook breakfast. Jane blows up her air mattress and hoists it up to the tree house. Folly settles herself in a chair, which she is not allowed to do at home in the city. Her conscience bothers her and she is uneasy, but not uneasy enough to give up the unexpected comfort. Herman blows out the lamps. The metal of the roof crackles a little with cooling. A twig snaps outside. A bird chirps once. Then deep quiet sheathes the grove.

In the stillness, the hypnotic scuttling of the sleepless stream is magnified. The stillness lasts until four-thirty in the morning when the cacophony of awakening birds goes off like a mis set alarm clock. Then quiet resumes until light bestirs the inhabitants of the grove, us included. Before I put my feet on the icy floor I watch a bright white full moon going down behind green trees in a bright blue sky, a very disorienting sight.

The bunkroom windows look out crown-high on the aspen woodland, a rich leafy green world. Here between the two streams the aspens are flourishing in their characteristically thicket-type grove. The water table is high, the ground permanently saturated within a few feet of the surface. The soil is deeper here than any place else on the land, largely washed into the valley from above, and too moist for the pine and spruce which normally would shade out the aspen. Most of the aspens that grow in with the conifers on other slopes are dead or dying. They stand attached by a root thread like the front tooth of a six-year-old, needing only a light tug to finish the job.

Aspens cannot reproduce in the deep woods, for they are intolerant of shade; they need nearly full light for root sprouts to develop into young trees. And none grow in the midst of the mature grove unless there is a small clearing where older trees have fallen, opening up the leaf canopy. Most saplings grow along the outer edges of the grove where sunshine is opulent, or near the lake. Once started, the sprouts make quick growth, for they have the advantage of a preestablished root system.

When we came to this land, the young trees near the lake were about shoulder high. Now they tower over my head. Old pictures show that the trees have grown about three feet in five years, and their trunks are beginning to hide the view of the lake from the cabin deck. None are over an inch in diameter, and all are leggy and awkward compared with the middle-aged stolidity of the mature grove.

The young grove arose from a previous group of aspens destroyed by beavers for their dam some thirty years ago. A few stumps remain, bearing the familiar chiseled conical shape made by beaver teeth. Beavers use aspen for both construction and food, storing up the tender stems against a long hungry winter. A beaver does not, as legend would have it, know which direction the tree will fall when he cuts it, but counts on alacrity to make up for lack of engineering expertise.

❧

These young trees sprouted in this area when it was suitable to their needs, just as the annuals and perennials invaded the bare ground of the meadows. The preparation was done by pioneer willows and sedges which created land out of marsh, and by beaver cuttings which let in the light.

As the young trees become established, they begin to infringe upon each other's needed space. Competition shows in the slenderness of trunk and paucity of leaf. Competition begins when the demands of the plants are in excess of the site's ability to fulfill them, and is keenest among plants of the same species which have identical requirements. Those trees which survive the competition will have about fifty years of rapid growth and a life expectancy of about one hundred years, rarely much longer.

This is one of the reasons aspen is considered a "trash" tree. Not being especially long-lived, the fallen trunks open the ground to erosion. To the lumberman, aspen takes up space that might better be used for more commercially desirable stands. By the time an aspen is large enough to cut for lumber, it is usually infested with heart-rot fungi and is therefore useless. We had to cut down a twenty-year-old aspen while surveying; rot had already begun in the heartwood.

Aspen is really useful only for smaller things; young trees make fine fence posts. Susan loves to carve it, and I still have a smooth satiny spoon she made years ago from sapwood. The sapwood in the tree we cut broke like gypsum. It was slippery wet and sweet-smelling with summer, a pale, creamy lemon-yellow.

Westerners have a special feeling about aspen that encompasses none of these ideas. It is the only tall deciduous grove-forming tree of the montane area. Alder, willow, dogwood, and mountain maple are all shrubs or shrublike trees and, on our land, are never over twelve to fourteen feet high. Conifers have a majestic monotony, like someone who is always right. They are too timeless to mark the seasons. But aspen has éclat, a glorious brashness in defiance of the rules, the flapper who does the Charleston in the midst of the grand waltz. The landscape would be dull indeed without them.

❦

The chalky gray bark of our young aspen is distinctive, leading many visitors to mistake them for birch. To obtain such a subtle gray would require mixing all the remnants of the palette with a dot of cadmium yellow and a touch of opaque Chinese white. The horizontal ridges make the bole look as if it were bandaged.

Being a self-pruning tree, there are many branch stubs and knots on the lower trunk which mark fallen limbs. Where each branch has detached is an "eye," a round black knot elongated by bark distortions on either side into a sometimes startling likeness of a human eye. When the leaves of the lower branches are shaded out by the top of the tree they receive insufficient sunlight for photosynthesis; the leaves fall and eventually the branch. The more intolerant a tree is of shade, the more rapidly self-pruning occurs, resulting in a tree that is very tall in relation to its breadth. Indeed, one of these aspens without the company of its fellows looks somewhat like a lion's tail, long and narrow, with a tuft at the end.

The aspen's growth habit permitted us to provide one of the joys of childhood at Constant Friendship. Since the leafing boughs of aspens do not begin until well up on the trunk, there was ample room for a tree house. About ten feet up, Herman lashed logs between four sturdy trees, upon which he and the girls built a house, complete with Dutch door and framed windows and big enough for two sleeping bags. It sways gently when the wind blows. From the tiny porch there is a bird's-eye view of the world below which reduces adults to their proper perspective.

✿

The high branches of the aspen allow the uninterrupted passage of the hummingbird. He shoots through the aspen grove as if it were a freeway, missing every tree, only the distinctive whirr of his wings telling of his passage. Hummingbird flight is much too swift for my eye to follow.

Before we had shelter and a wood stove, I cooked breakfast over an open campfire. Juggling a typical mountain breakfast for five—trout, eggs, sausage, fried potatoes, sometimes cornbread in a portable oven, and coffee or cocoa—meant eating in shifts. And it was with grateful appreciation that I would sit down in quiet long after everyone else had eaten and gone about their work. Looking out to the lake one morning, enjoying the freshness and quiet, eyes focused on the distance, a glass of tomato juice raised halfway to drinking, I was suddenly aware in the unfocused nearness of a very large bumblebee whirring in front of my nose. The "bee" backed off and came into focus as a broad-tailed hummingbird, iridescent in the cool light, green as chlorophyll, ruby throat changing color with the tilt of his head. The red-throat flash is caused by minute prisms in the feather surface

which break up the white light into colors and create an irides-
cent carmine patch, and the vivid greenness of the body comes
from the combination of yellow pigment and structural blue.

At another time one boisterous bird helped with the survey-
ing, darting through the transit tripod like a World War I
flying ace under a country bridge, prompting us to name him
the Red Baron. While we surveyed across the north stream, we
watched him perform a courtship dance for the female who was
well hidden in the thicket. He looped up, hung at the top,
swooped down again as if he were on an invisible roller coaster.
Over and over again, describing ovals and circles and elipses,
he was a most determined suitor. He rested for a moment on a
bush honeysuckle branch, the first time I had ever seen him
light on anything but a dead aspen twig. He pierced a closed
honeysuckle blossom with his tiny beak and was gone in an
instant.

Another male attacked the red pump handle by the sink
several times before he discovered that it wasn't full of nectar.
Hummingbirds are most responsive to colors in the red range
of the spectrum. We had to take down our red lantern, for he
preferred it to the less-bright red sugar water we hung from the
tree. One day he found my red enamel teakettle on the stove
and made several passes at it until we managed to shoo him out
of the kitchen. This boldness had disastrous consequences. While
we were gone he flew into the cabin through an open upstairs
window. We found him dead on a bunk—so small, even with
wings full spread he wasn't as large as my hand.

The feathers of the hummingbird's tiny wings are almost
transparent. The wing articulates mainly at the shoulder—in
flight, working somewhat like a paddle. To watch a hawk or
raven circling emphasizes the structural difference; in the larger
birds the flight feathers seem to curl and float on the trailing
edge. A hummingbird sculls the air, beating his wings continu-
ously and even flying backward by a downward scoop of the
tail and reversal of wings. He hovers with a wing beat so fast
it blurs in the sight. A hummingbird can neither glide nor walk.
The Red Baron perches for a moment on a dead aspen branch,
always a bare limb, never leafed, and then resumes his flight.

A hummingbird expends so much energy in flight during

·the day that he conserves energy at night by entering a state of torpor that is a form of hibernation. To maintain his metabolism, the hummingbird feeds on high-energy foods, mainly sugars from nectar; sometimes he finds tiny insects in the corollas of favored flowers. Each outer edge of the hummingbird's tongue is curled into a tube; the tongue is more or less fringed near the tip, forming a delicate brush. This construction efficiently serves the double purpose of sucking up nectar and flicking out insects from the deep safety of the flower.

Flowers in which the corolla is fused into a tube hold more nectar than open blooms, and these are the ones the Red Baron prefers. From the deck we watch him feed in the wild honeysuckle and gooseberry bushes, which he abandons for scarlet gilia and Indian paintbrush as they come into bloom later in the summer. He is an airborne jewel, a dart of green energy, and the aspen grove would be empty without him.

❧

The summer that we were building the second part of the cabin was a noisy one. We spent a great deal of time hammering and clattering about, metal ladders rattling, a small generator powering a snarling saber saw, galvanized tin roof sheets thundering in the wind—all very sharp, terribly mechanical sounds. In the midst of all this soliloquy of carpentering, there came a new sound, a sharp *rat-tat-tat-tat-TAT*. And there on the tin roof, head going like a jackhammer, was a yellow-bellied sapsucker, a species of woodpecker, pounding away.

He came back many times that week, attacking wood and tin with equal vigor. When we were inside the cabin it sounded like a Civil War Gatling gun. Outside we could hear him from the far meadows. Although the base of a woodpecker's skull is cushioned to withstand his drilling habits, we have always wondered if this one ended the summer with a blunted bill and a bad headache.

I watched him work on an aspen. His stiff tail feathers were braced against the tree trunk. He gave the tree four or five exploratory taps in rapid succession, much as one knocks on a door. Deciding that this was a good location for a hole, he began in earnest with a syncopated clattering. Chips sprayed out, falling to the ground. Within five minutes he had a hole well started which could be seen from thirty feet below. All day, through the grove, his persistent pounding punctuated the more intimate sounds of stream and aspen wind.

The woodpecker's bill hides a long tongue which hinges back up into the head. When looking for grubs or beetle larvae, he inserts his bill into a hole in the tree, unrolls his tongue and snaps up the borers. Black Hills bark beetles have caused thousands of acres of damage in Colorado, killing ponderosa and spruce. The woodpecker is the most efficient control, consuming thousands of beetles a day.

We hoped that he would nest nearby; there were certainly ample dead trees for his choosing. His drumming, so evident to human ears, also attracts a mate. A hummingbird makes himself conspicuous to the female by his roller-coaster dance; a wren sings; the woodpecker pounds. And he and his mate did raise a brood in the aspen grove, a boisterous bunch indeed.

❧

Only a few flowers bloom the day before spring at Constant Friendship, and these are adapted to take advantage of early sunshine; they grow not inside the aspen grove but in the open sunny meadows. There is no prevernal growth in the aspen grove because the ground is still too cold; below 40 degrees soil waters fail to dissolve the nutrient salts that plants need for growth. In late May, when I dig in the ground to plant some cinquefoil sprigs around the cabin, there is still ice five inches below the surface. The aspen grove remains grave and gray until early June, and the flowers which live in the grove are those which appreciate its protection from the bright summer sun: meadow rue, bedstraw, anemone, wild rose, shrubby cinquefoil.

Many shrubs, herbs, and grasses grow abundantly in the dappled shade of the aspen, for it is a bright shade and the light is little altered in quality as it filters through the interstices of the leaves. The number of vertical layers indicates the progression in succession from the meadow. In the earliest communities, such as those on the bare rock of the gate meadow, layering is measured in millimeters between crustose lichen and stone surface. In the meadow proper it is a layering of inches,

ROSE HIPS

WILD ROSE
(*Rosa woodsii*)

IN FRUIT

WILD GOOSEBERRY
(*Ribes inerme*)

IN FLOWER

Plate 50

between tall herbs, shorter herbs, and those on the ground. In the aspen grove it is a layering of feet, the forty-foot aspen towering over bushes and shrubs, lower herbs, and grasses of varying levels, down to the mosses which cling to the soil.

The soil in this valley between the two streams is the best on the land. Its greater fertility comes from a high water table, more incorporated organic matter, and the sediment which has been washed into this valley over the centuries. This ground between the two streams contains more water after a rain, and with its gentle slope retains it longer than the meadow's gravelly soils. But this too is considered an immature soil and has no clear B horizon.

❧

Wild roses grow in a tangled thorny thicket in the aspen grove; the thickness of the undergrowth in the grove is an index to the soil's fertility. The meadow's roses are mere sprigs; in the aspen grove they are luxuriant bushes, bearing big open blossoms varying from palest to deepest pink. Their fringes of yellow stamens are visited by a whirring of bees.

The fertilized ovaries of the wild rose ripen into red hips, first visible as a green swelling beneath the flower. When the petals fall, the sepals persist, drying and curling at the tip. By fall the ovary is a deep, shiny scarlet container, about the size of a hazelnut, the last spot of color in the deadening landscape.

Rose hips are extremely high in Vitamin C and excellent survival food. Why they are left on the bushes all winter long and not eaten by bird and rodent I never knew until I made rose hip jam. In the traditional way of making jam, I boiled the fruit and let the juice run through a cloth-lined sieve. The sieve turned black, as did the bright apricot-colored juice, with a smell to match.

When I seeded the hips to make a raw conserve, my fingers were sore from the almost invisible exterior spines. Because wild rose hips are largely seeds, this tedious task merely quartered the resultant quantity. Despite recipes to the contrary, it was very nearly inedible. It was a beautiful color however. Perhaps the variety of rose was at fault since rose hip soup is a prized Scandinavian soup. Maybe it was our pampered taste buds. But to have a natural food which is so nutritious left uneaten suggests that birds too may find it unpalatable.

On some rose stems are slightly elongated galls the size of a cherry, and on the tips of others are clusters of prickly round galls, rosy tan and red, more spined than the stems themselves. Both galls are caused by tiny flies. Like the schoolboy who brings home an interesting batch of eggs and winds up with a houseful of grasshoppers, I clipped some rose galls and tied them in a plastic bag until I should have time to draw them. When that time came, their time had come also; in the warmth of the studio they had hatched. The bottom of the bag was peppered with gall flies.

❧

Shrubby cinquefoil, another shrub of this layer, also belongs to the rose family. This is the only bush cinquefoil, the others being graceful herbs. "Cinquefoil" refers to the five-fingered leaves. Like the rose, the flower has five brilliant petals; its color is yellow right out of the paint tube, set against five green sepals, and a profusion of stamens. The shredded gray-brown bark, hanging in ribbons, and the dried sepals identify the shrub even without leaves. Cinquefoil is browsed by deer only when better forage is not available; wildlife biologists use it as an "indicator plant." If the cinquefoils are heavily eaten, the range is overpopulated with deer.

Squaw currant and gooseberry both have tiny pink flowers early in the summer, and they are easiest to tell apart when they bear their characteristic berries. Grouse are fond of them both for food, and the dried berries sometimes persist on the plant all winter long. Both shrubs send out long arching canes which root at the tip, and when growth is heavy in moist places, provide shelter for rabbit and bird.

❧

The blue grouse that adopted us one summer preferred wild currants to be held in the flat of the hand so that she could pick them up, one at a time. She appeared one afternoon early in the summer.

On a warm summer's afternoon it is sometimes very diffi-

SHRUBBY CINQUEFOIL
(*Pentaphylloides floribunda*)

Plate 51

cult for me to keep my mind on reading. The breeze disturbs the page, the birdsong disturbs my concentration, and all sounds combine to lure my eye away from the text. It is easy to lower the book, then turn it back up on my lap, and to look into the woods for·what is written there. It is often then, when the mind is receptive and relaxed, that one sees the most.

Out of nowhere she came, a small fowl, not much bigger than a football, half hopping, half walking. As she drew closer she appeared to be a young bird, still in speckled plumage. Terribly curious, yet not wanting to frighten her, I held my breath. She was the first grouse I had ever seen, and quite possibly I was one of the first humans she had ever seen.

Half an hour later I was still watching her, and she was contentedly poking about the rocks and shrubs. The voices of Jane and Sara as they came from swimming disturbed her not at all. Still she remained, walking around like a barnyard pullet. Susan came singing down the hillside, and hushed at our warning. And still the grouse stayed. She stayed for several weeks, all told, accompanying us on our hikes, being hand-fed, and treated like a member of the family.

Anyone who has read *King Solomon's Ring,* by Konrad Lorenz, the delightful account of how birds are "imprinted" by the first moving object they see after hatching, has probably surmised that to a degree this is what may have happened with the young blue grouse. Abandoned for some reason by her own mother, she came to regard humans as her family. From what we have read since, this situation seems fairly frequent with grouse.

She divided her time fairly between our neighbors, who called her Jenny, and us. She always appeared within an hour after we arrived from the city, and followed us out to the gate when we left, almost waving a wing goodbye, seemingly reluctant to be left behind. Folly was distraught. All she wanted to do was play with the new playmate and couldn't understand why she had to be tethered. The little bird had no fear of Folly, walking right under her nose.

Late summer came, and one day she didn't appear. Her plumage had been changing, feather by feather, and perhaps she left for other pastures. Perhaps even then the bobcat stalked

SEEDHEAD

BLACK-EYED SUSAN
(*Rudbeckia hirta*)

Plate 52

NORTHERN BEDSTRAW
(*Galium boreale*)

STAMINATE FLOWERS

ACHENES

MEADOWRUE
(*Thalictrum fendleri*)

PISTILLATE FLOWERS

Plate 53

the forest and found a small thing which had not been suffi-
ciently trained in fear. Or perhaps she found a mate.

It is still easy to see the speckled form in the spattered sun-
shine of the open grove, head bobbing as she walked, trusting
and companionable, good-natured and sweet-tempered, willing
to do what we did and offering in return her own impeccable
self to marvel at.

🌿

The summer that we first came to Constant Friendship there
was a field of black-eyed Susans along the road, scattered among
blue-green timothy. Its special beauty became associated with
coming here and the beginning awareness of mountain life.
That field is indelible in my memory, its brilliance and clarity
of form like those of stained glass. The memory has since been
overlaid with other stained glass images, each memorable in
itself. Over the years a resonance of color and meaning has
emerged, a knowing of this land, that transcend the simple sum
of the individual parts, symbolizing our mountain world.

The intense chrome yellow of the black-eyed Susan petals,
stained with gold or orange, always reminds me of this field.
With the emphatic black-brown raised center they are all ver-
tical and horizontal, softened by the curve of petal and enlivened
by the intensity of contrast—a flower I draw again and again.
The petals fall, leaving a cone-shaped seedhead subtended by
curling bracts, almost as handsome as the flower itself. Here
they grow sprinkled in the aspen woods, a pleasure of my sum-
mer. And the timothy, which flourishes best in cool climates,
bends and nods in the breeze. The slender seedheads remain
upright all winter, finely drawn lines of pale tan against the snow.

Beneath are smaller grasses and herbs, some with poetic
names like rue and valerian; others with interesting names like
orange hawkweed and death camas. Pale and delicate meadowrue
reminds me of Ophelia. The flowers are borne on graceful nod-
ding panicles, male and female on separate plants, looking like
tassels beneath the five-pointed sepals. The flowers are green and
modest, developing seedheads which look like smaller editions
of northern anemone, to which they are first cousin.

NORTHERN, or
MEADOW, ANEMONE
(*Anemone canadensis*)

GLOBEFLOWER FRUIT

GLOBEFLOWER
(*Anemone multifida* var. *globosa*)

Plate 54

The name *anemone* comes from the Greek word meaning wind, and their other common name is windflower. Growing in drifts among the grasses are the northern anemones. The flower head is formed of petal-like sepals, generally five, the size of a silver dollar in full bloom. The open cup is a glowing rich creamy white in which there are opalescent casts of yellow and pink and blue, sunshine and shadow. The slender flowering stem rises out of a whorl of lobed leaves, which show off the white flower like a green doily. The stems are fine, and up to my knee, and the flowers nod sinuously in the breeze. The delicate globe-flower blooms here also, bearing a tiny dark-red flower scarcely an inch across, less showy than the seedhead, which is woolly and white with easily windblown achenes that look like elfin cotton candy.

Yellow parsley blooms first in the gate meadow, a few inches high, and then here among the aspens, where it reaches its full height of fourteen inches, with each stem holding a flat topped cluster of tiny yellow flowers. Valerian blooms at the same time, a cluster of pink-tinged white flowers in a ball atop a thick green stem, often capped with a red admiral butterfly daintily sampling the sweetness of the flowers. The parsley ripens into small seeds like a miniature cow parsnip; the valerian produces tiny tufted seeds which sail on the wind.

High summer brings the showy daisies to flower. Their fine narrow petals are a deep lavender blue, thickly rayed in double rows about a flat yellow center. There are so many that their lavender heads form a halo around the edge of the grove and almost hide the fact that there are many other flowers in bloom. The early cushion daisies of the meadow cling to the soil to conserve heat; these tall daisies grow extravagantly, freed of the rigors of cold, repeating the summer sun in their golden centers.

Northern bedstraw begins to bloom beside the daisies, but the individual flowers are so small that they are scarcely noticeable in the wealth of other colors and sizes. The four-sided stems bear panicles of tiny, white, four-petaled flowers, resembling tiny dogwood blossoms. The common name comes from its use as a substitute for straw in mattress stuffing; tradition holds that the manger of the Christ Child was filled with sweet bedstraw.

Death camas send up stalks bearing open creamy white flow-

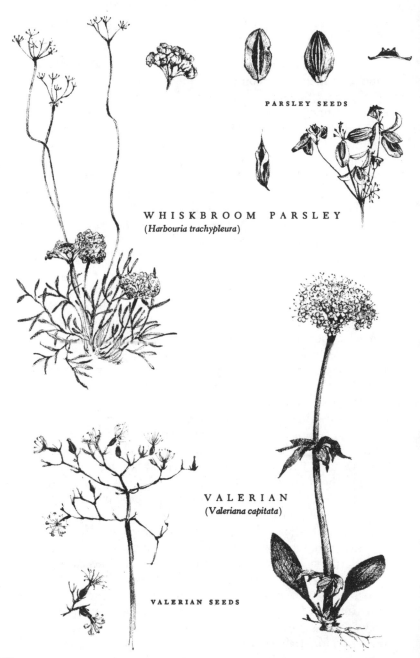

PARSLEY SEEDS

WHISKBROOM PARSLEY
(*Harbouria trachypleura*)

VALERIAN
(*Valeriana capitata*)

VALERIAN SEEDS

Plate 55

SHOWY, or ASPEN, DAISY
(*Erigeron speciosus* var. *macranthus*)

ers, each sepal and petal marked with a sticky green heart-shaped gland. As with grass-of-Parnassus, the markings attract insects. But hopefully not larger foraging animals—the whole plant is poisonous. Since the narrow green leaves appear early, they are easily mistaken for wild onions, which also grow here, small pink flowers nodding on a sunburst of stems. When the petals fall, the flower stems curl upward, splitting open to drop shiny black seeds.

This is a delicate grove in the summer, all green and yellow, pink and white, a three-dimensional Vivaldi concerto. In the back-lighting of early morning this is a gentle world. As a young friend of mine said, "I like to sit here on the deck and watch the grove waking up."

🌿

It was when the black-eyed Susans and showy daisies were in bloom that we took the indications of the aspen grove seriously: water was here. The well-developed understory of plants and the aspen grove itself are viewed by well-diggers as an indication of underground water.

Our mountain neighbor came by one Sunday and remarked that with the prevalence of water in the area it seemed foolish to carry water when we might dig a well. This sounded attractive to the female of the species, who, whether she be mosquito or human, is most likely to cause trouble. When I concurred with this suggestion for ready water, Herman struck a stance reminiscent of the Apollo on the west pediment of the Temple of Zeus at Olympia and said, "Dig!"

Susan and I began with pick ax and shovel. We hit water at twelve inches, and by the time we had gone eighteen, were well up over the ankles. The water was so cold that the first few minutes of digging were agony, replaced by a total numbness to the knees which suggested that you might chop off a toe and never know the difference until the water turned red. By the time we were waist-deep, other friends in sympathy and pity joined in digging our hole to China which finally reached seven feet, three feet in diameter, by late September.

Herman rigged a rope between two aspens and lowered three casings into the well with a chain hoist. The last casing

WILD ONION SEEDHEAD

WILD ONION
(*Allium cernum*)

WAND LILY
(*Zygadenus elegans*)

Plate 56

extended above ground so that no surface water could enter. He installed a pump and the necessary pipes, we all handprinted the cement around the edge (including Folly who could not have cared less), and then toasted each other with crystal-clear cold water.

❦

It was indeed a help not to have to carry water from town, and even though the well froze during the winter, there was bright and fresh water the next April. As Herman remarked as he held a glass up to the light, "Did you ever see such pure water?"

A week later it became painfully apparent that the beautifully clear water was mightily contaminated. Herman recovered quickly, but I spent a week in the hospital with a virulent salmonella infection contemplating the virtues of digging your own well.

When Herman dismantled the well he discovered that the weight of the cement had caused the bottom casing to drop while the top was held firm by its cement collar, allowing surface water to pour in. All attempts to patch it were a frustrating failure and that is how we met our first well-digger.

He came with his rig—as big as a fire truck—hard hat, big cigar, and witching stick. Many people have witched water in the aspen grove, and although we are not of the chosen who can feel the unmistakable tug of the twig as it bends downward to water, we know many who do. The well-digger spent two hours witching and then decided to dig within ten feet of the old well.

Of such ignorance adventures are often made, and we did not know that the County Health Department automatically considers any well within fifty feet of a stream to be contaminated. With rattlings of chains and wheezing of engine and the unmistakable painful pounding thump that well-digging drills make, the new well went in to twelve feet and no more, stopped by bedrock. Not having a hard-rock drill he could go no farther. So he folded up his rig and noisily chugged away, leaving silence and more contaminated water.

We carried our water from the city again and became a little touchy when someone asked us how the well was. Then we decided for one more try. The new well-digger came with a monstrous diesel truck—equipped with hydraulic jacks and interchangeable bits, a combination of delicate machinery and grinding power—and a cigar and a hard hat. No witching this time. "Just put a mark on the ground where you want the well."

The engine hummed and whined and the bit cut into the earth, spewing up dirt. As before, water immediately appeared and kept coming through twenty feet of gravel and gley. Then rock. And more rock. And still more rock. The decision had to be made, considering that well-digging is charged for by the foot, how far to go. Would there be a vein of water under this rock, or was it bedrock? One hundred and twenty feet later the answer was clear: straight Pikes Peak granite.

They pounded in casings into the top of the bedrock. An inner casing was fitted inside, slotted at the bottom, so water enters from beneath. It is filtered by the gravel, seeking its own level, and then is pumped up into the cabin by Herman's Rube Goldberg device of pipes and stopcocks, which allow it to be drained in winter. Every once in a while, on a very cold day, the pump stiffens even as we use it, and there is a great rush for hot water to keep it open. The water must be tested frequently. But it is pure now. For the moment.

❧

Summer is a glorious time of the year to have a party. The land flowers with people. The hum of pleasant conversation accompanies the conversation of the streams; human laughter is punctuated by birdsong. The deck is sunny and bright and no one sits inside.

But there are uninvited guests. Just as tick season is over in June, it is time to begin using food covers for the flies that come in July. Flies are the price we pay for summer. Houseflies are everywhere, bumbling against the windows, buzzing around the kitchen, littering the floor with their bodies, and having to be swept out every day. Their life cycle is fast and furious, completed in one to three weeks, depending upon the temperature.

As necessary a function as they perform in nature in the breaking down of organic matter, I still reach for the fly swatter when I see one. A housefly's proboscis is soft and spongelike so that it can mop up liquid food; if the food is not liquid to begin with, the housefly regurgitates the contents of its crop, hence its germ-carrying capacity.

The most annoying thing about houseflies, besides their reprehensible feeding habits, is that they are so difficult to swat. Like their antennae, all their bristly hairs are sensitive to the slightest movement of air. A fly's response to movement nearby is immediate; it requires only one-twentieth of a second to get airborne. In addition, there are three tiny ocelli, single-lens eyes, on top of the head, which receive rapid changes in light and thereby awaken and alert the fly's nervous system. Small nerves would transmit a danger message too slowly, so there are large nerve fibers which run the whole length of the nervous system.

The wings of a housefly are fast and powerful, their beating creating the familiar annoying hum of F in mid-range. If the temperature is too cool they sound flat. The fly's first pair of wings are short and broad and provide flight; the second pair have been modified into short- stalks, or halteres, which act like gyroscopic stabilizers. The halteres vibrate like wings during flight, helping to hold the fly's body in the same axis. One only needs to look at a drifting wafting cranefly to realize the efficiency of the housefly's flight.

There are always a few flies who remain inside the cabin in the fall, stupefied by the cold, rousing when the Franklin stove warms the room. They buzz irritably in the corners of the windows. When the temperature falls below 18 degrees, their bodies blacken the window sill like chunks of soot.

❧

Houseflies have one virtue; they do not bite. The biters are horse- and deer flies. At high altitudes where summers are brief, flies are inclined to be somewhat more dedicated than elsewhere to making life miserable for humans. Since the time is comparatively short in which to feed, they must consume more in a shorter time and hence are bold crapulous feeders.

Last summer I was bitten by an especially voracious female deer fly; my eyes were nearly swollen shut for two days and my face puffy for a week. Fast flying and not discouraged by being shooed away, deer flies are medium-sized with spotted wings and an iridescent body. The female is equipped with lancet-type mouth parts, which can pierce skin; she often makes several holes in one area, frequently choosing the hairline—perhaps attracted by perspiration. Deer fly larvae are vegetarian and have an insufficient supply of protein when they reach adulthood; the adult female must bite to get blood protein. The male deer fly, like the male mosquito, is an innocent vegetarian. I believe in motherhood but I draw the line at deer flies.

The other champion biter is the horsefly. These bumbling bombastic insects have a buzz as annoying as the chain saw. The large larvae are so cannibalistic that a collecting-jarful always ends up as one gorged larva. The horsefly's lancets are so large that the bite leaves a hole in the skin, sometimes with a drop of blood. The wound is made by flattened scissor-like mandibles, which literally saw through the skin. The maxillae, another mouth part, are plunged up and down in the wound, creating a pool of blood which is sucked up. When a horsefly bites, it hurts! Graf snaps, Folly yelps, I swat, Herman swears.

At 60 degrees horseflies breed continuously, the time from egg to adult completed in three weeks. It makes me glad, some summers, to see the first freeze of fall usher in fly-free days!

❧

Deer mice are as common as flies in the summer mountains. In the summer they forage in the cabin, nibbling the ends off foil soup packets and plastic lids off jars. In the winter they track the snowy grove. Deer mice are white-bellied and white-footed, big-eared and shiny-eyed. And they love a drawer of towels I have.

Another resident rodent of the aspen grove is the pack rat. After an absence of about a week several summers ago, we came back to the cabin. At that time it was still open like a gazebo. Herman let down the loft ladder to take up the children's sleeping bags.

Taking up half the area of the four-by-twelve-foot loft deck was a nest. Not just an ordinary nest but a conglomeration of everything loose inside and outside the cabin cozily pulled and patted and pushed and shredded and nosed into a heap, like the pile of fallen leaves that children pyramid and then run and jump into. A whole box of paper napkins, hundreds of aspen leaves, half a box of lavender tissue and a few colorful shreds of labels from canned fruit, disassembled pine cones, part of a pot holder and selected gnawings from a new tea towel.

The rat was nearby, caught behind a rafter—a pale gray, sleek, and elegant rat of indeterminate sex. But, as Herman remarked, were it a he, all that was missing were the etchings on the wall and he could have twirled a silken whisker and made the traditional bachelor's invitation.

🌿

Late last summer we noticed a pile of freshly pulverized brown dirt, about two feet across, quite near the cabin. There are so many burrows that come and go that we thought nothing of it, other than the fact that it was in the middle of the path and very noticeable. The hole, about a couple of inches across, was as neatly cut into the turf as if made by a bulb planter.

Later in the day Herman was cleaning out brush beside the cabin when he frightened a two-week-old baby rabbit, fully furred, about three inches long. The rabbit hopped up on a rock, stayed long enough for a telephoto portrait, and hopped away. Cleaning finished, Herman was reading in the cabin when he heard a thump against the side. He went out to look, and the tiny rabbit was back on the same rock, still warm, but very dead. There were no signs of an assailant. After watching for some time, he went back inside, glancing out some forty-five minutes later just in time to see a weasel whisking the rabbit into its hole.

In all, the weasel took three young rabbits that day, cleaning out the warren. The weasel poked its head out of the hole, looked around, and then slipped out to pick up the last rabbit it had killed. The weasel laid the limp body beside the doorway, backed in tail first, looked about again, and snatched the rabbit in and disappeared. The weasel was a beautiful caramel color, streaked with white beneath, long and slender. Its burrow was excavated where it commanded an unrestricted view of the aspen community—mouse-feeding stations, vole runways, and rabbit thickets.

🌿

Some of the random piles of brush visible from the weasel's hole contain rabbit families. The shrub understory provides the protection for larger animals and consequently the aspen grove is a busier place than the open meadows. The warrens are well ·hidden during the summer, but in the winter exclamation-point rabbit tracks make well-tramped highways that funnel to safety. There is one such highway near the Whale's Mouth, another along the brush of the south stream, and several in the aspen grove.

Each rabbit knows his own habitat so well that when he is frightened he is well on his way home before I catch sight of the small gray bundle that has erupted out of the path only a few feet away, white pompom tail making quick scallops in the air as he disappears with a characteristic leap and a bound. Ordinary feeding little affects the natural food supply. Only if the population increases too rapidly will rabbits damage seedlings and the bark of larger trees.

A rabbit's teeth are specialized, like those of the porcupine, gopher, and beaver; the incisors are large and sharp. Constant feeding friction wears them down, but since the pulp cavities of the teeth remain open, the teeth can keep on growing throughout the rabbit's lifetime. Plant materials are relatively difficult to digest, and rabbits have a large intestine harboring symbiotic bacteria, much as deer have, to aid in the digestion of cellulose.

A rabbit produces two kinds of droppings. The brown pellets that are familiar where rabbits have been feeding indicate that all the nutrients have been extracted. Rabbits also produce green droppings which are only partly digested. These are re-eaten and provide a rich amount of Vitamin B produced by the bacteria of the intestine. By digesting plant cellulose in increments, a rabbit derives the maximum possible nutrition from a limited source.

We found a nest, a depression prepared in the ground long before the young are born, covered with a fur coverlet made from the mother's pelt. There were no rabbits in the nest; had there been we might have heard the mewing sound the young make in response to pressure on the nest cover. The nest looked much like a mallard's nest; much the same signal-response action is used in feeding the young of both bird and rabbit.

Rabbits are quiet animals, but they have a peculiar high penetrating scream when caught. The first time I heard it, it sounded as shrill as a young child's voice, sharp and plaintive, a small squeal of total fear. Again it was the weasel, loping off across the stream. Rabbits also form a large percent of the bobcat's diet.

Yet they flourish because they use their defenses to the fullest and because they are able to reproduce rapidly. They have a staggering biological potential. Each time I feel soft-hearted about the tiny body lying so still by the weasel's hole, I remember that they could destroy the vegetation on the land within a few years' time were they not controlled.

And any animal catching a rabbit must be swift. As fast as Graf is, he is outrun and outmaneuvered by a rabbit. The last one he chased fled under the fence. Intent on the rabbit and not the landscape, Graf hit the barbed wire at full speed. Fence posts vibrated for fifty feet on each side. Susan brought him back to the cabin with a gash over one eye, much subdued, not very interested in chasing rabbits or anything else for the rest of the day.

❦

Fall comes at its own pace in this grove. Protected by surrounding ridges, these trees may not turn until the first week in October. All in a few days they become fired with blazing light, a torch holding back the winter frosts. On a Thursday they are still green; on a Sunday, they are golden. The leaves range from citron to copper, saffron to gilt, glowing with light. They shower down with each gust of coming winter, buttering the still-blooming lupine, catching the purple asters and the last black-eyed Susans. The mahogany-red rose bushes snag them. The juniper waylays them in needled branches, holding them upright in a card file of autumn.

The Danaän shower of gold enriches the ground. The sweet musty smell of fall is inches thick under the hammock. It is a fragrance of aspen dust and honey and sunshine. The air is golden, as rich and sweet and heavy as an old Chateau d'Yquem.

The trunks, reflecting the light and the fallen leaves, are gilded. The silence is soft and warm and full, between intermittent rustlings of gold tissue-paper wrapping up the glow of summer. Now, if ever, the sounds that hold human flesh within circumscribed familiarities dissolve in the permeating golden light. Nothing exists except motes of aspen dust glinting in a shaft of sunlight.

✤

When evening comes the mountain air chills rapidly. Herman rolls up the hammock, puts it away for another year. There is a psychological tightening of the mind in preparation for winter. We use each day as if it were the last before the guillotine of winter slices out the warmth. I go out, drawing all day long, trying to catch the last vestige of summer. Herman pulls in the raft and puts up the rowboat. He cuts another load of wood for the stove and the girls protestingly stack and fill the wood boxes. He replaces a broken window and paints the deck. Truly, Herman and I are the ant and the grasshopper.

The leaves are almost all down. They drop not because of the frost but because of the declining activity of the tree which takes place regardless of temperature and is initiated by the tree's response to the lengthening nights. By the time low temperatures hit, the tree must be safely dormant in order to escape damage. A layer of tissue forms between leaf twig and stem. As water is cut off from the leaf by the tree, the chlorophyll of the leaf is not renewed; it breaks down and disappears, revealing the yellow pigment beneath. The cells at the base of the leaf stem disintegrate and the leaves fall in descending helices.

A gust of wind, impatient with remnants, sweeps the last leaves out of the treetops—an irritable housewife shaking a mop. A late rain or an early snow mats the quilted ground, the branches stretch and whine, the trunks sway and creak. The days grow short so quickly. Colors leach out. On the ground, yellow leaves fade to tannin-brown, grass to bronze-gray. The boles are opaque milky-gray, the early snow cold blue-gray. The empty branches are charcoal-gray against a sky bleak-gray. Only forms remain, drawn in soft pencil on rough paper.

Something small, black, and horizontal moves in the brush,

just enough to catch my eye. It is the tail tip of a magnificently camouflaged animal, pure white washed with pale yellow on the belly like dead leaves, two shoe-button eyes, an inquisitive triangular face. It is the weasel in his winter pelage, a fur so distinctly different from his summer coat that it is called ermine. A black triangular dot above each eye enlarges the eye area so that he seems to have a winsome Pierrot mask.

The change of coat is triggered not by cold but the shortening hours of autumn days. The amount of light registering through the eyes is thought to affect the pituitary gland which in turn indirectly triggers the whitening of the pelt. The weasel stood there, curious, evidencing no apprehension, his hypersensitive nose quivering with our unfamiliar scent. He moved only slightly and was gone, and it was a moment before I could pick him out again in the random pattern of blacks and whites and tans.

❧

In the winter the aspen woodland is a thousand eyes. When the wind blows, the trees of the grove rock in unison, keening over lost summers. Empty black branches, formed like clutching hands, scratch at the sky. The boles are pallid in the white winter sunlight, gleaming like bleached bones, only a shade darker than the shadowed snow at their bases. At the foot of each trunk is a tiny crescent of open ground, facing the sun. The warmth reflected by the light-colored trunks warms the snow and opens the turf to foraging by the deer mice who live in the community.

A deer mouse hunts at night and his tracks through the aspen grove form cat's cradles from one tree to the next. The amount of tracking shows this to be a busy grove. Perhaps it is still warm enough in December to find bark beetles or a few late sluggardly insects. The seedhead of a black-eyed Susan lies shredded. And then the neat precise tracks lead to a sprig of wild timothy. Here the dried stem is bent down by two tiny forefeet—the seeds nibbled, and chaff spilled on the new snow. And then tiny paired footprints hop on, incessantly searching for food to keep body heat up in the below-zero nights to come.

But others are hungry too, for at this altitude and this season there is no abundance of food. Surface feeding habits make the mouse easy prey. In the middle of one of the long ladder of tracks is a scurry of snow. The weasel's tracks, wide-spaced with hurry, lead into the thicket next to the big rock where it has a den.

✤

When the January snow showers come, all outlines are obscured by white filaments. I see the aspen grove amorphous and remote, framed in the paned windows of the cabin. It is like being on the inside of a cocoon looking out. The cabin is steely cold before the stoves are lighted.

But even in the middle of winter the top branches of the aspens are studded with the buds of spring to come. The smaller leaf and larger flower buds are covered with a tiny resinous reddish-brown scale like a beetle's back that protects the bud from cold and desiccation, from the destructive rapid freezing and thawing of frigid nights and hot winter sun. The bud scales protect more against drying than the cold, for the cold is necessary for deciduous trees to stimulate renewed growth in spring. The aspen must be below 40 degrees for several months in order to open leaf and flower in spring.

Even on the darkest winter day the buds on the leafless branches give a faith in spring to come, an assurance we sometimes are much in need of when night closes in at four o'clock and the streams are totally covered with snow and even the birds seem to be stilled by the breathless cold. The land seems unnaturally quiet, as if someone had just said "Shhhhhh" and in the sudden hush you can hear your heart beat.

The winter birds are all the more welcome because they come at a time when the world is bleak and gray. We host a small mixed flock of gray-headed and slate-colored juncos which completely undo the usually vociferous jays. Never once do the jays attempt to scatter the smaller juncos in what we have come to consider as typical jay pugnaciousness. They simply sit and watch the juncos feed, shifting miserably from one foot to the other.

Outside the kitchen window, on the big rock, the juncos feed happily. They are gone by spring, on their way to high

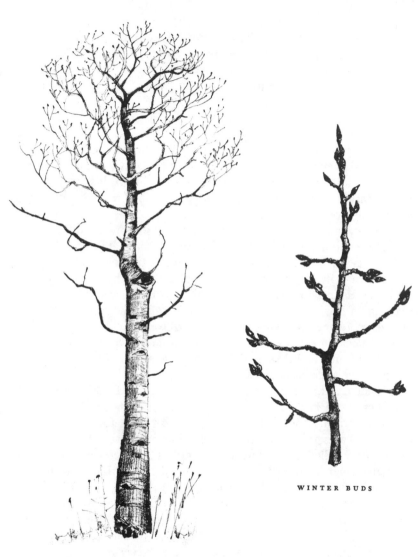

WINTER BUDS

WINTER ASPEN

Plate 57

summer-breeding grounds, but winter finds them visiting a regular route of food stations, of which our rock is one. Migration provides birds with a longer daylight period in which to find food for nesting young, and a better food supply elsewhere for winter. These little birds range from the far north to New Mexico, living mostly in coniferous forests. The gray-headed junco has a cinnamon-brown triangle on its back; its gray is the color of dead wood or winter rock, the brown of dead pine needles.

Junco bills are short and broad, adapted to seed cracking. Their busy feeding makes short work of the day's dole, to the jay's discomfiture. Sara gives them an extra ration of seed and they are unconcerned by her presence. They chatter with a sharp metallic clacking, a sound like a stick hitting along a picket fence.

These are flock birds and they signal danger by a flash of white on the tail. Inconspicuous on the ground, they are easily seen in flight. One bird taking off signals the rest of the flock to lift—an automatic reaction, just as the whole flight of ducks clatters off the lake if one leaves.

This winter the birds were joined by a new guest. A half-grown rabbit discovered the scattered seed and crouched in the snow like a pussycat, eating as fast as he could. He was so hungry that he was oblivious of Sara's comings and goings and Herman's camera shutter's snapping. By an accidental hop he found the cleared space on top of the rock where Sara had dumped a whole panful of seed.

His nose quivered with the ecstasy of plenty. All the while he fed, his ears turned this way and that, like a radar antenna, sampling the sounds of the woods. The jays sulked on the nearby branches, not daring to come near. But one of the juncos landed tentatively a few inches away. When nothing happened, he pecked at the seed, pausing now and then to eye the rabbit, each small creature uneasily aware of the other but enduring the discomfort for the sake of a full stomach.

🌿

Even smaller than the juncos are the mountain chickadees. Fat, round little Friar Tucks, their feeder is within inches of another kitchen window. When we come to the land in the win-

SEED PODS

LUPINE
(*Lupinus argenteus*)

Plate 58

ter, they are silhouetted against the tops of the aspens like enlarged animated buds. Their chittering and chattering fills the woods.

They are always terribly busy, seldom silent except when eating, feathers fluffed against the cold. They eat with staccato gestures, as if life were too short to waste any time, holding a seed in one foot and pounding it with a jackhammer beak. Mountain chickadees have a black line over each eyebrow, giving them a rakish mask. Along with the aspens they are the gossipers of the forest, and nothing is more cheery than their optimistic report on the seed situation on a bleak February day.

❧

In the center of the aspen grove is a small clearing, scarcely big enough to be called a meadow, which in summer is sweet and soft with white clover and edged with black-eyed Susans, lupines, and fleabanes. It is open and sunny and level, large enough to put up a badminton net or for playing volley ball. Herman mows it, bemoaning the fact that without any care it is an impeccable lawn and that his carefully manicured city frontyard often doesn't look as well.

Like the aspen grove itself, it is a people place, and because it is much lived in and played in, some of the happiest memories of Constant Friendship are tied to it.

Some years ago several families with young children planned an old-fashioned Fourth of July with us, to be shared with other friends who enjoy the out-of-doors. A bachelor brought a boiler-size watermelon. He chose to sleep on the raft in the middle of the lake and nearly congealed in the early morning dews and damps. He was just getting to sleep in the warmth of the sunshine when Herman shot off his carbide cannon announcing breakfast and a glorious Fourth.

There were watermelon-seed-spitting contests and fishing (which was largely unsuccessful due to the noise); there was a one-legged race and a treasure hunt. Susan and her house guest Jean planned a flag ceremony which the younger children carried out. They requested silence as we crossed the footbridge to the flagpole. Small hands struggled with stiff latches and stubborn grommets. Then slowly and carefully they raised the American flag to catch the morning breeze in a Colorado sky. Beneath it flew the bright blue flag of Constant Friendship with its blazon of five aspen leaves. The dignity and propriety of the boys, stilling the giggles of the girls, invested the mountain clearness with ideals and hopes. There are those moments that we remember with clarity because they epitomize a time or an awareness, that by caring for the things close to us we are able then to care for a larger world. No one had to ask for silence back across the footbridge.

The children wove in and out of the day on their own errands. It was as if the adults watched from the wrong end of a telescope trained on a section of stage landscape. Periodically figures came into view, a frieze of youngness running across the set, first from one wing of aspen, then the other of pine, diagonally upstage or down, sometimes stage front, sometimes behind a scrim of aspen leaves, sometimes swiftly, sometimes in a pavane. They belonged to the land that day, not to their parents. They were small sprites of the substance of leaf and shadow, interweaving with the patterns of flickering sunlight. The figures seemed to pause briefly, then rearrange—moments of stop-motion alternating with moments of movement.

Once a tree is grown there is no return to the seedling stage, and so the adults who watched could only remember and see arabesques of life and sunshine and unaware grace as natural as a flower or branch in the varying small figures. Even out of sight, the sound of their voices came carried on the aspen breeze. They were small exotic creatures at home in a world of wind and light. Here in these mountain meadows and groves they were all Peter Pans.

And then dinner, complete with fried chicken, corn-on-the-cob, baked beans, salad, sliced tomatoes, cucumber and watermelon pickles, homemade bread, coconut cake decorated with a red, white and blue pennant, all the good things brought and all the good things remembered from an Indiana Fourth of July. After darkness we went up to the ponderosa hill overlooking the lake. Herman set off fireworks from the lake rock, each shower reflecting in the blackness beneath, hissing upward to drop sizzling into itself. When the last rocket fell, it was hard to know whether it was fireworks or a shooting star.

6 ❦ ❦ The Forests

There are many mountain smells at Constant Friendship: the pungency of sage, the elusive honeysuckle breath of columbine, the pineapple aroma of wild camomile, the sweet-dry smell of aspen, the cool damp fragrance around a fern-sprigged rock, the elusive mushroomy smell of lactarius and russula.

But the odor that dominates is that of the ponderosa. The smell of the needles and the resinous sap is familiar, pleasanter than turpentine, yet still sharp. The sap springs out of every twig and needle and coats my hands with its odor. It emanates from sticky drops hanging from trunk and branch. It is an evocative smell of cleanness and fresh air. It is neither sweet nor cloying. It does not assault the senses. It is straightforward and clear, changing with damp or dry weather, but always retaining its essential clarity and identity. It is unmistakable, just as the conifer itself can be confused with no other tree.

No matter where I look I can see ponderosa pine on the land. There is a pure stand on the sun-struck slope above the lake. Ponderosas are gregarious and wind pollination is more efficient within a grouping of trees. Another grove grows farther to the west, intermixed with Douglasfir. Other ponderosas range over a low ridge and into a narrow valley so full of summer fungi that we call it Mushroom Valley. In the Douglasfir forest on the north-facing slopes a few ponderosas subsist, thin and ill-needled, simply enduring with no hope of reproducing and already being phased out by the thick shadows of the spruce.

Ponderosas are big trees, well deserving the name given to them by David Douglas, the young Scottish botanist who identified them in the far Northwest. The trees had been recognized as a new species by Meriwether Lewis but he collected no specimens or seeds, and it was Douglas who marked the tree a quarter century later, sending seeds back to England for study and planting.

The bark of older trees is very distinctive, layered with rust and gray-brown plates, pulling off in perforated sheets like mica. On an old tree the bark thickens and only the innermost layers expand with growth. The outer furrows deepen and widen into the distinctive patterns which I can flake off into thin, crisp plates.

The needles grow on arching branches in clusters of twos and threes; when the wind blows, the long needles shine silken in the sunlight. New spring growth is encapsulated in paper-like brown wrapping; by July these caps are all over the ground like small brown bugs. If I roll a needle between my thumb and forefinger I can feel the shape: the three-sidedness makes it roll more easily than the two-sided needles of the Douglasfir. The olive color of ponderosa needles is the somber green of the spruce suffused with sunlight.

❧

Within the Montane Zone—between 7000 and 9000 feet in our area—there are two different stands of conifer forest: on the south-facing slopes, receiving ample sun, are the ponderosa pines. On the north-facing slopes, shaded and damp, are the Colorado blue spruces and an occasional Engelmann spruce. Douglasfir may intermix on either slope. Even from the highway the two growths are distinguishable: spruce and fir are dark green, sharp-pinnacled; ponderosa is olive-green, bushy-needled, round-topped.

The difference between the two slopes is even more marked on a walk. If I stand at the top of a ridge I can see two dif-

STAMINATE CONE CLUSTER

FIRST-YEAR CONE, SPRING

DEVELOPING CONE

PONDEROSA PINE
(*Pinus ponderosa*)

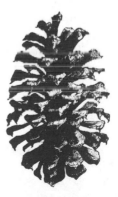

MATURE CONE

Plate 59

ferent forest worlds, one on either side, for conditions change abruptly and clearly. Walking down the north-facing slope the world darkens, dampens, and deepens into a dense growth of spruce mixed with Douglasfir—the setting for a Gothic novel. The deadfall on the forest floor makes walking difficult and muffles the footsteps. Mosses grow in the secretive shelter of logs and rocks at the top of the slope; at the base they fur the ground in mats. Climbing the south-facing slope the world becomes sunny, ponderosa bristling against a flat blue sky. It is open walking, though not always easy when the slope is both steep and graveled.

The topography of the Front Range with its predominantly east- and west-running ridges, produces these alternate north-facing and south-facing slopes. In the northern hemisphere, slopes facing south receive a higher concentration of sunlight than those facing north, with the result that south-facing slopes have warmer soils, higher air temperatures, less moisture, and less snow cover. South-facing slopes carry a plant population largely intolerant of shade and this sometimes includes desert plants, such as our pincushion cactus. Exposed to the full heat of mountain sun, the soil of the south-facing slopes where ponderosas thrive is well drained and dry, especially in winter. To convert such a soil to the cold damps of the north-facing slopes is an impossibility because it is the aspect, not the parent material, which determines the soil type here. Our entire land is underlaid with Pikes Peak granite; the tilt and direction of the slope determines the kind of soil which has formed on its surface. Trees requiring warmth and dryness climb to higher altitudes on slopes facing the sun which may be ten to fifteen degrees warmer, and those demanding lower temperatures and greater soil moisture extend to lower altitudes on the shaded side.

❧

The evergreens keep the land from being totally bleak in the winter. Unlike deciduous trees, evergreens do not put vast amounts of food and energy into leafing out. By retaining modified leaves all winter long, they can begin photosynthesis when the temperature reaches the minimum at which food-making can proceed.

To hold a pine needle, slender and sleek, and an aspen leaf, flat and heart-shaped, is to see the obvious differences between deciduous and coniferous trees. A single vein runs up the center of the needle to carry water and nutrients; the net-veining of an aspen leaf is neither necessary nor possible for the needle. Between the vein and the outer surface of the needle are food-producing cells and ducts containing wound-healing resins, unnecessary in deciduous leaves which are not out in cold weather. The high content of resin, instead of watery sap, in the needles acts like antifreeze, lowering the freezing point and preventing damage. The walls of the leaf are porous but thick, well adapted to survive cold and desiccation; pine needles do not wilt as deciduous leaves may.

Conifers are, as a matter of fact, deciduous, but not in the seasonal sense. They lose their needles when they are too shaded to perform photosynthesis. This may occur throughout the year, not only at the end of the growing season. The triangular form of an evergreen tree is the result of this growth pattern, the most efficient shape for exposing the most needles to light. Like a magnified dandelion rosette, the branches are usually evenly arranged around the main stem. Only at the outer edge is there sufficient light for food-making; the inner needles brown and fall off. The lower the branch the more it must stretch out toward the light, producing the familiar silhouette.

❦

The word "conifer" derives from the Latin word for cone. Seeds are borne on cone scales rather than inside an ovary, as rose seeds are. Male flowers grow at the tip ends of the branches, sulphur-yellow with pollen about the last week in June. Pollen dusts the needles and puffs out in clouds if I brush against a branch.

It requires two years for the fertile cone to develop; the female flowers are not fertilized the year they appear but develop only into small tight cones, light brown, about the size of an egg. The second spring, the cones open their scales while the pollen is blowing, closing after fertilization. The cones grow to four or five inches during the summer. Each cone scale holds two winged seeds on its dark-brown shaft. I handle them cautiously because each scale has a recurved sharp prickle of light brown at the tip which marks the first year's growth; the dark-brown shaft marks the second year's growth. I sometimes pick up a sackful from the ground to put in a basket beside the Franklin stove or to fill with peanut butter and birdseed for the birds. On the way back to the cabin I shake the seeds out along the way like Johnny Appleseed.

The cones rattle with the dry seeds. Conifer seeds are so widely utilized by so many animals that the trees must set a large number of seeds in order that a few will survive. When seed production is poor, the tree's whole seed output may be consumed by birds and rodents. The oily seeds have no protective shell to keep them intact or viable in the digestive tract of an animal, and so they are destroyed by all who eat them: mountain chickadees, blue grouse, Steller's jays, nuthatches, sparrows, woodpeckers, porcupines, tree and ground squirrels, mule deer and mice. Ponderosa seeds germinate best if only lightly covered with soil; if they are buried even an inch below the soil surface by a winter-conscious rodent, the seeds will not sprout. When seed production is curtailed by unfavorable weather, the animal population suffers proportionately.

There are some tiny ponderosas rooted in the most unexpected places; ponderosas often root in granitic or other rocky soils or on cliffsides where soil is almost nonexistent, thereby avoiding competition with other trees. But however tolerant the seedling may be of poor soil, it is intolerant of shade. It cannot grow beyond the first year without full bright sun. For this reason the ponderosa cannot reproduce in the depths of the spruce forest. This intolerance characterizes the mature tree: the silhouette of a ponderosa is that of a cone of empty branches tipped with whisk brooms of needles sweeping the sky.

At least half of the ponderosa's volume is underground. Roots have been found forty to fifty feet deep, following rock fractures. Root competition is most telling in poor soils, such as that of the grove above the lake. The ponderosa's ability to survive dry conditions gives it undisputed tenancy here, with no competition from other trees. There is, however, severe root competition between the pines themselves because of the limited amount of growth materials. Competition between individual root systems determines how close each tree may grow to its neighbor. These trees stand with their lower branches just touching, spaced as carefully as children at dancing school.

❦

The floor of the grove is dry and full of sunshine. Where the floor levels off it is clean, covered with a springy layer of duff, puddled with kinnikinnik and wild geranium, and early in the spring, white dots of candytuft. A ponderosa grove manages to give both sun and shelter, sound and silence. The trees spear light on their needles, tangle wind in their branches, changing the empty meaning of noise to song. The wind plays on the needles like a giant's child humming through the teeth of a comb. But after the layering of plants in the aspen grove, or even in the meadow, the floor of the ponderosa grove is empty. The top layer is formed by the trees, the bottom by low-growing ground cover.

The amount of shade beneath the trees does not necessarily preclude a rich herb layer, but the type of soil does. The constant rain of pine needles from twigs and branches permeates the soil with an acidity that is unacceptable to many plants. There are no plants which grow here only because of the pines' shelter, unless it is the saprophytic pinedrops, which are common in the pine forests of lower altitudes. Many of the plants which grow beneath the ponderosas are able to grow also in the dry meadows and on other open slopes. The food and water requirements of the ponderosas themselves are so extensive that an area thirty to forty feet around a tree may be too devoid of moisture to allow herbs to begin growth.

The soil beneath the ponderosas is largely undifferentiated and young. The first four inches is a light layer of gravel; beneath this the soil is just beginning to "podzolize"—the soil minerals are being leached out of the upper layer by acid water draining through the pine duff. *Podzol* is a Russian word meaning "ash beneath," since the soil eventually becomes gray and ashy-looking.

MOUNTAIN MAHOGANY
(*Cercocarpus montanus*)
IN FLOWER

MOUNTAIN MAHOGANY
DEVELOPING FRUIT

MOUNTAIN MAHOGANY
MATURE FRUIT

MOUNTAIN JUNIPER
(*Juniperus communis*)

Plate 60

❧

The commonest shrub within the ponderosa grove is the ubiqui-
tous low-growing mountain juniper, which also grows in the
aspen grove and the spruce forest and a little bit of everywhere
else. The berries begin as a pale, frosted green and ripen to
dusky dark blue. I immediately picked a sprig to draw and
thereby painfully discovered that the needles are exceedingly
sharp-tipped. They stud the branch in whorls of three, bent at
the base. They are short and the bush has a bristly aspect which
is well deserved.

Mountain juniper grows widely throughout the Montane
Zone, in both light and heavy shade. It indicates no specific en-
vironment but rather that hardiness and widespread tolerance
depend upon growth pattern. Needle-leaves and low stems leave
more energy for reproduction. This juniper wastes no time or
energy on being deciduous or strengthening upright branches.
It simply insinuates itself a little further each year, tortoise
fashion.

❧

I drew the seeds of mountain mahogany long before I knew what
they were. Mountain mahogany frequently grows near and some-
times under the ponderosa if the grove is open enough, for it
needs the sandy well-drained soils that are often on south-facing
slopes that host the ponderosa. The shrub blooms with thick
pink bells which phase into showier seeds. The pink part of the
"flower" is actually a calyx tube; "calyx" is a collective term
used for all the sepals, here fused into a cylinder. The seeds
appear in late summer, attached to three-inch-long quixotically
quirked tails which help to auger the seed into the soil.

Mule deer are especially fond of mountain mahogany. It
has high forage value all year, and deer eat the seeds, the new
twigs, and the leaves; it forms from ten to twenty-five percent
of their diet and must be well established before deer will in-
habit an area. It grows more widely farther south, where it is
called *palo duro* by the Spanish-Americans because of its heavy,
dense wood.

❧

After the wild candytuft blooms, scattered like late snowflakes on the graveled ground, I find the first wild geranium leaves, their notched lobes rimmed with red. In the aspen grove they form graceful plants twelve to fifteen inches high, abundantly flowered. In the pine woods they are very low-growing, only one or two to a hillside, with fewer small flowers, but still as resonantly pink-petaled, hair-lined with red.

The design of the whole plant is based on fives: seed pod, ovary, petals, and leaves all have five component parts. One of the devices with which geraniums and many other plants assure cross-pollination is the successive ripening of the stamen and stigma of each flower. The anthers of a single flower ripen and shed their pollen before the stigma elongates to receive it. By the time the stigma is ripened in one flower it will receive pollen from another flower or another plant.

The fertilized ovary ripens into an intricate slender pod, from which the popular name, "cranesbill," is derived. The seed pod has five compartments, each of which carries a single seed attached by a filament to the outer wall. When ripe, the wall dries and contracts, curling the seed upward. If this occurs quickly, the seed is flipped several feet away, removing it from the area of competition with the parent plant.

❦

On the ground, pussytoes and kinnikinnik enliven the variegated browns and pinks and grays of the forest floor. Kinnikinnik is a creeping shrub, widespread and well loved throughout our mountains; it is a circumpolar species. We use its sprigs at Christmas time, the red berries and shiny leaves being more available than holly and somehow more appropriate. It grows near ponderosas and other native conifers, usually on dry poor soil. It scrambles across the dry meadows but does not appear in damp moist soil. Also known as bearberry, it was used as a tobacco substitute by Indians and early settlers. Cooked, the berries make palatable survival food, important because they persist all year long. The common palindromic name comes from the Algonquin-speaking Indians.

Kinnikinnik scraggles along the ground, the bark gray-brown and shredded, the new twigs green and slender. The root sys-

FRUIT

SEEDS

WILD PINK GERANIUM
(*Geranium fremontii*)

Plate 61

PUSSYTOES
(*Antennaria parviflora*)

KINNIKINNIK
(*Arctostaphylos uva-ursi*)

IN BERRY

IN FLOWER

Plate 62

tem is very shallow and under no stress of competition with deeper-rooted trees or grasses. The evergreen leaves are a glossy dark-holly-green, divided by a principal vein down the center; they grow on a short twisted leaf stalk which enables them to reach upward even though they may be attached to the bottom of the branch. The leaves are able to withstand the dryness of air and climate because of the thick waterproof cuticle which coats each leaf. The leaves turn a rich coppery hue in fall, resuming their greenness with spring.

Beginning in late April in the meadow and on through May in the woods I can find their small clustered pink bells, almost hidden under the leaves. Translucent pink, scallop-edged with deeper rose, each tiny bell is the size of a quarter-inch bead. By hanging down, the corolla protects the pollen supply from rain damage. The flowers develop into shiny green berries, which ripen to deep bright-red, often persisting several seasons.

Tiny rosettes of pussytoes have already finished flowering in the meadow when they begin in the ponderosa grove. Pussytoes are one of the mistakes I made in a wildflower garden I had several years ago. Given a little encouragement, they simply took over, sending out stolons that blanketed the garden.

Like the juniper, they are widespread plants of the mountains, growing in several different habitats; their hardiness and adaptability makes them one of the few plants of the ponderosa underlayer. But even they grow sparsely here. As with many montane plants, the low rosette form provides protection against spring cold while at the same time achieving the greatest exposure to light by a minimum of overlapping. The wedge-shaped leaves are thick and softly hirsute, giving them a soft-gray-green color; the undersurface can be so densely hairy that the green of the chlorophyll is completely hidden.

The flowers rise two or three inches out of the patch, resembling the tender pads of a kitten's paws. They lack ray flowers; the tiny petal-like pink circlets surrounding the white tubular flowers are bracts which persist after flowering, so that pussytoes seem to be in bloom all the time.

❦

At the edge of the mixed ponderosa-Douglasfir grove above the north stream is the only place on our land where yucca grows large enough or vigorous enough to flower. Small plants grow up the dry hillside of the grove itself—not yet old enough to bloom, sharp splays of green many feet apart with only empty soil between. I am constantly amazed that they can grow on such precipitous gravel slopes.

The young plants are nibbled and browsed. But some of the older plants, perhaps more woody and less succulent, have a stalk or two of pendent creamy-white blossoms, topped with pink-flushed buds. The presence of yucca here indicates the presence of the yucca moth, without which yucca cannot be pollinated. The female emerges with the flowering of yucca in July. She lays four or five eggs in the pistil of a flower, inserting a ball of pollen on top. To each flower she distributes a new ball of pollen, systematically fertilizing each ovary. As the seeds ripen, the moth larvae feed upon them, destroying only a few of dozens. The majority of seeds survive to sprout into new plants to provide food for future generations of moths.

Another striking large flower of the mixed dry woods is the white evening-primrose. This, like the yucca, grows on the driest, best-drained slopes. The plants hug the ground, forming colonies on steep slopes where water will not stand in their close-packed leaves. They extend in patches, rootstocks snaking along under the surface to sprout in a nearby rosette.

The soft-haired leaves form a background for the enormous stemless white flowers; some are more than four inches across. They contain no white pigments, only air between the cells just as air beaten into egg whites makes them snowy white. The flowers turn pink as they wither, lasting but a day.

These are long-day plants, not blooming until there are fifteen or sixteen hours of daylight. I had some in the garden for many years. One evening I happened to cup my hands around the four long, narrow rose sepals which cover the bud. In response to the heat of my hands the flower opened against my fingers. It was a mysterious sensation.

❧

WHITE EVENING-PRIMROSE
(*Oenothera caespitosa*)

Plate 63

New discoveries are the delight of Constant Friendship. I had never seen pinedrops before, except in books. Late one afternoon a low shaft of sunlight shot through the forest, spotlighting their rusty-rose stalks. Pinedrops are saprophytes, plants living directly or indirectly on other plant production. They are not parasitic because they neither destroy their host nor weaken it, and do not subsist on living organisms. The pinedrop's roots form irregular mats associated with the fungi that decay deadfall. The clump of rose stems in the dusks of the forest reminded me of an underwater scene, the sooty shadows and un-green leaves belonging to another world.

Mistletoe is parasitic. One becomes conditioned to the growth pattern of the ponderosa: sturdy trunks bearing branches empty toward the center, tufted with brushes of varnished olive-green needles at the end. Against this familiar pattern, on infected trees, are short gnarled tangles, chunky and clotted, obstructing the lines of the branch. The smooth waxy stems of dingy yellow-green spread in fanlike clusters, rooted in the branch of the tree. This mistletoe looks nothing like the one under which one stands so hopefully at Christmas.

Mistletoe germinates through breaks or injuries in the bark: porcupine scar, wind damage, frost crack, needle scar. It has some chlorophyll and can proceed with partial photosynthesis, but depends upon its host for water and minerals. It sends haustoria (derived from the Latin word meaning "to drink") into the heart of the wood. Infected branches require more food and water from the root system, starving out healthy branches and eventually starving the rest of the tree as infestation grows.

The berries of late summer and early fall are eaten by blue grouse, rodents, robins, and mule deer. The seeds are mucilaginous and they cling to a bird's bill. In cleaning himself the bird may scrape the seeds off against an uninfected branch with a lesion in which the seeds may germinate. If not eaten, the seeds are sometimes expelled forcibly by the plant, shooting out thirty to forty feet, although it seems to me the chances of their landing on another ponderosa branch are slim. In a sense, mistletoe is a consumer of the ponderosa. There is no control except cutting the tree. There is no end except death.

PINEDROPS
(*Pterospora andromedea*)

MISTLETOE
(*Arceuthobium vaginatum*)

Plate 64

❦

Especially typical of the ponderosa woodlands are the Steller's jays, named for George Steller, an early European explorer after whom a mountain in central Alaska is also named. The only time the jays don't visit the cabin is when they are nesting. One pair built their nest of twigs, needles, and mud in a huge ponderosa just above the Whale's Mouth, exploding out of the branches whenever anyone came near and completely undoing the unwary hiker.

Tarzan appears within half an hour after we do at the cabin, squawking like a squeaky gate. He is a faithful trencherman whom we named Tarzan because of his robust size and the jay's typical manner of descent. He starts at the top of one tree and descends to the rock in short arcs, swinging down from tree to tree to bush to bush to rock. His midnight-blue feathers are as elegant as formal evening wear, his cockatoo topknot waving in the wind. Head-on, he has two sharply defined white marks, accents *grave* and *aigu*, one over each eye. On the near-black head they make him look like a medieval headsman.

Sara puts seed or bits of bread out for him on the big rock by the kitchen window. A jay is not a busy incessant feeder like the juncos, but a mouth-stuffer. Tarzan lands, grabs seeds or scraps of bread, picking up four or five pieces, his mouth so full that his beak can't close, and takes off as if there were springs in his feet. He seldom eats on the rock. He is too skittish and prefers a private picnic elsewhere.

For all his brashness and size, Tarzan is timid and scatters at the slightest movement or new sound inside the cabin. He flies to a nearby branch where he perches, shifting his weight from one foot to the other, looking about uneasily, waiting for his world to return to normal. The quiet *ssip* of the camera shutter is enough to send him sweeping off, refusing to return as long as Herman remains on the deck with the camera.

At first, only one Tarzan came, then two, then three, and now sometimes seven or eight: a cacophony of jays.

❦

Our one confrontation with a porcupine was without incident, but not because we didn't try his patience. He had made himself known by long claw marks in the mud at the edge of the lake long before we found him in the quill. He was wedged in the wall of a branch house that Susan had made for a dressing room. No amount of prodding could dislodge him. He stared at us with expressionless dull eyes, unperturbed, totally lethargic. The next day he was gone.

Conspicuously light against the dark bark near the top of many ponderosas are the ravagings of a porcupine. The animal generally peels the tender bark of the younger branches. Even when it is not fatal, the girdling hinders good growth and makes the tree vulnerable to mistletoe or beetle infestation. A porcupine chips off the corky outer bark to reach the sweet cambium which lies just beneath. These layers contain a large amount of sugar and starch, which provide body heat and nourishment for the cold months, the only time live trees are stripped.

A porcupine never attacks but backs into a corner or crevice. When his enemy comes too close he makes a rolling lunge or turns around and bats with his quilled tail. But porcupines are vulnerable, as is proved by a bobcat. A bobcat either backs the porcupine out onto a limb or turns him over with a swat of the paw, exposing the unquilled underside. Jane found a tiny skull one summer that was formed with a thin sharpness that was nothing like the rotund creature in the branch house.

Porcupines tend to leave us alone as we do them, fitting themselves into the general scheme of mountain life. But they are not the thing for unwary and pugnacious Graf to confront. A quiver of quills can make surgery necessary. The point of the quill is paved with microscopic diamond shaped scales which work like barbs, going in easily but catching when pulled backward. But then it is the dog, not the porcupine, who is the intruder in the mountains, and so far Graf hasn't found a porcupine.

Abert squirrels are also characteristic inhabitants of the ponderosa woods, never living elsewhere. The tufted ears in winter and charcoal-gray coat make them quickly identifiable. These are the only squirrels in Colorado protected from being hunted.

Their nest, or dray, is built in the crotch of a ponderosa. The squirrel constructs a foundation of sticks and branches into which he interweaves smaller branches. Mountain squirrels, unlike squirrels of warmer climates, use their nests all year round, making them waterproof with grasses and frayed bark and lining them with moss and roots. One perches near his nest and gives me a few choice comments about invading his woods.

Squirrels are major seed eaters, varying their diets with the cambium layer of ponderosa twigs. No matter what time of year there are always squirrels active in the woods, a fat tail disappearing behind a tree or an irritable chirping indicating their displeasure at human company. Frequently I find a stump littered with pine-cone scales, the debris from a gourmand's feast.

❧

The large trees provide shelter for the largest animals of our woods, the mule deer. I most often see deer when I am sitting sketching in the ponderosa wood. I suppose that, seated quietly on the ground, dressed in tan jeans and an old sweater, I am as camouflaged as they are. The flickering sun and shade dapple their coats and obscure their outlines; the high branches allow easy passage beneath. Here they find safety, shelter, and food. When we were surveying in these "open woods" I often could not see the transit twenty feet away. The woods are more protective than they may seem.

It is improperly anthropomorphic to describe a mule deer as "gentle." It is not a quality a deer has and one he would probably find useless if he had it. Yet, in the slender legs, soft coloring, swift grace, and wide limpid eyes there is a quiet innocence that can only be described as gentle. As common as they are in our area, it is still of moment to see one, and we still talk about the day eight appeared in the aspen meadow. They epitomize all wild and shy things, and their immobile stance as they watch the strange two-legged animal stirs compassion for such fear and bewilderment. Even as I watch, they melt into the backdrop of the woods. But we find them also strangely curious about us, at a distance. While Herman was rowing the boat last May a young doe came down to the water's edge and simply watched him. Mule deer have enormous ears, which are usually at the alert, hence their name. Their coats are gray-brown in winter, becoming more cinnamon in summer. As they walk away the white triangular rump patch shows, covered with a short tail. At a sudden noise they all take off with a typical bounding gait, all four feet coming down together to make a four-leaf clover track. When they flick their tail, the white rump patch shows as a signal to the rest of the flock of danger, and the group responds immediately.

Deer are ruminants like cows, with the canines and incisors of the upper jaw replaced by a pad against which vegetation is pulled instead of bitten. Since they do not chew their food, deer must have complex stomachs with a series of digestive processes to break down plant food and extract maximum nourishment. Bacteria, in the digestive tract, or commensals, act on plant cellulose. The deer's ability to try new forage at different times of the year is vastly affected by the presence or absence of such bacteria. If the deer are near starving and in poor health, no amount of free feeding is successful because there is not enough time or strength for the proper commensals to develop. High-quality feed, such as alfalfa, put out to prevent starvation in winter months, is ineffective and deer are often found dead with a full stomach.

Deer must eat all year long since they neither hibernate nor store food. The only seasonal change for winter is the growth of hollow hairs which trap warm air against the body. They search for food, sometimes desperately, in all seasons, over a large range. They feed in the higher mountains in summer, going lower for winter food where the snow is not so deep.

They browse many plants. Mountain mahogany and other twigs and grasses in the spring provide a high protein boost to an impoverished winter diet. In the summer, with a wider choice, their diet reads like a list of plants at our land. One spring I found a willow by the lake with all the new twigs shredded off. Beside it was a large matted bed in the tall timothy.

Antlers are pure bone, reappearing each season, almost always on the male. They are fully formed by mating season, when they are used in fighting. When antlers first sprout they are flexible, enclosed in a covering of "velvet" which eventually peels off. Charging through the woods with a full rack has been compared to having a coatrack glued to the forehead with no hands allowed for protection or balance. Size and branching increase with each successive sprouting until the buck passes his full prime. Then they diminish. As soon as the rack is shed, the new growth begins, continuing rapidly, hardening by the end of summer. This rapid growth of bone makes high nutritional demands on the range, another reason for large wilderness areas for deer herds.

❦

The deer pass through our land going downward in the fall, taking the last vestige of summer with them. Sometimes a fawn follows a parent. Sometimes only the does pass silently through. After the aspen leaves are gone, the deer are gone too. Their hooves make no sound on the padded ground.

Frost, a sharp line in the otherwise stately gait of the seasons, silences the sounds of summer. Noontime sun is warm but the mornings are chill and quiet. Ripened rose hips and garnet currants are set in thorny branches. The muted golds and browns of the landscape are the colors of the deer's coat. The last yarrow adds its frothy dusty white. Imperceptibly plant life is slowing with cooler nights and shorter days. And the deer, following the passage of summer, fade with the shadowed leaves.

Only the ponderosas seem untransient, unchanged by the season that transforms so many living things, caught in the sibilance of their own silence.

❦

When we first came to this land we talked about cutting our own Christmas tree come December. December came, and Herman and I suggested that the children might like to come with us to choose a tree. I think we had in mind establishing a sentimental family tradition. However, the temperature was near zero, a sharp wind was blowing snow arrows, and Jane and Sara were notably unenthusiastic. Herman and I got into boots, coats, scarves and mittens. I carried the saw, he the ax.

We walked for half an hour. Every tree that Herman liked I found too tall, too short, too skimpy, or misshapen. Every tree that I liked Herman found too tall, too short, too hard to get at,

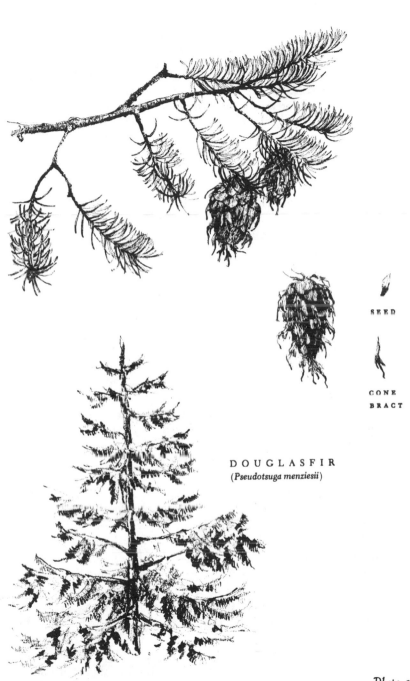

SEED

CONE
BRACT

DOUGLASFIR
(*Pseudotsuga menziesii*)

Plate 65

or too uneven. Finally we settled on a lovely Douglasfir, cut it, and Herman carried it back to the cabin while I carried the ax and saw, walking a respectful distance behind and getting poked in the eye with the tree because I was cold and in a hurry to get back and didn't watch where I was going.

Halfway back, Herman stopped. He had figured that for twenty Christmases we would cut twenty trees, and wished to impart this information to his blue-faced wife. The thought of the girls sitting in the warm cabin while I suffered with snow in my boots, trees in my eyes, and a philosophizing husband was too much. We have bought our trees since and consider it well worth the cost.

❧

The Douglasfir was named for David Douglas, the young Scottish botanist who traveled in the Northwest country between 1825 and 1834. I have always felt an empathy toward this explorer the Indians called the Grass Man because he thought grasses "the most striking and graceful objects in nature."

The lower branches of a Douglasfir droop gracefully while the top ones lift upward, terminating in a sharp, clear spire. The tips of the upper branches splay upward like the extension of a Siamese dancer's hands. The branchlets along the boughs are slightly drooping, creating a feathery aspect. The needles are dark yellow-green, much darker than those of the ponderosa and without the blue cast of the spruce.

Some years, at the end of May, new cones, a striking rosy red, form at the tips of the branches, soft alizarin miniatures of the crisp brown cones of fall. These tiny cones remind me of the red flowers on a sweet shrub. Behind the single cone on the branch tip are many tiny cone-like male flowers, their profusion the safety factor insuring a sufficient supply of wind-borne pollen to fertilize the many ovaries contained in the cones. At the end of June the new growth tips every branch with new green, just freshly unsheathed. The change in color brightens the whole forest.

The cones are distinctive. Tridentate light-brown bracts extend from between darker brown scales, as if a tiny brown mouse had just dived inside for safety, back legs and tail still stuck out behind. The cone matures in a single season. A tree is capable of dropping two million seeds in a good year. The seeds are rounded triangles, encased in wings. Because they are light they are able to blow beyond the immediate area, enabling the sprout to escape competition from the parent grove and to migrate into new areas.

There are no pure stands of Douglasfir here. According to the slope upon which they grow, they associate with ponderosa or spruce. Their seedlings need more light than spruce seedlings but less than those of the ponderosa, so they grow more freely with the latter at our land, and the tallest Douglasfirs are those in the ponderosa groves.

🌿

Beside a noble Douglasfir I found the fairy-slipper orchids, named *Calypso bulbosa* for the beautiful sea nymph with whom Ulysses became enamored, and the bulblike corm. It was a delightful surprise, a Christmas in June. The orchids grew in a neat row alongside a decaying Douglasfir log—a characteristic habitat—brilliant deep-pink with a lip that is pointed and thrust forward like that of a pouting child. There is only one leaf per year, fading as the flower fades. Then a new leaf greens, lasting the summer and winter, beside which next year's flowering stalk appears.

The other lovers of deep shade are the small wintergreens. Unlike the orchids which seem to appear and disappear in a short fortnight, the wintergreen's pace is measured, opening a few blooms at a time. The green-white flowers hang like white jade globules from the stalk. The fruit is a berry, pendent and globose, shaping at the base of the stalk which is still in bud at the top. The leaves are leathery, varnished shiny dark green, protected in much the same way as pine needles and like them, able to withstand below zero temperatures. They are hidden secretive figments of the forest floor.

🌿

Although I may have started out early in the morning with definite plans to go further afield, it is simply too much of a temptation to stop and watch the ants. They cope with such

**FAIRY-SLIPPER
ORCHIDS**
(*Calypso bulbosa*)

WINTERGREEN
(*Pyrola virens*)

SEED POD

Plate 66

tremendous burdens, dragging pieces of food as large as they over log-sized pine needles and around skyscraper mushrooms, poking and pushing with such dedicated persistence that I, who complain about carrying wood for the stoves, feel like a sluggard.

Often the ant that I watch is yards from home. At leaving the nest, the ant receives the image of the sun at a point on its retina. By keeping the image in the same place as it travels it manages a straight line. Like Hansel and Gretel, it lays down a trail for the return journey, a path of formic acid which it can smell through its antennae. I draw a finger across the soil in front of the ant, destroying the continuity of the smell-path. The ant pokes about, probing with its antennae, until it stumbles on the homeward way.

Some hills are almost a yard across and half a yard high. Pellets of excavated earth form cone-shaped mounds surrounding the nest entrance. These hills are inhabited by members of a species of *Formica* who make their passageways near the surface, burrowing deeper in winter to cluster in a compact heat-conserving ball. Mound-building is typical of Western ants. The orienting of the hill entrance toward the greatest amount of incident sunlight utilizes all the available solar heating. A glance shows that none are built on the opposite heavily shaded slope.

Banding together as a colony helps to assure sufficient food since all members contribute to the food supply. The social organization of a colony gives ants greater efficiency and even control over other insects or situations which might otherwise destroy them. In each colony there are several egg-laying females. The first eggs hatch into sterile workers, fed on the saliva of the queen. The worker caste, as with bees, seems to result from an inadequacy of protein during larval life. The stratification of a caste system engenders a high degree of sterility.

While watching the ants clambering around the hill out of the corner of my eye I see a tiny drift of sawdust falling out of the bottom of a large log. The mound is only an inch or so high, but tiny fragments of wood drop with hour-glass persistency on the ground. The large black carpenter ants are also at work in the early morning warmth. They operate on old logs on which the bark is loosened but the wood still fairly firm. Unlike termites, they do not eat the wood they excavate for living quarters, but carry each bit out to the entry, dropping it on the ground. They feed on nectar, and must find a heady harvest in this small valley.

Watching the peregrinations and excavations of the ants reminds me of Henri Fabré, an eighteenth-century French entomologist and teacher, whose fondest hope was to own a parcel of land where he could observe "his insects." He made up for his terrible personal poverty with richness of observation and insight. He wrote a delightful account of ants over a century ago and the tiny tireless foragers of the forest have meaning for me because of what he wrote.

❧

The ant hills are near the beginning of a small narrow forest valley, which is exuberant with wildflowers and velvet with grass, widening and opening into the lake around the corner of the ridge. The floor of the valley is kept moist with runoff from the flanking slopes. Tall trees weave the wind in their branches, so that the soil is slow to dry out.

The valley begins narrow, pinched between two ridges. It is as full of deadfall and juniper, as carpeted with pine needles and kinnikinnik, as the forest floor of which it is part. Dog lichens curl in patches on the ground, gleaming green-brown in the spring damps. Pussytoe rosettes medallion the earth and an occasional strawberry makes tentative growth.

Small valleys like this one are characteristic of the dendritic drainage system of the area in which all the valleys feed into a central runoff system, as the branches of a tree funnel into the trunk. As the valley widens the grasses become denser and higher. A dozen or so good-sized aspen, four to eight inches in diameter, scatter across the periphery of the narrow meadow, taking advantage of the sunlight. An alpine butterfly uses them for pylons in its slow acrobatic flight. A white-breasted nuthatch makes his way down an aspen, headfirst. He blends into the shadows—black crown the size and color of an aspen eye, blue-gray back the cast of a shadow, white breast reflecting the color of the trunk. Slowly and deliberately he proceeds down the trunk, testing at every step for grubs under the bark.

In the summertime a whole vocabulary of Western mountain wildflowers grows here—false Solomon's seal, green gentian, columbine, Indian paintbrush, lavender gentian, graceful cinquefoil, lupine, bedstraw, and still others. One of the reasons for this unparalleled variety lies in the comparative fertility of the soil, neither acid nor alkaline, which is called a chestnut brown for its color. Decomposition over the years has enriched and darkened the soil. A bed of gravel lies within the layer of rich clay loam and aids in drainage. The soil is several feet deep before hitting the Pikes Peak granite substrate. The surrounding hillsides drain into the little valley, bringing not only moisture but washing down organic and inorganic materials from above.

Snow is an extremely important source of moisture. Shaded throughout the winter and spring by the flanking slopes, the ground remains blanketed late, the melting snow seeping slowly downward, and coming just before sprouting time when plants are most in need of deep moisture.

❧

When I sit on the grass, picking up bits of wood or moving rocks on the soil surface, it is somewhat like watching a flea circus. Soil forms a friendly habitat for those who live in it, with abundant raw materials and a climate which does not change sharply as that above ground does. Springtails appear on top of the soil and pop to safety out of my hand. A pinpoint of a red mite skitters across a crack in the dirt. A millipede scuttles under a piece of bark. They are active in the pleasant days of spring and fall, becoming dormant during heat and cold. Millipedes are one of the decomposers of fallen leaves and bark. The exquisite skeletonized aspen leaves are largely their work. I lift a rock and two centipedes filter back into dark safety. A black carpenter ant runs back into the log where its colony had been excavating, finding some difficulty in crawling over a red strawberry runner which has tied into the soil with a new plant at its tip.

There is a busy society of infinitesimal creatures beneath the surface. Bacteria, fungi, and algae predominate; earthworms and other fauna make up the rest. The living components of the soil are miniscule in proportion to the total volume, but they dominate because of their high rate of activity. Peter Farb, in

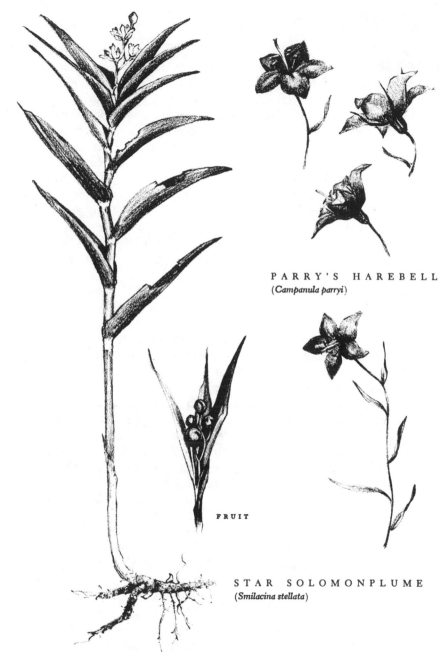

PARRY'S HAREBELL
(*Campanula parryi*)

FRUIT

STAR SOLOMONPLUME
(*Smilacina stellata*)

Plate 67

GREEN GENTIAN
(*Frasera speciosa*)

his fascinating study *Living Earth*, estimates that a teaspoon of temperate-zone soil has five million bacteria, twenty million fungi, one million protozoa, two hundred thousand algae, and assorted leftovers. They engage in such fierce activity in the top six inches of soil that the energy per acre equals ten thousand humans living and working there. For all the numbers involved, nature controls competition below ground just as precisely as above, by balancing the increase of one organism with the means of terminating its multiplication either through food limits or increased predation.

❧

Strawberries lace the valley floor with red runners, taking root at the node with a miniature sprig of leaves. The white flower is a reduced replica of a wild rose, the center full of gold stamens. Strawberries have been known since Roman times but were not cultivated until the fourteenth century in France—their popularity shows in the affection with which their delicate tendrils are illuminated in the margins of medieval manuscripts.

Finding a wild strawberry fruit is somewhat of a prize, for they are eaten as quickly as they ripen by grouse, chipmunks, mice, and Susan, Jane or Sara, all of whom know a good thing when they find it. I have been known to release sharp-eyed strawberry-laden daughters from table-setting in return for a handful of fruit. It is incredible that a combination of fruit ethers, sugars, and fruit acids can taste so good. Izaak Walton, in *The Compleat Angler*, quotes a Dr. Boetler as saying, "Doubtless God could have made a better berry, but doubtless God never did."

The flavor develops with cold days. Warm-weather berries look good but taste like sawdust. The berries must ripen at least a week in a daytime temperature of 50 degrees, common at high altitudes. Wild strawberries are not much bigger than a child's fingertip but of such concentrated tart sweetness that a store-bought berry tastes like pulp by comparison.

Some years ago I brought a few shoots down to the city garden. Since then they have multiplied unconscionably, creating a thick mat of leaves, many blooms, and enough berries for a couple of memorable breakfasts. They bear twice, once in early June and again later in the summer, while mountain berries bear only once. The red runners proliferate all over the city garden wall, setting out in good faith across cement deck. No such vigor exists in the mountains; they grow and fruit but not profusely.

The fruit is not a true berry but a receptacle on whose surface the seeds are embedded. Numerous fertilized pistils ripen into seed and remain attached to the receptacle, which develops somewhat like the rose hip, first small and green, turning bright red when ripe. They hang beneath a canopy of toothed leaves, just deer-mouse height.

❧

Columbines float over the strawberry-webbed ground, the large flowers seeming to hover without visible stems, deserving their name of dove. Another of the diverse buttercup family, the columbine achieves its grace by the five lavender sepals alternating with the palest-yellow petals which roll into extended lavender spurs. This is the state flower of Colorado, more tenuous and finespun than the Eastern red and yellow variety.

Numerous golden stamens depend upon insect pollination to carry pollen from one plant to another. If anything, columbine is overspecialized. Nectar, concealed in the tip of the petal spurs, is apparent in the slight bulge at the tip. Nectar can be reached only by an insect with a long proboscis, such as a butterfly or hummingbird moth. But certain bees, being as resourceful as any, frequently nip a hole in the end to avoid the work of getting nectar through usual channels, and so forestall fertilization and pollination.

Columbines are further limited in their propagation by the propensity of the selfish who do not hesitate to pick the flowers, leaving the plant with limited or no seed production. Picking has been made unlawful in Colorado in an effort to preserve the remaining columbines, which grow in great luminous drifts along mountain meadows and woodlands.

Columbines grow in their optimum environment here, blooming profusely and producing an abundance of five-compartment seed follicles. When I sit to draw them, they smell sweet, somewhat like honeysuckle—a delicate elusive fragrance

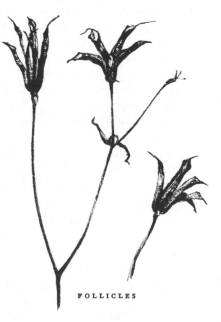

COLORADO BLUE COLUMBINE
(*Aquilegia caerulea*)

FOLLICLES

Plate 68

often lost in the big brassy smell of the summer-warmed pine woods. To sit there, head-high in columbine, is a heady experience in which one finds familiar responsibilities fading in a response to the permeating wonder of soft sunshine and hypnotically flickering pale patterns. The blooms seem suspended above the green leaves like tiny birds, and tremble in the slightest breeze. Their lavender is the depth of aspen shadow, their yellow that of the first sunlight. Crystallized with dew, a flight of columbines in early morning is the essence of our inherited memory of Arcadia.

❧

A blurred pale shape visits each blossom, ignoring the fact that I am there, working across the hillside. A blur of wings hovers before each bloom and then moves on, operating like a hummingbird. Furry, heavy-bodied, the sphinx moth resembles a hummingbird in its daylight habits and method of feeding. The hairiness of the thorax gives thick insulation for the powerful musculature needed for hovering and feeding on the wing. The upper end of the long proboscis contains a bulblike sac, which works like a syringe, pumping nectar back into the stomach.

At rest, the soft colorings of the wings blend into the mineral colors of the granite. This is the only time of the year that the sphinx, or hummingbird, moths frequent Constant Friendship; they come for the columbine nectar the way oenophiles visit the Burgundian countryside during wine-tasting.

There are other echoes of ancient worlds here. Gentians were named for Gentius, a king of ancient Illyria which lay in the northwestern part of the Balkan peninsula. The flowers of the little gentian are a gracious soft lavender-blue, paler toward the base of the corolla. The petals open out starlike to reveal the distinctive fringed crown.

Just how ideal this habitat is for their development can be seen by comparing one here with a gentian from the gate meadow which is only two inches high, with a single stalk topped by a single modest bloom. Here they are well branched and flowered, growing in stately groups, a paler, more delicate version of the well-known blue gentian.

Clematis is the diminutive of the Greek word which means

LITTLE GENTIAN
(*Gentianella amarella*)

GROWING IN SHADE

BISHOP'S CAP
(*Mitella pentandra*)

GROWING IN SUN

Plate 69

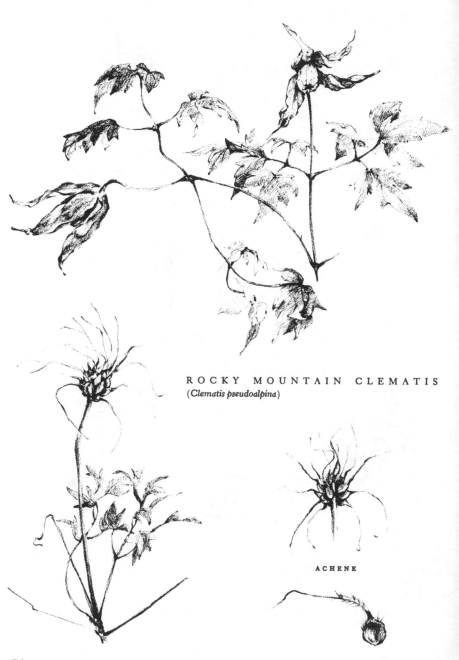

ROCKY MOUNTAIN CLEMATIS
(*Clematis pseudoalpina*)

ACHENE

Plate 70

"vine-branch." The thin and wiry clematis vines tangle over a tree and some juniper bushes at the edge of the clearing. Climbing plants are most abundant in deep shade since they cannot endure the harsh light or competition of the open meadow. The stem is only a conductor of food and water, without the strength of support.

The clematis flowers are large lavender pendent bells, which seem to grow from the juniper rather than their own concealed stems. Their growth is rapid; one day the juniper bush is just juniper and the next it is bedizened. Virgin's-bower clematis, another form of the same plant which grows low on the ground, has the same flower on a short green stem—these are flowers which seem to have strayed from a hothouse, an anachronism in the rugged woodland. In the East, clematis is a plant of sunny meadows. Here it prefers gentle light and damp corners.

One April, Jane and I were looking for the new leaf buds on the clematis vine. The stems were so wiry and brown that they looked like dead twigs caught in the juniper. When we finally found the leaves, we saw they were maroon and furry to hold the spare spring warmth. In order to mark the place I picked up a piece of wood about six inches long, and inadvertently uncovered an ant nursery. The wood was the roof, warming the soil beneath and protecting the larvae from rain.

Each nurse ant immediately picked up a tiny white grain of rice larva. With no confusion each nurse took one larva back into the earth and returned for another and then another. There seemed to be two or three charges per nurse. It was done within minutes. Then the slight hollow in the dark earth was empty, no different from the rest of the forest floor. We replaced the wood carefully and marked the clematis with a dead branch instead.

Such Lilliputian activity seemed to be very proper in this Persian miniature world, where moths nuzzle columbine, hummingbirds sip of scarlet gilia, and small children believe that fairies dance on midsummer's eve. After all, the circles of graygreen lichen on the rocks mark where a fairy tripped and spilled a bucket of moonbeams.

❦

Our first years at Constant Friendship were dry years, and mushrooms were not plentiful, or perhaps I did not have the eyes to see them. The dry years were followed by an exceedingly wet summer, marked by an unpleasant plentitude of slugs in my city garden and a burgeoning variety of mushrooms in the mountains.

The first boletes that I saw growing beneath the ponderosas were so huge that I called the children from swimming to see them. The dry tan caps blend with the dry pine needles and dust, and they grow on such short fat stems that they cast no shadows. But there they were, dozens of them. The barefooted swimmers tiptoed gingerly upon the needled slope, hesitancy giving way to flatfooted dashes as they discovered more and more, and bigger and bigger mushrooms the size of saucers, the size of salad plates, and one gargantuan specimen as big as a luncheon plate!

Boletes are mushrooms which drop their spores not from gills but through tubes. If I cut one vertically the finely packed tubes, ending in thousands of minute holes on the underside of the cap, are visible. These boletes spring almost full blown from the ground, swelling two to ten times underground with summer moisture until the right amounts of heat and dampness command their emergence. Then, growth mainly accomplished underground, they arise, fat and meaty and majestic.

Because this species of bolete is closely related to the prized steinpilz, some mycologists suggest that it is also edible. I break open many caps to find them already inhabited by myriads of tiny feasting fly larvae, black heads poking out in distress at the sudden fresh air. These are offspring of fungus flies, which lay their eggs in the mushroom often before it rises above the ground. The eggs hatch into larvae surrounded by an opulent food supply.

These tan-capped mushrooms occur wherever there are many ponderosas on the land, and it is possible that this is a mutualistic relationship, or an example of mycorrhiza. The threadlike hyphae of the fungus may either invade the root hairs, as is the case with orchids, or may encase the root hairs, as is true with conifers. Pre-Carboniferous ancestors of present-day evergreens had mycorrhizal roots; it has clearly been a long and successful association.

A normal conifer root tip is capped by a whitish thimble which augers through the ground, pushed by the zone immediately behind it in which rapid cell division takes place. This is the only part of the root that elongates. Behind is a section covered with thousands of root hairs through which the root feeds. The hairs live only a few weeks, constantly replaced by new ones; one inch of root may have fifty thousand hairs. It is these root hairs that are encased by the fungal hyphae, sometimes ninety to ninety-five percent of the tree's roots being involved. Mycorrhizal roots appear short, thick, and nubbed in contrast with normal fine roots. Many mycorrhizal fungi produce hormones which stimulate new root growth and promote more areas on which fungus may grow. The roots in turn secrete substances which encourage fungal growth.

The fungi make more food available to the tree since they are more efficient in absorbing minerals from the soil than the roots themselves. In return the fungi derive part of their nourishment from the carbon products of the tree's photosynthesis. It has been conjectured that the presence of mycorrhizal fungi is one of the reasons pines grow in inhospitable, substandard soils; they are forced to grow there because such areas are the preferred habitat of the fungi.

❧

Where the mixed ponderosa-Douglasfir woods come down to meet the high beginnings of the lake meadow is Mushroom Valley. At the end of July a new set of mushrooms seems to pop out of the ground each week—flora without bright petals and green leaves, without seed pods or pollen, but with an incredible range of subtle colors and shapes.

We soon learned where to look for this muted flora: an old cow pat, a dead log, an open moist patch of ground. And for us each year there has been the pleasure of finding new species. One of the most knowledgeable, accurate, and sensitive portrayers of mushrooms was Beatrix Potter of *Peter Rabbit* fame. She kept a journal of her work which was as observant scientifically as artistically, ending one entry by noting: "There is complacency in finding a totally new species for the first time." I concur heartily.

Nearly all of our Colorado mushrooms round into being in the woods, where shade prevents desiccation and provides a more uniform environment. Mushrooms must have the same appropriate nutrition, adequate moisture and temperature as green plants. But they need relatively little light since most of their life is spent within the darkness of the soil. Fungi have no chlorophyll and do not make food by photosynthesis, and so they thrive here in the shuttered light of the pines and Douglas-firs, making food out of already dead organic matter with which the soil abounds.

When conditions within the soil allow, the mushroom spore sends out a threadlike hypha, derived from the Greek word meaning "tissue" or "cobweb." The microscopic hyphae elongate and branch, making rapid growth that is concentrated in the tip end; a new branch can be produced in half an hour, invading the soil a half-mile per day when conditions are optimal. Occasionally the mass of gossamer threads clump together and become visible as coarse strands or clumps called mycelium. Mycelium must build up a reserve of food before fruiting can begin. It may persist underground for years, fruiting when possible, remaining dormant when not.

On a warm moist day in summer the floor of the valley suddenly begins popping with mushrooms. The tightly packed bud packages underground have merely been awaiting the proper trigger to emerge into the familiar above-ground configurations. And appear they do, in clusters and drifts and splendors, a munificence of mushrooms.

Mushrooms are the fruiting bodies which can loose, hour after hour, day after day, as many as five hundred thousand spores per minute. Sara brings the caps inside and puts them upside down on a paper in a quiet corner of the studio. The next day there is a powdered diagram of gill and pore in colors ranging from white through cream and buff to dark brown and black. Left in the woods the spores permeate the air in invisible clouds, which account for their almost cosmopolitan distribution.

They fall with surprising slowness, floating to the far corners of the woods, drifting on to leaves, dusting twigs, blanketing mosses and lichens, sticking to rain-wet bark, coating and floating and sifting.

🌿

As a city housewife used only to buying white mushrooms with brown gills at the grocer's, I couldn't believe the variety of wild mushroom shapes and colors. Clitocybe caps are funnel-shaped with a hole down the center of the stem. The white gills are thick and widely spaced, uneven in edge and length. A collybia has a twisted cartilaginous and slightly furry stem, indicated in the common name of velvet stem. The whole mushroom is a glorious golden cinnamon-brown. Chanterelles are sparse here, but the orange contorted cap and shallow forked gills are unmistakable. Called *Pfifferling* in German, they are widely prized for eating, and even ours, woody though they are, have a delightful aroma of warm apricots. Shiny yellow-capped *Hygrophorus conicus* gleam in the grass; shaggy hedgehog mushrooms bear their spores on toothlike gills.

All sizes and shapes spring up, from fat round puffballs to open cups. The last look like crumpled tees for a volleyball-sized golfball. Heavily veined and white-felted beneath, soft velvety brown on top, they appear to have no spores whatsoever. But a wisp of wind or a soft breath sends up a cloud of silver dust which glistens in the sunlight. The saddle mushrooms are brown pieces of suede folded awkwardly on top of a semihollow stem. They carry their spores in the same way as the open cups, but are raised two inches above the ground, enough to allow the wind better access.

A cluster of panacolus sprigs out of an old cow pat which dates back to the time when this land was used for grazing. Slender pale-brown caps, spotted with deeper brown, top tall graceful stems. As they mature black spores dust the gills and stem. Remnants of a veil hang in shreds at the cap's edges. Spores are discharged into weeds and grasses which are eaten by animals; these spores pass through the alimentary tract unaltered and fall to the ground in dung, which provides ideal

Paxina acetabulum   SADDLE   *Hygrophorus*
                             MUSHROOM   *conicus*
                             (*Helvella infula*)

HEDGEHOG   VELVET STEM   *Panaelous*
MUSHROOM   (*Collybia butryacea*)   *campanula*
(*Dentimum repandum*)

Plate 71

Russula emetica

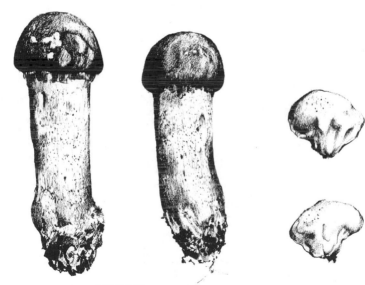

STEINPILZ
(*Boletus edulis*)

PUFFBALLS
(*Lycoperdon pyriforme*)

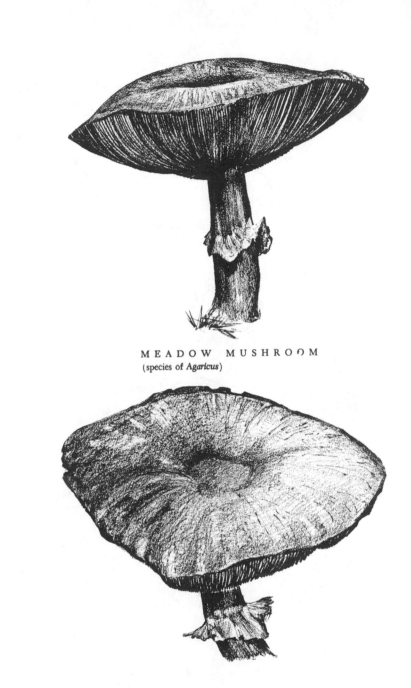

MEADOW MUSHROOM
(species of *Agaricus*)

Plate 72

nourishment for them. For humans, eating these mushrooms causes an extremely unpleasant and instantaneous reaction, which is not too different from a severe overdose of alcohol.

The most poisonous mushroom, and probably the best known, is the fly mushroom or fly amanita. Many cultures have made use of its peculiar properties. Decoctions causing intoxication or hallucination were used in certain ancient prophesying ceremonies. Eating the mushroom straight proves to be sixty to one hundred percent toxic. The only known antitoxin is atropine. The poison acts on the nervous system within one to six hours after eating. A minute fragment can be fatal. The most deadly amanita, called the destroying angel, does not produce any symptoms until enough time has elapsed for the poison to have fatally pervaded the system.

The red-capped and white spotted fly mushroom is one most frequently used in fairy-tale illustrations. On our land it bears a soft yellow cap verging on buff, encrusted with the warts of the dried veil. When young, button amanitas are indistinguishable from the eminently edible and luscious puffballs. Only by dissection of the mushroom is the gourmet preserved for other meals. The puffball is even all the way through, like foam rubber. The amanita shows the nascent stem and gills all enveloped in a universal veil. When the stem elongates and the cap opens like an umbrella, the veil shreds. Remnants fringe the cap and blotch its surface with white. We also have found one of the few edible varieties of amanita, but its pale gray clamminess discourages even the most experiment-minded.

Some of the largest mushrooms in the valley are the lactarius, so called because of their milky juice. The climate of the mountains is so dry that the genus as a whole does not show drops of white liquid upon cutting. The most common, the delicious lactarius (*Lactarius deliciosus*), stains a brilliant turquoise upon cutting. A blush of salmon pink suffuses the milk-orange cap, which is ringed with concentric circles of deeper tan. The narrow neat gills grow downward onto a thick short stem. The cap is usually slanted like some jaunty tam o'shanter. It is delicious when baked in a closed dish. When the lid is lifted the aroma is Elysian. All that is needed in preparation is a little olive oil or sweet butter, a sprinkle of *fines herbes*, and a few dried bread crumbs over the top, with a thick slice of home-made bread toast to mop up the juices.

Less common are the lavender-brown cortinarius mush-rooms. They are small and often hidden but so attractive that they are worth looking for. A webby veil binds cap to stem, enveloping the young button and drying to a persistent thread-like webbing. The gills are dark brown as is the cap when aged, but when young the cap is as lavender as a love gentian, a muted amethyst of the forest.

Within the radius of sight are ochers and hazels and hennas, lavenders and fawns, and here and there a trace of pink or yellow. In the acid soil the fungi decompose animal remains, the dead tree branches and the dried grasses, breaking them down in series—bark first and wood last—to the simple components which green plants need to combine with sun and water and chlorophyll to produce new growth.

❧

August evokes the ruby-red russula. For weeks I look and find none; then one day I find dozens. The dry scarlet caps catch pine needles and duff in the swiftness of their rise, which may take place within an hour. Pure white beneath and having a pristine stem and narrow even-set gills, they are the cleanest and most precisely composed of mushrooms.

They have a less pleasant aspect, however. Their scientific name, *Russula emetica*, describes their effect on humans. They contain muscarine, a chemical which affects the nervous system and is also the active poison in the fly amanita; it causes nausea, vomiting, and diarrhea. *Russula emetica* has been found in mycorrhizal association with oak, and it is possible that it may grow here in this manner with the spruce.

Since the soil is so acid, decomposition must be provided largely by fungi. Primary decomposers are the sugar fungi, and last are those which attack the plant cellulose and lignin. Lignin is an organic woody fiber which overlies the cellulose of plant cell walls. It is more inert chemically and biologically than other plant materials and more difficult to decompose. Fungi are more effective in breaking down newly fallen needles and lignin than bacteria.

Every scrap of wood I pick up is furry white with mycelia on the underside. An ounce of forest soil may contain two miles of fungal threads, a growth so dense in some spots that it actu- ally holds the particles of soil together and prevents them from rolling down the steep slope. Not only do the fungi decompose dead wood and leaves, but they add their own decaying structures to provide fresh basic food supply for green plants.

Some fungi produce fruiting bodies that encrust logs and stumps. Engelmann spruce and aspen are both subject to a fomes rot, a common rot of the temperate zone. Most stumps bear the shelving fruiting bodies, tough and dirty-white. Some branches and twigs have scabs of bright-orange rind, *Dacrymyces stillatus*, a fungus especially prevalent on dead aspen twigs on the ground. There are no common names for these fungi, which suggests that man is not as aware of them as he ought to be. The world could not exist without green plants, neither could it exist without fungi. Decomposition would be slowed to such an extent that there would be an insufficient amount of basic minerals for green plants to exist.

❧

That I cannot find more varieties of mushrooms high on the slope may be because some species produce antibodies that are toxic to other species, and also because of the low-moisture, low-temperature environment there. In a kind of fungal version of territoriality they poison the ground for invading spores. There may also be a lack of available space. Small mushrooms are like icebergs, with vast streams of mycelia below ground. Sidestep ping down the steep slope I have to look hard to find the few modest mushrooms which are easily lost in the shadows.

There are puffballs and earthstars, brownish to off-white, making up in profusion what they lack in size, small nuggets which fit themselves in where they can. Puffballs consist of two layers, the outer layer disintegrating as the mushroom browns with age. These are the stomach fungi in which spores are formed inside the inner layer. At the base of the slope, nearing the stream, they are profuse. Sprinkled among the puffballs on sandy spots are earthstars. They look like puffballs with petals, formed by the peeling back of the thick outer skin. On a dry day the petals close upward over the inner sphere; when the day is damp they reflex to allow the escape of the brown spores.

Both puffballs and earthstars emit their ripened spores when a drop of rain hits the container. The sudden change in inside pressure causes an explosion of brown smoke, sometimes millions of spores in a puff. Since they are released during wet weather the spores are often rain-carried, assured of falling on damp soil. Needless to say, visiting children are adept at spotting them, for they retain a tremendous amount of spores and release a brown puff whenever squeezed.

Along with the puffballs and earthstars at the foot of the hill there are also delicious lactarius and hedgehog mushrooms. These are shaggy with teeth, instead of gills, upon which the spores are produced. The whole mushroom is pale buff, the cap often growing off-center and tilted.

There is a particular and pleasant anticipation coming back to the cabin from a late afternoon walk in the cool of the spruce woods with a pocketful of puffballs. They are so simple to prepare and so good that I can hardly keep from eating them while they are cooking, burning both fingers and tongue. Sliced and sautéed in butter, they have a delicate ephemeral flavor and aroma. The warmth of the wood stove is pleasant in the chill evening. The watercress for salad drains in the sink. The oil lamps soften the shadows. The land is quiet. The kettles of hot water hiss comfortably on the back of the stove. It is good to be reminded every now and then that the most pleasant things in life are, after all, the simplest.

❦

Even in the wilderness, humans establish patterns of existence, enjoy certain walks, relish certain places to sit, places to which they return again and again, a human need for the familiar. Along the shadowed bottom edge of the north-facing slope below the dam is one of those walks that I find myself returning to.

It may be that there is always a greater variety to be found here: deer or rabbit tracks, puffballs or earthstars, a pile of shredded spruce cones at the doorway to a burrow, lush mosses and lichens, secluded violets. Or perhaps it is the eternal fascination of the human with the mysterious depths of a dark woods, remembering Hansel and Gretel or Norse myths and Russian fairy tales.

For this is dark woods, full of deadfall which crackles and snaps underfoot. Tree branches break off in my hand if I use them for support. Pewter-gray dead aspen fall at a touch. There are secretive ivory flowers, emerald mosses and ruby mushrooms, worth a mountain king's ransom. Scrambling up the slope is difficult, for the ground is soft and gives way beneath my feet. Only deadfall, which forms haphazard steps, makes it easier. Ascent has to be made diagonally. It is almost impossible to go straight up.

While we rest at the top of the ridge, Graf finds pine cones, drops one, chases it down the slope and then pants back up to the top again to drop another. The slope is so steep that he seldom catches one before it bounces on the bottom path, his swiftness trammeled by the obstacle course of trees he runs.

From the sunlit top of the slope I can look down into the close-packed profusion of Engelmann and blue spruces and Douglasfir. In the wintertime the slope is covered hip-deep in snow, persisting sometimes through May. In the summer the woods are cool, a little clammy, a little dank, always several degrees cooler than anywhere else on the land except the Whale's Mouth. Even on an August evening the forest is chill, psychologically or physically or both, even though the forest keeps the air warmer than that of the open meadow at night. The brightness of day is blotted by interwoven branches, the wind is trapped far above my head, the odor is of damp dirt and musty fungus, not unpleasant but not cheerful either. Broken branches snag my clothing. Twigs snatch at my hair and eyes. Deadfall suddenly confuses my footing. On dark days the forest is a woodcut by Kirchner or Munch.

❧

Two fifty-foot Colorado blue spruces rise like sentinels near the dam, their ruggedly perfect spires pendent in the lake—a trademark of Constant Friendship. Several small spruces, none more than two feet high, are scattered across the floodway to the edge of the deep woods. With plenty of water and light both large and small spruces grow evenly and form an almost perfect cone. But most of the spruce grow on the dark shaded slope.

Blue spruce resembles Engelmann spruce so closely in the wild that the only easy way to tell them apart is by the cones. Those of Engelmann spruce are under three inches, those of blue spruce larger, up to four and a half inches. Engelmann spruce also has a fine pubescence on the needles, the "blue" being caused by glaucous coating on the new growth. In our area and at our altitude the two spruces often intermingle and probably hybridize.

Spruces have very sharp-pointed needles, growing stiffly on the branch. Trimming a spruce Christmas tree is not my idea of fun. Each inch-long, four-angled needle is borne singly on a short brown woody stem which angles the needles to the branch, tending to crowd on the upper side. When the wind blows, ponderosa needles wave on their branches but spruce needles scarcely move. A dead spruce shows the underlying spiky delicacy of structure. The ends of the branches form an outspread hand, flat in plane, fanned out at the end with new growth.

Spruce cones are oval and cylindrical, dangling from the top of the tree like so many Christmas tree ornaments, neat and as tightly packed as the needle-clogged branches. They seem constructed of brown wrapping paper, each scale carefully and neatly crimped and overlaid in a precise shingling. The cones shed small seeds during the late fall or winter, each set into a broad oblique wing which carries them on the winter wind.

But more likely, according to the evidence beneath the tree, they have been feasted on by the rodents of the forest. The scales of many spruce cones do not open when they fall, and the mice and rabbits and squirrels shred them off, leaving a pile of discarded scales as high and disordered as a plateful of artichoke leaves.

Spruce root systems are relatively shallow, growing only to eight feet even in deep soils, so the spruce is subject to wind throw. Growing in a closed stand minimizes the wind effects, but when one tree goes, evaporation increases so tremendously that the transpiration of adjacent trees is affected and others may fall, taking out a chunk of forest as effectively as a fire. In the new light, ponderosa and aspen and Douglasfir begin a new succession, making good growth, only to be shaded out eventually by the returning spruce.

❧

At this altitude spruces are most abundant on north-facing slopes, where temperatures and soils are cooler and moisture more prevalent. At Constant Friendship, ferns grow only near the streams or within the spruce-Douglasfir forest, indexing the amount of dampness held within the air here. Although more Engelmann spruces grow at higher altitudes, some grow here on these darker slopes. Neither spruce does well in sandy or gravelly soils; both grow where there is a moderately deep well-drained silt and clay loam.

Although spruce seedlings must have greater soil moisture than other conifer seedlings and deplete the available moisture faster, they can also better endure moisture loss. This is crucial in the winter droughts of high altitude where frozen soils give up little water. The spruces are more resistant to winterkill than Douglasfir and ponderosa, but less able to withstand the dry August of a drought summer.

❧

The amount of deadfall and undecomposed litter on the ground of a spruce-Douglasfir forest is a fire hazard. When the summer is dry we watch the storm clouds build up at noon, hoping that they carry rain, not just thunder and lightning. Fire has always been a part of the forest world. Sometimes fire is totally devastating, but sometimes it is beneficial in cleaning out diseased trees, clearing the forest floor, aiding bacteria in decomposition, providing light and space for new forest growth. But when man enters the forest, so enters the fear of fire, for we are unable to accept the perspective of nature which is that of centuries. Fire is not compatible with the life span of man and he does everything he can to prevent its spread. And just how little that can be, we found out several years ago.

Early in the afternoon of a July day, a very dry July day, there was a typical summer mountain storm, a few drops of rain but lots of *Sturm und Drang*. There were fourteen lightning strikes within our general area, and one of them hit in our spruce-Douglasfir forest, near the top of the ridge above the lake. We were building the cabin addition and Herman had gone back to working on the cabin roof after the storm was over. From the vantage point of a rafter he noticed a wisp of smoke rising insolently above the tree tops. A tall Douglasfir had been hit, lightning snapping down the trunk and leaving a washtub-sized hole where it hit the ground.

Herman carried water, a bucket at a time, up the steep slope and tried to dampen the smoldering duff. At 8400 feet this is debilitating work. The duff continued to smoke. He trenched around the base of the tree, digging down eight inches to solid soil to prevent the fire from spreading under the surface litter. When duff is sun-warm and dry, the great danger is a subsurface fire, snaking through dry needles and twigs, fanning to flame with wind. Protected by the trees above, it can only be put out by an unusually long heavy rain.

Herman dug and trenched until the light gave out. The next morning he and Sara, who was camping with him, awoke to the sound of the Forest Service fire-plane circling the cabin. The smoke had begun to rise again. They spent the rest of the day digging and smothering, finally exhausting the fire and themselves, coming home smelling of smoke. The soil is still blackened there, a macabre reminder of natural destruction and the feebleness of man's attempt to control it.

❧

When the rain does come, it runs down tree trunks and drips incessantly off branches, and the forest soaks it up like a sponge. In contrast, the south-facing slopes have quick runoff, water sparkling in the after-sun as it ribbons across the rocks. In our weather pattern these are quixotic summer showers, over almost as soon as begun, sun shining through the raindrops brought by vagrant winds and updrafts and air-moisture patterns.

The dark slopes of the north-facing ridges hold the rains of summer and the snows of winter longer. The blanket of snow prevents deep freezing of the soil surface, so that the pores between soil particles are not filled with ice. When melting begins, there are spaces through which the water can work instead of running off a frozen surface. A deep reservoir of soil moisture is built up, protected from evaporation by the heavy cover above. When the gate meadow soil is dusty in the hand, this soil is spongy and cool.

The thick duff floor is typical of a conifer forest. On top is a layer of litter, made up of twigs and insect cases and pine needles, all in recognizable form. When it has begun to decompose it becomes darker in color and more amorphous and is called duff. As surface water percolates through the needle debris and duff, it leaches out the soluble basic salts, especially calcium carbonate. The soil becomes acid; no bases remain to neutralize the acid from the continuous pine-needle droppings. Nitrifying and nitrogen-fixing bacteria are intolerant of acid soils. No clovers or lupines or vetches—legumes which foster these bacteria—grow here. Other bacteria are replaced by fungi. Earthworms cannot live here and there is little intermixing of soil. It may take three or four years to decompose the duff into leaf mold. This is accomplished in two years in a beech or oak grove.

The dense growth of Douglasfir and spruce, soil acidity, and the darkness of the slope suppress the undergrowth severely. Of the larger plants, only kinnikinnik and juniper manage to grow here. The juniper sets many berries and seems undeterred by the supremacy of the trees, but the kinnikinnik is often barren. Shade-tolerant mosses and lichens creep along the ground. If the undergrowth, such as it is, were removed, there would be no essential change in the forest. If the spruces were removed, the entire area would show an immediate dramatic change.

❧

At the edges of the spruce grove enough light enters to allow a spatter of shade-tolerant plants to bloom. Against the darkness of the forest background small clematis grow, and miterwort, displayed against the black velvet of the forest floor. Sometimes these venture into the deeper woods. Then the clematis' lavender sepals are paled nearly to white, and its finely divided leaves are as fragile as tissue paper.

There are many rocks studding the slope here, clustered in crumbling castles. In their crevices there are ferns and mosses, some embossed with spotted saxifrage. The word *saxifrage* comes from two Latin words meaning rock and break, referring to the habitat of many saxifrages. The tiny pointed saxifrage leaves grow in rosettes, cluster upon cluster, forming a green mat like an enlarged moss cushion. In the warmth of July they send up threadlike stems topped with half-inch six-petaled flowers, dotted with tiny specks of magenta and orange. Their wiry stems are invisible a few feet away and the flowers seem to hang poised in the air, a summery mobile.

Farther up the slope there is a level spot where it is pleasant to sit. An old log forms a bench and another a footrest. There are many mosses tucked beneath a rock or beside the log—meadows for the insect minutiae which tramp the turf. Lichens toast the summer with gray goblets, unfurl in ruffled circles, and tuft out of logs in wisps and snippets.

All forms of lichen grow within the radius of my reach here. Crustose lichen coats the rock thinly. Foliose lichen rises from the surface in furls and curls, the center parts clinging to the substrate. The fruticose lichens are attached at one end only, forming a shaggy tassle like reindeer moss, or arise in upright stalks from a froth of green thallus like the pixie-cup lichen.

Pixie-cup lichen ices the soil. From a pale green thallus cluster, curling to show the white underside, the stalks rise almost half an inch. Another lichen of the same genus sends up slender gray pegs which seem bent in an unseen wind. A third species produces hollow stalks, rising out of each other in stories. The cup margins proliferate with brown-tipped points, which are the fruiting bodies containing spores. The light-green granulations on the surface of the gray stalks and flared rims are clusters of algal cells.

Within an arm's reach is a large foliose horizontal dog lichen, bright glossy-green with dark-brown fruiting discs around the edges. A more common dog lichen grows next, outer edges raised and recurved to reveal the veining of cottony rhizomes on the underside. The ends of the lobes are curved shut like a fist; when the spores are ripe, the fist opens to show the shiny brown surface beneath. On the rocks are ruffled green fingers splaying outward from the center—a fruticose lichen found on granite all over the land. The fruiting bodies vary in size, dark chocolate-

SPOTTED SAXIFRAGE
(*Saxifragia bronchialis*)

species of *Hypnum*

species of *Grimmia*

Plate 73

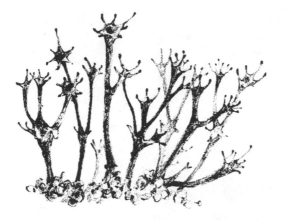

LICHEN
(*Cladonia furcata*)

Plate 74

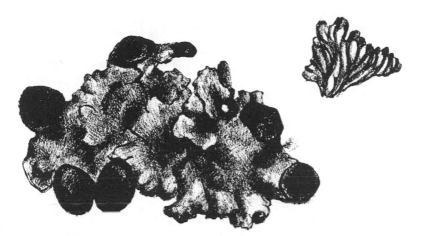

HORIZONTAL DOG LICHEN
(Peltigera horizontalis)

DOG LICHEN
(Peltigera canina)

FRUITING PROCESS

brown in the center, rimmed precisely with gray-green, clustered in the center of the patch. None of these nonflowering plants exceeds two inches; most are much lower.

The spruce and Douglasfir shade the duff to the exclusion of all other herbs; a spindly daisy or a frail goldenrod are the exception, not the rule. The forest floor is soft not with grasses but with the tatami mats of pine needles. The flora is of Lilliputian proportions. Only the exquisiteness of it compensates for the hands-and-knees difficulty of viewing it.

🌿

A chirping red squirrel scolds at me, sounding like a child's toy wound up to the limit and running down with a clattering, clacking impertinence. He is usually just out of sight and generally just out of temper. He rattles like a jay, screeching about the pass to which things have come when unknowns can enter his forest. He feeds largely on spruce seeds, along with Douglasfir seeds and bark, cutting and storing them in caches between scolding sessions. He sometimes feeds totally on conifer seeds, and in a year of limited seed production a large population of squirrels can seriously hinder tree reproduction.

This red squirrel goes by many names: chickaree, pine or spruce squirrel, Fremont's squirrel. The last commemorates the Pathfinder, who was not only an explorer and ambitious politician, but an acute observer of nature. Our wild pink geranium also bears his name—perhaps a more lasting memorial than his political achievements.

🌿

When Herman cuts wood for the stoves and I dutifully stack it, I am always fascinated by the hieroglyphic tunnelings and meanderings on the bare underbark surface of the wood, the abandoned paths of boring beetles. The most destructive are the Black Hills bark beetles, which infect mature and overmature conifers. Engelmann spruce are often riddled with Engelmann bark beetles.

When I walk in the woods I sometimes try to visualize the life beneath the bark. So much of the forest world is so busy, yet so quiet. The female beetle burrows into the tree, followed

CONKS ON ASPEN STUMP
(*Polyporaceae*)

BORING BEETLE TRAILS

ORANGE FUNGUS ON ASPEN
(*Dacrymyces stillatus*)

Plate 75

by the male. Together they hollow out a vertical gallery in the living inner bark, producing one gallery per season, usually about seven inches long. In it they lay their eggs in midsummer, emerging afterward. The eggs hatch in two weeks. After the larvae feed on the inner bark at the edge of the main gallery they set out on their own horizontal excavations. They remain dormant during winter months, resuming feeding when June warms the trunk. They are full grown by midsummer, when they pupate and emerge as adults. There are few controls: woodpeckers are the best control, followed by sharp weather changes which upset breeding habits, or an extremely low temperature. But the bark of the tree is an effective insulator. Only the voracious appetite of the woodpecker controls the desecration.

Both Douglasfir and blue spruce are attacked by a spruce gall aphid, which is equally common on city trees. The tip of a new branch is weakened at the point of infection, causing it to bend downward and finally to die. The turned-down browned tips still retain their needles fused to the stalk. They are especially noticeable on younger trees where they contrast markedly with the burgeoning growth.

❧

The true animal of the dark forest is the solitary predator who finds within its shelter the total cover which allows attack with the element of surprise. The predator is an animal without a shadow, crouching to blend his size and shape into the broken outlines of the forest, or of such swiftness and skill that his coming is unfelt until the flash of claw on hide. The ultimate predator is the silent mover, the patient waiter: the soft-padded bobcat or mountain lion, the stalking wolf, the watchful weasel, the soaring eagle.

Before we came to this land, I had the common erroneous notion that predators were "bad." Now I have come to realize that predators are a conserving element in nature, eliminating the weaker members of a family or herd to maintain the larger unit at a level the land can support. The population of predators fluctuates with that of their prey, flourishing when prey is plentiful, starving when prey is scarce. The long-term effect of predation is moderate, sometimes neutral, and generally beneficial. Disease, severe climate and nutritional difficulties may become more deadly than predators. Without a weasel the forest would be overpopulated with rabbits and mice. The pines would likely suffer from overbrowsing and die out. Willows would be eaten to the ground. Thousands of small animals would starve or flee from the mountains to find food elsewhere.

When I walk beside the bobcat's tracks in the snow, my footsteps paralleling his, I can feel his restless hungry searching. He averages five to six miles of travel a night, cat eyes glowing in the darkness, ranging through forest and grove, crossing the snow-covered lake many times in his search. His winter range may be ten to fifteen square miles, for his appetite is large. His favorite method of hunting is by stalking or crouching in trees which are chosen along familiar game trails. His den is in a fallen log or windfall of trees. Not a large animal—he weighs about eighty pounds—he is a stocky cat with broad jaws and sharp teeth and claws. He creeps close when a deer is resting. With one spring he lands on the back or neck, sinking sharp canines into the jugular. Or he pounces on a feeding rabbit, who is busy cracking open pine cones and never hears the pad of silent feet. Or he rolls over a porcupine to reach the unprotected underside and clamps it with lethal paw. The hunting is incessant, for a bobcat will not eat putrid meat. Kills which are not completely consumed, even though covered with brush or snow for later feasting, are often discovered and finished off by scavengers before his return.

🌿

We traditionally spend Thanksgiving at Constant Friendship. We arrive early in the morning in order to fire up the wood stove and cook the turkey. When we came a year ago we noticed crows and magpies circling the lake—unusual at any time of year and especially in winter. We found a young mule deer doe trapped in two-inch thick ice, about eight feet offshore from the dam. The hindquarters, under water, and the head were intact, held together by the limp bare backbone. Pieces of scapula and cartilage were scattered about the crest of the dam. Carrion-feeding birds had mixed the new snow pink with blood and their three-toed tracks. Clearly imprinted in the fresh snow were the tracks of a bobcat.

We traced cat and deer tracks up the south hill where bright blood and disturbed snow showed she had been jumped. She had fled down the slope, out of the frightening forest, her hooves slipping in a frantic irregular path through the snow onto the lake. The thin ice had held her weight for a few feet and then she had broken through. Her futile attempts to swim were marked by black slots of open water. Near the shore she had become trapped by the thickness of the ice and the terrible cold. There the cat had snarled out onto the ice, disemboweled the deer while she was still alive, torn out and dragged the front quarters away. The sense of death was still in the air although the cat was gone.

We hauled the carcass out of the lake and down behind the dam where it would not foul the water. All afternoon the scavengers skirled and squabbled, an incessant foreign obtrusive sound against the usual winter quiet. The sounds ceased abruptly. We looked out the cabin window.

Into the silence, wings full spread, wheeled a bald eagle, so much larger than ordinary birds that he was out of scale to the whole landscape. He alighted in the top of a Douglasfir, his weight swaying the slender spire. The magpies and crows made a conspicuously quick exit and the eagle floated down to feed.

Less than a week later there were no traces, not a bone, not a scrap of hide, left of the deer. But bobcat tracks still weave through the forest, a reminder of hunger on swift silent feet.

7 ❧ ❧ The Lake Rock

When I need my sense of order restored, I sit on the lake rock. It sums up all I have learned about this mountain world. Connected to the shore by a narrow, somewhat unstable catwalk, the rock is just big enough to sit on comfortably. It is a pebble dropped into the water, the center of widening rings of montane life, beginning with the life of the lake itself and culminating in the evergreen forests, where the succession that is taking place is mapped in the communities that I can see. The rock is a place of order, reason, and bright mountain air.

Encircling the rock is the community of plants and animals which can survive only in the water. Small motes of existence, they float with its currents, cling to underwater supports, or burrow in the brown silt of the lake bottom. Some I can see as I sit here. Others have to be corralled under a microscope lens. I watch a fat trout lurking in the fringed shadows of the sedges. All around the edges of the lake, where water meets land, grow willows, sedges, and rushes, predicting a time when amber water will be green plant, the lapping sound of small waves the sly whisper of grass stems.

It is a busy place with a constant spin of insects, punctuated by the pursuing green arcs of leopard frogs. The south stream enters the lake through willows and cow parsnip and a pile of logs placed there when the lake was built to prevent silting. The north stream's entrance is hidden in elephant-foot-sized clumps of bulrush which change sheen in every breeze. Tangles of willows forecast spring in their catkins. Yellow or red branches identify them even in winter. The streams are the one constant in this landscape.

The circle widens. Behind the lake edge, to the north and west, the land rises into the lake meadow, drying as it slopes upward. Blue grass and brome grass crowd every square inch. I see chipmunk and ground-squirrel burrows, haloed with dandelions. Hundreds of wildflowers grow in this meadow, perennials whose coming I look for each year. A few aspens tentatively grow along its edge.

The established young aspen community between the two streams contains small slender trees, growing almost a foot a year. Still gangling and adolescent, they will in a short time obscure the view of the mature grove behind them. Leaves flicker celadon in spring, viridian in summer, clinquant in fall, tallying the sovereign seasons, graying and greening to reiterate the message of snow and sun.

Wider still, the north edge of the lake meadow steps upward over its granite base. Where it levels off, the ponderosas grow, big and sturdy and full of cones. They stand staunch, widely spaced, allowing sunlight to filter through for wild geranium and kinnikinnik and tiny wild candytuft that crosses the dusky duff.

The south slope of the lake curves away from the shore, becoming more spruce-shaded as it retreats. This area is the first to be snow-covered, the last to be clear. Shade-tolerant plants root in the precipitous hillside; from here I can see a few late orange-red Indian paintbrush and the stalks of monkshood and larkspur. Dark-red strawberry blite ties down an old log with the help of raspberry and rose bushes. A few last aspens mingle with the spruces, their trunks thin and pallid, most of their branches down from insufficient light. Above them the Douglas-firs and spruces grow close together, presenting a solid wall of black-green.

The ever-widening circles of montane life culminate in

WILD CHRYSANTHEMUM
(*Bahia dissecta*)

INDIAN PAINTBRUSH
(*Castilleja miniata*)

Plate 76

these evergreens which intrude visually into the lake. Even in winter, when the India-ink reflections are gone, the uncompromising contrast of black and white still commands the eye. In the spring, when the air is heavy and laden with late snows, the lake reflects their pendent spires, solid as a German Expressionist woodcut. In the summer the reflections shimmer in the breeze, slotted with blue sky, an animate Monet. In the fall they form a moving mosaic with the aspen when the wind fragments the surface to create tesserae of emerald and gold leaf—a Byzantine pavement.

It is impossible to look at the land and not be aware of the evergreens. In all seasons they dominate, unchanging in color, towering in size. Their spires crenelate the sky. Their opacity of color, depth, and density create a background against which are measured the brightness of aspen leaf, iridescence of dragonfly wing, scarlet of gilia, and gleam of lake. The ponderosa, spruce, and Douglasfir are the reminders of an end point of succession for this land, for there is no other vegetation that will replace them, short of catastrophic climate change.

These trees change the environment to fit their needs, making an acid soil which is inhospitable to other plants, attracting rain by the massiveness of their own transpiration. At the beginning of succession, moss and lichen grow a few centimeters above the ground and a few below. At the end of succession, for this land, trees tower many feet into the air and send their roots through the ground, demanding the most that the environment can give. These conifers will be there in decades, in centuries, to come. They will shade out other trees and brighter flowers, intrude into the deepening soil of the meadows. Succession is an inexorable progression which may be altered or disrupted but which will eternally begin again and again to achieve the same end. No emotional pleas or moral inducements will change it; to understand this is to accept the irrevocableness of nature.

❦

The knob of granite forming my tiny island rises three feet above the water on the lake side, stepping and sloping down to a few inches above on the land side. The surface breaks off and crumbles into sharp gravel in my hand with the ease of Pikes

Peak granite. Near the waterline on the east, the plants grow in independent patches, on a nearly vertical face. On the rise and tread of the protected step they grow more thickly. Green pincushions of moss are softer to sit on than the gravel. At my feet, on top of one mat of moss, are a few square inches of blue grass, neatly trimmed by the wind. Through this nest of stolons and roots and rhizomes grow cinquefoils, wild strawberry, white clover, an ubiquitous dandelion, asters, wild chrysanthemum, rosettes of scarlet gilia and bright pink wild geranium.

Strawberry and geranium seeds may have arrived via the droppings of a gluttonous chickadee. The tiny leaves, replicas of normal-sized leaves on shore, bear the imprint of limitation. Composite seeds came on efficient parachutes, sometimes air-borne, sometimes as a flotilla sailing across the water and snagging in a crack. Porter's asters and wild chrysanthemums give the final touch of yellow and white to the rock; golden asters are one of the most tolerant plants of the mountains, flourishing in a wide variety of habitats in a wide variety of altitudes.

Bush cinquefoil cliff-hangs at the southernmost edge of the rock; fully exposed, they set brilliant blooms against the darkness of the lake's pine-tree reflections. Although the bushes are small, their leaf and blossom size are the same as those of shore plants. Looking around the lake shore, I can see these same flowers and shrubs in the meadow or the aspen grove, usually where there is some protection and, at the very least, more soil.

I take a mental walk along the rim of the parent rocks of this island which form the south-facing slope at the edge of the lake. There, large boulders of Pikes Peak granite form a crumbling cliff with the ponderosa grove at the top and the lake at the base. Below the dam, the rim of granite drops sharply to the runoff stream. Facing almost due south, the slope receives the full intensity of mountain sunlight, especially in the winter when the low sun hits at a ninety-degree angle and keeps the slope snow-free.

In the weathered gravel which forms talus-like patches between the rocks, some plants have rooted. Water drains most quickly from a gravel slope, making colonization exceedingly difficult. Decomposed rock has little stability, and the steepness of the slope causes it to roll easily. Nonetheless there is a fairly even growth of penny-cress, shepherd's-purse, butter-and-eggs, amaranth, and buckwheat. Considered as being noxious weeds at lower elevations, they provide soil hold here, and even their propensity for forming myriads of seeds has not given them unchallenged progress. They simply find the growing conditions too difficult to make nuisances of themselves.

Towering over the annuals are the exclamation points of mullein, huge stalks of this year's green reiterated in the browned stalks of last year's pods. *Candelaria* is the descriptive Spanish name, and indeed they seem like huge candelabra, verdigris in summer, bronze in winter. With a few scarlet gilia, some small-flowered blue gilia, and white thistles, these are the only biennials. An early narrow-leafed mertensia is the only perennial herb. There are some rose twigs, but to call them shrubs would be presumptuous.

Farther down this same slope, on top of a large level rock which the children used to use for a stage, are a few pincushion cacti. Some also grow in the loose gravel nearby, tucked at the foot of another boulder near sprigs of pin cherry. Cacti have extremely shallow and spreading root systems, which cover such a large area that they can take full advantage of even a light rainfall. Leaves, like those of the conifers, have been narrowed to needles; stems are thickened to a sphere covered with a heavy cuticle. The stomata are closed during the day when evaporation is high and opened in the cool of the night. These devices hinder water loss so effectively that cacti are most common in desert areas. And this is very nearly just that: there is no shade, the rocks catch and radiate the full heat and glare of high-intensity altitude sunlight, and solid rock lies just beneath the surface. Growing conditions are hard indeed; the delicacy of the early pink flowers is almost incongruous.

Still farther down the slope, on another large rock table, is a cluster of stonecrop. Like the cactus, its succulent leaves are thickly cuticled and the root system is shallow and wide. Tolerant of a wide soil range, stonecrop grows on many montane rocks and dry slopes. It blooms profusely in June and July, brilliant six-pointed stars visible as puddles of yellow many feet away although no single blossom exceeds half an inch in diam-

NARROW-LEAVED
MERTENSIA
(*Mertensia lanceolata*)

PINNATE-LEAF
GILIA
(*Gilia pinnatifida*)

Plate 77

STONECROP
(*Sedum lanceolatum*)

SAND CHERRY
(*Prunus besseyi*)

Plate 78

eter. Its vitality is in no way diminished by conditions other plants would find impossible.

❧

To compare these rock environments with the lake rock is to see what water can do to alter the vegetational pattern. Cactus, stonecrop, and mullein could not grow on the lake rock, for they require a dry situation. Other conditions are the same: Pikes Peak granite base, exposed site, close enough to receive identical amounts of sun and rain. The difference in vegetation is caused by the surrounding water, and is indicated not only in the type but the increased variety of plants. The measured relative humidity on the rock is consistently nearly double that of the shore rocks. In the winter the rock is ice-locked and generally snow-covered over the plant line, protecting the plants from the extremes of thaw and freeze and desiccation that the shore plants must endure.

Water is the most important single factor in this succession. The lake has made possible a local condition with local vegetation, just as the stream running through the dry prairie makes possible the phalanx of trees along its banks. The two extremes exist side by side.

The lake-rock community has progressed as far, in terms of plant succession, as the meadow community, and in a measurably short time—since the lake was built some seventeen years ago. It had and still has many aspects of a pioneer community. Much of the growth is isolated, a hand-span or more apart. The soil is minimal and undifferentiated. Layering is narrow, and the environmental factors almost totally control the plant life. The predominant growth here is that of perennial herbs, characteristic of a more advanced stage of succession than that which exists on the shore rocks before me. None of these plants are limited in range or in need of special conditions on this rock. Tolerance and hardiness mark the pioneers.

❧

A succession of animal life accompanies the succession of plant life. The animals who busy themselves by the lake rock are insects, mostly transients who can fly. No mice burrow here, no deer browse, no birds perch. The blue damselfly frequents the rock as a passer-by. Flies make a noisy nuisance of themselves but lay their eggs elsewhere. Only wolf spiders leave dots of white cotton egg cases. The lake rock is isolated from the shore, the water as effective a barrier as if it were a mile across, and the sparse plant cover provides no shelter for larger animals.

But when the lake has finally been absorbed, and the rock is surrounded and covered by soil, then perhaps larger animals will come padding and pawing and nosing about, their ancestors even now roaming the woods. I would like to think so. But perhaps they will not, for by then they may already be gone from here, as the wolves, wolverines, and grizzly bears are already gone, pushed to extinction by man's narrowing of the wilderness.

❧

We have tried to understand the patterns of the land at Constant Friendship. We have hoped to change it as little as possible. After all, we are only visitors to this mountain land. But to keep this land untouched has meant that we have had to partially fence it, with a fence almost as much psychological as physical. And this, incongruously, seems to be the only way in which wilderness lands can be saved. Only within the periphery of the fence is there time to learn, to understand, to cherish. My interest in the vast world of nature began when we came to this land, with the finding of a new world, a sense of discovery, a sharing. But somewhere in the learning came commitment, the realization that in the understanding of this natural world comes the maintenance of it, that with knowledge comes responsibility.

At Constant Friendship we chop down a dead aspen that might fall on the cabin during a wind storm, destroying the chance for it to be home for bird or insect or weasel. It makes good firewood, we say, thinking of our creature comforts. But we have cut down no masses of trees, leaving open scars to erode. We have polluted no streams, shot no marauding bobcat for bounty, no deer for sport. But by our presence we do cause the balances of nature to be readjusted.

Because we can and do manipulate our environment, we are then charged with the responsibility of our acts, for if we are to survive we must insure that this best of all possible worlds survives with us.

❦

The lake rock is a microcosm, and here I find stability and order, and an understanding of my own place in an impeccable design. From here I can reach out to my less orderly world beyond. From here I can see the seasons chain together in a continuity that runs through our lives. Each one of us has sat here, at one time or another, almost as much a part of the landscape as the lake rock itself, absorbing a sense of strength from the granite and a sense of freedom from the sky.

This rock in winter is a handy place for Sara to put her ice skates on or for me to rest from the altitudinal exertions of shoveling snow to make a rink. I can look down and down through pellucid ice into a silent deep world where air bubbles are trapped in crystal. It is so cold that the snow creaks and crunches with our footsteps and sparkles as if it had mica in it. If there is no wind and the sky is clear, the sun shining through the thin atmosphere is gloriously warm. But if there is a January wind cutting out of the north, the rock is untenable. The warmth of the cabin is more than welcome; it is a necessity.

The lake rock awakens to spring in small ways. Tiny wolf spiders spew out from under the moss cover which is just greening underneath. A ladybug staggers along the unbalanced boulders of gravel on top of the rock. Among the deep-red strawberry leaves of last year is a cocoon of unfurled fuzzy leaves, not yet ready to face the frosted mornings. Clover leaves are folded in origami patterns of pale green. The lichen, usually dry as a cornflake, is pliable with the moisture of spring. I look up to see a flight of robins leafing the aspen below the dam. By now a wide rim of black water circles the rock, contrasting with the milky rotting ice. The snow patches at the edge of the lake are granulated and shiny on top from daytime thaw and nighttime freeze. Herman stands on the dam, listening to the spring runoff pour down the standpipe, reassured to know that the lake is coming alive again, and that the rainbow trout are getting fresh oxygen.

In summer the sun is hot on the rock, but the persistent mountain breeze and high altitude keep the air cool. If you sit very quietly and dangle your feet in the sun-warmed surface of the water, a rainbow trout, nibbling from the submerged rock ledge, may also nibble upon a toe. I watch Susan watching the world beneath, finding her own order in her own way. Iridescent dragonflies, bluer than the blue lettuce or the penstemons flowering in the lake meadow, dart a busy halo above her head. A horizontal line of golden banner is a band of sunshine marching across the dam.

As soon as she leaves, Graf brings out three precisely equal sticks, of a significant length known only to him. He lines them up neatly and pushes them one by one into the water. Then he dashes down the catwalk, around the shore, and plunges in to capture each of the flotilla in turn. Sometimes he tries to reach the floating sticks from the lake rock itself, feet slipping on the loose graveled surface of the south side, barking hysterically when the currents edge the sticks just out of reach. He finally tires of his game and goes in search of Herman, who is chopping firewood and will welcome him not at all.

Folly trots out to watch one of her beloved humans in the rowboat. Jane rows over and coaxes her to jump in. Folly ducks and bobs her head in basset indecision and cries and whines, but she won't jump. She stands woebegone and forlorn when Jane rows away.

One summer's day when I came out to the rock, a large creamy-white crab spider, with two handsome maroon racing stripes on her back, lay in wait in a chokecherry bush near the catwalk. Half an hour later when I returned, a butterfly dangled from her clutches.

On a warm sunny autumn day I sun on the lake rock like a turtle. A damselfly wings by, late-starting and slow-flying. The chill nights cramp its style. Having escaped trout and swift, the damselfly will not escape the predation of winter. Its hesitant flight tells of summer's going.

I pull up the swimming ladder and it smells like the back corner of a Florida beach, pungent and fishy. Plumatella are clustered on the underside of some of the steps. Caddisfly cases are attached to another. Snail eggs glisten gelatinously along the side. Algae and green protozoa enliven the yellow-brown of the

SEED HEAD

BLUE LETTUCE
(*Lactuca tatarica*)

BUTTER - AND - EGGS
(*Linaria vulgaris*)

Plate 79

FIREWEED
(*Epilobium angustifolium*)

Plate 80

underwater growth. Flies appear immediately, busily exploring the rapidly drying surface.

A small snail makes its way down the still-damp ladder into a puddle formed by dripping water, and insinuates itself over the edge of the rock and down the side into the water. The snail will survive, but not the minutiae attached to the steps. They seem to retreat within themselves as the sheen of the water evaporates. They will be dead within the day, the heat from the sun drying them into lifeless crusts. But they are preserved in the statoblasts and seeds and spores and bits of pieces of continuity drifting slowly to the lake bottom.

The late asters and wild chrysanthemums bend and twist in the sharp freshening wind. Fireweed's cottony seeds skitter across the lake's surface, diagramming the darting gusts. The chillness of the wind stiffens my hands and tugs at the page of the paper, so that I cannot draw. An aster seed blows into the lake, joining a fleet of aspen leaves. Cinquefoil, geranium, and strawberry leaves are burnished bronze-red. On the south shore a few aspens hold the last golden leaves. The rhythm of their quavering is doubled to semiquavers by the lake's reflections. The year is on its way to ending.

It is time to go back, light the wood stove, and begin supper.

GLOSSARY

Achene A fruit type that is small, dry, one-sided, and remains closed
at maturity, borne by such plants as buttercups, avens, and ane-
mones.

Alternation of generations One generation reproduces sexually, the fol-
lowing asexually by spores, which develop into the sexual genera-
tion. Ferns, mosses, liverworts, and horsetails reproduce in this
manner. (Flowering plants also undergo the same process but have
telescoped it into a single plant which bears sexual and asexual or-
gans at the same time.)

Annual A plant, grown from one seed, producing flowers and fruit in
one growing season, such as pennycress.

Anther The pollen-containing part of a stamen.

Biennial A plant producing leaves the first year, usually in a rosette,
flowering and fruiting the second, then dying; examples are mul-
lein and scarlet gilia.

Bract A modified leaf, usually reduced in size and subtending a flower
cluster, as in angelica; sometimes vividly colored, as in Indian
paintbrush.

Bulb An underground modified bud, made up of a basal stem covered
by fleshy scales and functioning for asexual reproduction; onions
and lilies grow from bulbs.

Calyptra The cap covering the green capsule in most mosses.

Calyx The outer part of the floral envelope, composed of sepals.

Capsule The spore-container of a moss; a type of fruit that is simple dry, dehiscent, and usually several to many-seeded.

Catkin A pendulous deciduous cluster of inconspicuous flowers, usu ally of one sex and without petals, characteristic of the Poplar anc Birch families to which aspen and willow belong.

Chlorophyll The green pigment in plants which is required for photo synthesis to occur.

Climax vegetation Vegetation in an ecosystem or plant community in relatively stable equilibrium with the environment, and able to reproduce there, e.g., spruce and pine in the high country. Climax vegetation will remain the same over long periods of time unless strongly disturbed.

Community The biological segment of the ecosystem made up of the plants and animals living there.

Corm A modified, thickened underground stem, often bearing scale-like leaves; some orchids grow from corms.

Corolla The inner set of floral leaves made up of petals.

Ecology The study of the processes that operate among plants, animals, and their environment.

Ecosystem A recognizable unit of the landscape composed of plants and animals that tend to characterize the area, the environmental factors operating, and the environment and organisms interacting.

Environment The total physical factors that affect the plants and animals making up a community, e.g., climate, parent soil material, topography, solar factors.

Follicle A fruit type which opens along one edge only, as in columbine.

Food chain The series of organisms through which food energy and materials move, beginning with a plant producer and generally ending in an ultimate predator.

Fruit A ripened ovary.

Gley A soil formed under poor conditions of drainage, often gray in color, frequently found in low areas of temperate and cold climates.

Habitat The specific type of site in which a plant or animal lives.

Halteres The knoblike stabilizers that have replaced the second pair of wings in flies.

Horizon The layer of soil designated by a letter: A (top), B (containing materials washed down from the top layer), and C (decomposed, disintegrated, and parent material).

Hypha A single fungal filament.

Legume A type of fruit that consists of one carpel, usually splitting at maturity along two sutures; lupine and locoweed are examples.

Montane Pertaining to mountains; the Montane Zone in central Colorado is between 6500–7000 and 9500 feet.

Mutualism The relationship between organisms living together with mutual benefit, as that between an alga and a fungus in the formation of a lichen.

Mycelium A visible mass of hyphae.

Mycorrhiza A mutualistic relationship in which the fungal mycelia of "fungus roots" surround and/or invade the roots of a green plant; most common with orchids, conifers, and oaks but known in a wide range of plants over the world.

Nymph An immature insect having undergone incomplete metamorphosis. For example, the grasshopper nymph looks like an adult but is wingless and has no resting period before assuming its final form; also, the aquatic young of some insects, such as dragonflies and mayflies.

Ovary The basal portion of a pistil in flowering plants which contains one or more ovules; after fertilization each ovule becomes a seed. An orchid has thousands of ovules, a grass plant but one per flower.

Panicle A kind of inflorescence that is elongate with compound branching, as in some bedstraws.

Parasite One organism dependent upon another host organism for food to the detriment of the host; mistletoe and ticks are parasites.

Parthenogenesis The development of an egg without fertilization, as in certain generations of aphids or *Daphnia*.

Petal One of the parts of the corolla, often colored but sometimes missing. A rose has petals, but a Pasque flower has none, having instead colored sepals.

Perennial A plant living many years, dying down in winter and sprouting each spring from an established root system.

Photosynthesis The complex process of making sugars from carbon dioxide and water, incorporating light energy into the compound through the agency of chlorophyll.

Pioneer The plant or animal beginning a new stage of succession; lichens and mosses are often pioneer plants.

Pistil The female reproductive part of a flower.

Quadrat An area, delineated by an ecologist as a study plot, used to examine plant and animal populations, succession, etc.

Rhizome A modified undergound stem which roots at the nodes, usually growing horizontally; blue grass and iris spread by rhizomes.

Root That part of a plant usually below soil surface, which anchors, absorbs, and stores food. Not all subterranean plant parts are roots; some may be modified stems, such as rhizomes.

Saprophyte A plant without green color that depends upon dead organic matter for food, as pinedrops and most fungi.

Seed A fertilized ripened ovule, composed of a young plant and stored food, enclosed in a seed coat.

Sepal One of the parts of the calyx, or outer set of floral leaves, usually small and leaflike, outside the petals; if petals are missing, the sepals are often colored, as with various anemones.

Soil The combination of mineral and organic compounds forming a growing medium, developed by hundreds of years of interaction of organisms and environment with the parent substrate.

Spermatophore A sperm package, simplifying sperm transferral, used by dragonflies, springtails, etc.

Spore Typically a one-celled asexual structure which can develop without fusion into a new plant; produced by mosses, ferns, and fungi.

Stamen Male pollen-producing segment of the flower.

Stolon A modified above-ground horizontal stem that may root at the nodes and apex producing new plantlets, as strawberries do.

Stomata Pores in the leaves and stems of green plants through which water vapor, carbon dioxide, oxygen, and other gases may pass in and out.

Stigma The part of the pistil on which pollen adheres and germinates.

Style The stalklike middle portion of the pistil usually connecting the stigma and ovary.

Succession In an ecological sense, the change in vegetation at a given place over a period of time if disturbance has taken place, as in the case of a meadow succeeding toward climax woodland. Succession is termed *primary* if it begins on barren rock or where no plant life has existed previously; *secondary* if it begins on disturbed ground where there has been life before.

Symbiosis See *Mutualism.*

Thallus A plant body not differentiated into stems and leaves; often characteristic of lower plants such as algae and liverworts.

Transpiration The giving off of water from a plant, mainly through the leaves.

Umbel A type of inflorescence in which the flower stems radiate from a central point on the stem, in a manner similar to an umbrella, characteristic of the Parsley family; blooming usually proceeds from the outside in.

Vegetation The plant cover of an area.

❧❧ SELECTED REFERENCES

This is a selected list of references about the southern Rocky Mountain region that would be of help in identifying flora and fauna of this specific area; field guides of more general focus that have been found to be useful here are also included. Even though many books cited are out of print, they have been included nevertheless because they are of such basic interest for this region; they are often available locally or through secondhand book dealers. Paperbacks are marked with asterisks.

FLOWERING PLANTS

*Berry, James Berthold. *Western Forest Trees*. New York: Dover Publications, 1964. Concise, informative, illustrated.

*Carter, Jack L., and Harry M. Stover. *Key to the Gymnosperms of the Pikes Peak Region*. Excellent mimeographed material, available locally.

Clements, Frederic, and Edith S. Clements. *Rocky Mountain Flowers*. New York: Hafner Publishing Company, 1963. A reprint of a classic by two Rocky Mountain botanists who did a great deal of research on Pikes Peak, literally; extensively illustrated with Mrs. Clements' beautiful color and line drawings; contains botanical descriptions as well as plant-name derivations. Excellent for the immediate area.

*Craighead, John J., Frank C. Craighead, and Ray J. Davis. *A Field Guide to Rocky Mountain Wildflowers.* Boston: Houghton Mifflin Company, 1974. A handy and basic identification book, well-illustrated, although perhaps better for the northern Rockies.

Fassett, Norman C. *A Manual of Aquatic Plants.* Revised appendix by Eugene Ogden. Madison, Wisconsin: University of Wisconsin Press, 1966. Comprehensively illustrated book on these often ubiquitous plants.

*Harrington, H. D. *Edible Native Plants of the Rocky Mountains.* Albuquerque, New Mexico: University of New Mexico Press, 1968. Exquisitely illustrated with line drawings, written in a pleasant readable style; includes recipes, plants to avoid, etc.

*———. *How to Identify Grasses and Grasslike Plants.* Denver: Swallow Press, 1977. By far the larger percent of our flora is grasses, sedges, etc.; this is a helpful guide to identifying the less showy but infinitely more important members of our flora.

*———. *Manual of the Plants of Colorado.* Denver: Sage Books, 1954. The definitive botanical reference for Colorado; out-of-print copies can occasionally be found at secondhand bookstores. Without illustrations, it is not a book for the layman.

*Harrington, H. D., and L. W. Durrell. *Colorado Ferns.* Fort Collins, Colorado: Colorado A. and M. College, 1950. Good local guide, unfortunately out of print.

*———. *How to Identify Plants.* Denver: Swallow Press, n.d. Invaluable for checking unfamiliar botanical terms and for determining just how to describe the unknown plant before you; excellent glossary.

*Herzman, Carl W., et al. *Handbook of Colorado Native Grasses.* Fort Collins, Colorado: Colorado State University Extension Service Bulletin 450-A. Indispensible.

*Hitchcock, A. S. *Manual of the Grasses of the United States,* 2 volumes. Second edition, revised by Agnes Chase. New York: Dover Publications, 1971. The definitive book on grasses, includes distribution maps, thoroughly illustrated.

*House, Chuck. *Trees of the Pikes Peak Region.* Fort Collins, Colorado: Colorado State University, U. S. Department of Agriculture, and El Paso County, n.d. Available locally and well done.

*Knobel, Edward. *Field Guide to the Grasses, Sedges and Rushes of the*

United States. New York: Dover Publications, 1977. Good to use with Harrington's book on the same subject.

*Long, John C. *Native Orchids of Colorado.* Denver: Denver Museum of Natural History, Denver Museum Pictorial No. 16, 1965. One of a series of small attractive booklets published by the museum; because there are so few orchids, this one is more comprehensive than most. Illustrated with color photographs.

*McKean, William T. *Winter Guide to Native Shrubs of the Central Rocky Mountains.* Denver: Colorado Department of Game and Fish, 1956. For cross-country-skiing winter botanists! May be out of print but sometimes available locally.

*Marr, John W. *Ecosystems of the East Slope of the Front Range in Colorado.* Boulder: University of Colorado Press, University of Colorado Studies Series in Biology, No. 8, 1967. The best source for the ecology of the immediate area, and what plants are to be expected where and why.

*Nelson, Ruth A. *Handbook of Rocky Mountain Plants.* Estes Park, Colorado: Rocky Mountain Nature Association, 1969. An up-to-date revision of a classic; a must for this area.

*————. *Rocky Mountain Plants from Canada to Mexico.* Tucson: Dale Stuart King, 1969. Mrs. Nelson has a gift for composing keys to various plant families in layman's terms which makes identification a joy.

*Peattie, Donald Culross. *A Natural History of Western Trees.* Boston: Houghton Mifflin Company, 1953. More inclusive than an identification book; now out of print.

*Pesman, Walter. *Meet the Natives.* Denver: Denver Botanic Gardens, 1975. A color-cued book for easy identification. Descriptions are skeletal and illustrations relatively few, but still the most-used guide for this area and the easiest introduction to Colorado plants, although not necessarily the most accurate.

*Petrides, George A. *A Field Guide to Trees and Shrubs.* Boston: Houghton Mifflin Company, 1972. One book in the consistently good Peterson Guide series.

*Preston, Richard J., Jr. *Rocky Mountain Trees.* New York: Dover Publications, 1968. Handy identification guide, lots of illustrations.

Ramaley, Francis. *Colorado Plant Life.* Boulder: University of Colorado, 1927. Although superseded by more thorough guides, this is a basic, readable book written from an ecological viewpoint by one of the pioneers in Colorado plant studies. Now out of print.

*Roberts, Rhoda N., and Ruth A. Nelson. *Mountain Wild Flowers of Colorado.* Denver: Denver Museum of Natural History, Denver Museum Pictorial No. 13, 1978. A small but very useful beginniner's book, somewhat limited in species but containing the most common plants of the mountains.

*Roberts, Rhoda N., and Harold D. Roberts. *Colorado Wild Flowers.* Denver: Denver Museum of Natural History, Denver Museum Pictorial No. 8, 1978. Good photographs; same format as above.

*Rydberg, R. A. A. *Flora of the Rocky Mountains and Adjacent Plains.* New York: Hafner Publishing Company, 1954. A reprint of the 1922 classic of Colorado plant manuals.

*Spellenberg, Richard, Susan Rayfield, and Carol Nearing. *The Audubon Society Field Guide to North American Wildflowers,* Western Region. New York: Alfred A. Knopf, 1979. Copiously illustrated with photographs, arranged in color groupings, but missing some of the common species in our area.

*Sweet, Muriel. *Common Edible and Useful Plants of the West.* Healdsburg, California: Naturegraph Company, 1962. Small paperback, profusely illustrated with line drawings, containing much interesting information.

*Thornton, Bruce J., and Harold D. Harrington. *Weeds of Colorado.* Fort Collins, Colorado: Colorado State University, Bulletin 514-S, n.d. Of more than local interest as most weeds have continental distribution. Because each example is illustrated this is a useful identification guide, since many plants called "weeds" are also wildflowers, depending upon your point of view. Out of print.

Weber, William A. *Rocky Mountain Flora.* Boulder: University of Colorado Press, 1976. The current authoritative guide for this area. The paucity of line drawings somewhat limits its usefulness for the layman, but it is absolutely indispensable for accurate identification and current nomenclature. Dr. Weber is curator of the herbarium at the University of Colorado.

NONFLOWERING PLANTS

*Bigelow, Howard E. *Mushroom Pocket Field Guide.* New York: Collier Macmillan Publishers, 1974. Can be used in conjunction with more limited local guides.

*Coffin, George S., Catherine B. Hammond, and Margaret H. Lewis. *Twenty Common Mushrooms and How to Cook Them.* Boston: Brandon Press, n.d. Easy to carry into the field, well illustrated with good diagrams of mushroom structure, and good rules for gatherers as well as recipes.

*Conrad, H. S. *How to Know the Mosses and Liverworts.* Dubuque, Iowa: William C. Brown Company, 1956. This *How to Know* series has excellent keys and plentiful, albeit small, illustrations. It is a pity that many of the titles are out of print, including this one which opens up a whole new world of delight to someone with curiosity and a hand lens.

Grout, A. J. *Mosses with Hand Lens and Microscope.* Bennington, Vermont: J. Johnson, 1972. A bountifully and beautifully illustrated reprint of a classic; a big book that's a joy to pore through.

*Hale, Mason. *How to Know the Lichens.* Dubuque, Iowa: William C. Brown Company, 1969. Excellent pictured key as well as general background information; since lichens are often ubiquitous, many species included here are common in the West.

*Kreiger, Louis C. C. *The Mushroom Handbook.* New York: Dover Publications, 1967. Just that—very helpful.

*McIlvaine, Charles, and Robert K. Macadam. *One Thousand American Fungi.* New York: Dover Publications, 1973. Lots of information and line drawings.

Nearing, G. G. *The Lichen Book: Handbook of the Lichens of Northeastern United States.* Ashton, Maryland: Eric Lundberg, 1962. Even though out of print and not specifically for the Rocky Mountain area, contains ingenious keys which are most helpful to the amateur fascinated by the variety of lichen species, many of which are also western in distribution.

*Shuttleworth, Floyd S., and Herbert S. Zim. *Non Flowering Plants.* New York: Western Publishing Company, 1967. One of the series of inexpensive brightly illustrated paperbacks, small and light to carry. What they lack in depth they make up for in breadth of information.

*Smith, Alexander H. *A Field Guide to Western Mushrooms.* Ann Arbor, Michigan: The University of Michigan Press, 1975. Besides color photographs of most mushroom species, includes chapters on where to expect to find them and poisonous species; glossary and bibliography.

Thomas, William Sturgis. *Field Book of Common Mushrooms.* New York: G. P. Putnam's Sons, 1948. Small, easy-to-carry guide with an imaginative and useful key to mushroom species, a great help to the amateur; plentifully illustrated.
*Wells, Mary Hallock, and D. H. Mitchell. *Colorado Mushrooms.* Denver: Denver Museum of Natural History, 1966. Although somewhat limited in scope, contains good color photographs.

INVERTEBRATES

*Bland, Roger G. *How to Know the Insects.* Dubuque, Iowa: William C. Brown Company, 1978. Spiral bound, exhaustively illustrated, with all kinds of identification aids; thorough.
*Borror, Donald J., and Richard E. White. *A Field Guide to the Insects of America North of Mexico.* Boston: Houghton Mifflin Company, 1970. Contains an excellent pictorial key and copious illustrations; indispensable.
Brown, F. Martin, with Donald Eff and Bernard Rotger. *Colorado Butterflies.* Denver: Denver Museum of Natural History, 1957. Although definitive, this book has only black-and-white photographs, so it is best used in conjunction with other guides with color. Out of print.
*Chu, H. F. *How to Know the Immature Insects.* Dubuque, Iowa: William C. Brown Company, 1949. Well keyed for identification and thoroughly illustrated; unfortunately out of print.
*Fichter, George S. *Insect Pests.* New York: Western Publishing Company, 1966. More thorough than many Golden Press guides because of the narrowness of the study; again, "pest," like "weed," depends upon your point of view.
Gregg, R. E. *The Ants of Colorado.* Boulder: University of Colorado Press, 1963. A definitive text with much ecological information; the introductory section is one of the best reviews of the stringent Rocky Mountain environment.
*Holland, W. J. *The Moth Book.* New York: Dover Publications, 1968. A reprint of one of the only books totally devoted to moths; amply illustrated.
*Jacques, H. E. *How to Know the Beetles.* Dubuque, Iowa: William C. Brown Company, 1951. And Colorado has some beautiful ones!

Lutz, Frank E. *Field Book of Insects.* New York: G. P. Putnam's Sons, 1948. Although originally written in 1937, it is still of real use and very good reading; lively and informative.

*Mitchell, Robert T., and Herbert S. Zim. *Butterflies and Moths.* New York: Western Publishing Company, 1964. Another handy and handsomely illustrated Golden Press guide.

Morgan, Ann Haven. *Field Book of Ponds and Streams.* New York: G. P. Putnam's Sons, 1930. A basic handbook of great usefulness, illustrating well the variety of life in aquatic environments; also includes plants and vertebrates.

*Needham, James G., and Paul R. Needham. *A Guide to the Study of Freshwater Biology.* San Francisco: Holden-Day, 1966. Loads of line drawings with no text to speak of; good descriptions of collecting techniques; primarily for identification.

Pennak, Robert W. *Freshwater Invertebrates of the United States.* New York: Ronald Press, 1953. Definitive for the Rocky Mountain region as well as elsewhere.

Swann, Lester A., and Charles S. Papp. *The Common Insects of North America.* New York: Harper and Row, 1972. Charles Papp did the hundreds of drawings; species descriptions and illustrations are like-numbered, making the book easy to use.

VERTEBRATES

*Aiken, Charles E. H., and Edward R. Warren. *The Birds of El Paso County* (Colorado), 2 parts. Colorado Springs: Colorado College Publication, General Series No. 74–76, Science Series, Vol. XII, No. 13, May, 1914. Photographs accompanying lots of good local information and observation.

Bailey, Alfred M., and Robert J. Niedrach. *Pictorial Checklist of Colorado Birds.* Denver: Denver Museum of Natural History, 1966. Big, definitive, expensive, but worth it; full-page color plates of all the birds of Colorado.

*Beckman, William C. *Guide to the Fishes of Colorado.* Boulder: University of Colorado Museum, 1963. An invaluable booklet, unfortunately out of print.

*Beidleman, Richard G. *Guide to the Winter Birds of Colorado.* Boulder: University of Colorado Museum, 1963. A reminder that all nature studies don't have to take place in the summer; well written by a fine zoologist and teacher. Out of print.

*Burt, William H., and Richard P. Grossenheider. *A Field Guide to the Mammals.* Boston: Houghton Mifflin Company, 1976. Completely illustrated, including distribution maps; indispensable.

*Jones-Burdick, W. Harry. *Guide to the Snakes of Colorado.* Boulder: University of Colorado Museum, 1963. Precisely useful but unfortunately out of print.

Lechleitner, R. R. *Wild Mammals of Colorado.* Boulder: Pruett Publishing Company, 1969. Thorough and useful; out of print, but occasionally available.

*Murie, Olaus J. *A Field Guide to Animal Tracks.* Boston: Houghton Mifflin Company, 1975. Indispensible for hikers, especially handy in winter when tracks and scats may be all you see; also includes other animal signs.

*Niedrach, Robert J., and Robert B. Rockwell. *The Birds of Denver and Mountain Parks.* Denver: Denver Museum of Natural History, 1959. Very good for the immediate area.

*Peterson, Roger Tory. *A Field Guide to Western Birds.* Boston: Houghton Mifflin Company, 1972. THE bird book; indispensable.

*Robbins, Chandler S., et al. *Birds of North America: A Guide to Field Identification.* New York: Western Publishing Company, 1966. Easier to use than Peterson's guide because distribution maps and descriptive text are opposite each illustration; text is good and to the point.

*Rodeck, Hugo G. *Guide to the Mammals of Colorado.* Boulder, Colorado: University of Colorado Museum, 1966. Another fine guide of this series.

*State of Colorado, Department of Game, Fish and Parks, has issued a series of booklets which are illustrated and written for the layman: *Game Animals of Colorado* (Educational Pamphlet No. 5); *The Fishes of Colorado* (No. 3); *Game Birds of Colorado* (No. 2); and *Furbearers of Colorado* (No. 4).

*Stebbins, Robert C. *Field Guide to Western Reptiles and Amphibians.* Boston: Houghton Mifflin Company, 1966. Definitive, handsomely illustrated by Stebbins himself.

*Udvardy, Miklos D. F. *The Audubon Society Field Guide to North American Birds,* Western Region. New York: Alfred A. Knopf, 1977. Totally illustrated with photographs, with species grouped "according to an obvious similarity in shape or appearance . . ." Text descriptions are arranged by habitat.

*Yocom, Charles, *et al. Wildlife and Plants of the Southern Rocky Mountains.* Healdsburg, California: Naturegraph Company, 1966. Especially useful because it includes plants as well as animals for each life zone, it is probably the best source for an overall view of this specific area. There is a companion guide for the northern Rockies.

*Zim, Herbert S., and Hobart M. Smith. *Reptiles and Amphibians.* New York: Western Publishing Company, 1961. Another commendable Golden Guide, more general in nature than Stebbins but very applicable to the West.

❦ ❦ INDEX

About the Author

ANN ZWINGER is the 1976 recipient of the John Burroughs Memorial Association Gold Medal, awarded for *Run, River, Run*. In this work as in her other books, she combines her abilities as writer and illustrator with the dedication of a nature lover. She makes her home in Colorado Springs.